The Prime Minister
and the Cabinet

Methuen: Canadian Politics and Government

The Prime Minister and the Cabinet

W. A. Matheson

Brock University

Methuen

Toronto • London • Sydney • Wellington

Canadian Cataloguing in Publication Data

Matheson, William A., 1932-
  The Prime Minister and the Cabinet

Includes index.
ISBN 0-458-92020-7 bd.
ISBN 0-458-91780-X pa.

1. Cabinet system — Canada. 2. Canada —
Politics and government — 1867 —
3. Prime ministers — Canada. I. Title.

JL97.M38   354'.71'05   C76-017020-7

Printed and bound in Canada

1 2 3 4 5   80 79 78 77 76

TO MY PARENTS

Acknowledgements

A large number of people have assisted in making this book a reality and I gratefully acknowledge their help. The late Dr. R.O. MacFarlane of Carleton University provided guidance when the book was still a Ph.D. thesis. After his death, Dr. K.Z. Paltiel assumed responsibility for supervision. In this capacity Dr. Paltiel proved to be a conscientious, demanding, and stimulating supervisor and I am most grateful for his assistance and advice. Dr. R.J. Jackson of Carleton University and Dr. Michael Stein, formerly of Carleton University but now at McGill University, provided useful advice and encouragement in the early stages of the book and my colleagues at Brock University have been helpful as the work proceeded. I am also deeply indebted to many cabinet ministers, past and present, civil servants, party officials and others who gave so generously of their time during the numerous interviews that I conducted in connection with my research. I have respected the anonymity of these interviewees by not quoting them specifically by name. Dr. Thomas A. Hockin of St. Andrew's College and York University read the penultimate draft and provided both encouragement and helpful criticism.

At various times Bonnie Bellows, Marilyn Kaplan, Marilyn Koop, Eileen Legace, Ann Pidwinski and Anne Soroka have taken on the difficult task of typing the manuscript. Mr. Geoffrey Burn of Methuen Publications has provided much encouragement and advice and The Canada Council has been of assistance in providing a doctoral fellowship.

All of the above have contributed to whatever merit this book may have; responsibility for its shortcomings rests with the author alone.

Contents

Introduction

The achievement of stability in a democracy, despite a fragmented political culture, economic and geographic regionalism, and disparate religious and language groups, may be brought about through the efforts of the various elites to accommodate the divergent interests and demands of the subcultures. To fulfil such a key role, the elites must have the ability to transcend cleavages and to join together with one another in a common effort. This is possible only when there is among the elites of the subcultures a commitment to the maintenance of the political system and an awareness of the perils of political fragmentation; that is, there must be a *fundamental consensus* on the need to keep the system stable and operating. Such a democracy — one with subcultural cleavages tending to immobilism and instability, but one that is deliberately turned into a stable system by the leaders of the major subcultures — may be described as a *consociational democracy*.

In Canada, one of the chief mechanisms of accommodation has been the federal cabinet. Adherence to the representation principle first introduced by Sir John A. Macdonald in 1867 has brought together the elites from the various subcultures and provided them with a means whereby they can work together to stabilize the Canadian political system. Thus in the Canadian context the cabinet has filled a dual role, for in addition to exercising the usual functions of executive leadership, the cabinet has provided an arena in which the elites may counter the dysfunctional and unstabilizing effects of cultural, regional, and religious fragmentation.

Because of his key role as builder and master of the cabinet and as leader of the majority party, the Prime Minister's position is pre-eminent. Because he brings together the political leaders of the various subcultures and keeps them together, he is the one person who becomes a truly national (i.e., pan-Canadian) figure. The necessity of accommodating divergent interests has placed a heavy burden of responsibility on the Prime Minister and has led to a style of politics characterised by prudent leadership and moderate policies.

The pre-eminent role of the Prime Minister and his status as a national figure have made him the most powerful figure in Canadian government. In recent times this has led to the creation of a separate source of policy influence and policy input in his personal entourage, distinct from the traditional sources. This development may in future alter the method by which the politics of accommodation will be practised in Canada.

The cabinet in Canada is the centre and mainspring of Canadian government and of Canada's pluralistic society, the source from which flow statements of policy, legislative pronouncements, and quasi-judicial, administrative, and political decisions. Because government action now penetrates deeply into all aspects of our society, the role of the cabinet has altered greatly since 1867, and its responsibilities have increased enormously. It now dominates Parliament. To some extent this dominance is not surprising, since many areas of concern to contemporary governments are well beyond the competence and knowledge of individual Members of Parliament who frequently find it difficult to understand much of what governments are trying to do, let alone control such action. This increase in complexity and the development of strict party discipline has encouraged the independence of the cabinet and altered traditional notions regarding the cabinet's responsibility to Parliament. In spite of apprehension over its growing power, however, it may well be still correct that "Cabinet Government is the best instrument that has yet been devised for the daily conduct of national affairs."[1]

In spite of the dominant role of the cabinet, it remains an institution almost wholly unknown to the laws of the land. This is because the cabinet has evolved over a long period of time, adjusting itself as time and circumstances demand and always retaining a degree of flexibility it would never possess if it were constitutionally defined. Mr. Arnold Heeney, after many years of experience as cabinet secretary and as Clerk of the Privy Council, has noted: ". . . no one who has not had some personal experience of the day to day affairs of government can appreciate the degree to which flexibility of method is characteristic of the Cabinet system."[2] In an age when pragmatic rather than ideological considerations determine governmental policies, the need for flexibility would seem to be increasing in importance.

What follows is an attempt to describe the cabinet system as it operated in Canada up to 1972, both in theory and in practice. It is a large subject and it would be impossible to cover it completely, but it is hoped that at least a basis will be provided for future study.

NOTES

[1]Lord Oxford & Asquith, *The Genesis of the War*. (London; Cassell & Company Limited, 1923), p. 3.

[2]A.D.P. Heeney, "Cabinet Government in Canada". *Canadian Journal of Economics and Political Science*, Vol. XII, No. 3 (August, 1946), p. 282.

Chapter I

Cabinet Government in Canada

The cabinet, dominated by the Prime Minister, stands at the apex of the parliamentary system of government in Canada. It usually controls Parliament and thus the law-making process; it determines policy, originates the legislation giving effect to policy, and supervises the carrying out of these policies. It has over the years assumed a degree of independence from Parliament that has given many observers cause for alarm. To some extent this independence is not surprising, since many of the activities and interests within Canadian society that are influenced and regulated by government policy are frequently so complex that the average Member of Parliament lacks the knowledge and experience necessary to understand and control the cabinet's action. In addition, the growth of the convention of strict party discipline has encouraged the independence of the cabinet.

In spite of its dominant role, the Canadian cabinet remains an institution not described or mentioned in any law of the land. There is no law or document that specifically defines the cabinet or its responsibilities, because the cabinet has evolved over a long period of time, adjusting itself as time and circumstances demanded and always retaining a degree of flexibility it would never have possessed if it had been constitutionally defined. This flexibility is characteristic also of the Canadian cabinet's prototype, the British cabinet.

The Origins of Cabinet Government

The British cabinet originated in the Privy Council, the king's private council, which advised him on policy, assisted with administrative duties, and performed some judicial functions. The Privy Council had in turn developed from the Curia Regis, a council of advisors to the king. The Curia Regis eventually divided into two parts; one part, which met in the "Star Chamber", became immersed in judicial matters and was thus unsuitable for advisory and executive action, especially since it was unable to accompany the king on his travels. The second part consisted of a small group of advisors who could travel with the king. This body was the one he usually consulted on political matters and which eventually became known as the Privy Council. This group did not conduct its

1

business in public, and to describe it as "privy" was merely a statement of fact.

In time the Privy Council itself became too large, and the king utilized only a section of it. Because its size made it ineffective, a group of its more important members gradually formed themselves into a smaller or inner council for the purpose of effectively dealing in secret with important matters. In this way there developed a body forming a part of, and yet distinct from, the Privy Council. There are some references to it at this time (approximately 1625) as the Cabinet Council. The term *cabinet* originally meant small room. Cabinet counsel implied secret counsel and Cabinet Council meant those people who gave such advice in the king's own cabinet.

William III (1688-1701) began the practice of using small working parties consisting of the most important office holders to deal with specific matters. The most important of these standing committees of the Privy Council dealt with foreign affairs, but it soon became responsible for all important affairs of state, both domestic and foreign.

There developed a growing distinction between the Privy Council as a whole and the more powerful "efficient" part of it that was responsible for providing advice to the monarch and for implementing policy. Most of the members of this inner circle occupied offices of state that in effect required them to be aware of and to be consulted about the more important acts of government. Under William's successor, Queen Anne (1702-1714), this inner group met frequently to prepare material and recommendations for the full council. The queen, like her predecessors, attended all such meetings and personally made all appointments to the council, which was responsible to her.

The Hanoverian George I (1714-1724) rarely attended full council meetings and, as a result, the inner circle, now known as the "Select Lords", moved into a commanding position; by 1720 it was the chief advisory body on domestic and foreign matters. Important decisions were taken in the king's absence, and by this time one finds the term "cabinet" frequently used to describe what in fact had become the decisive executive body. It must be remembered, however, that the influence of the monarch was still important, and he could always veto any decisions made by the cabinet.

Over time, the membership of the cabinet increased and by 1739 it numbered about twenty men. This increase led to the development of an "inner" and "outer" cabinet. The inner cabinet consisted of the First Lord of the Treasury (Walpole), the Lord Chancellor, the Lord President and two Secretaries of State. It normally met at the home of Sir Robert Walpole, 10 Downing Street, with Walpole assuming a leading role because of his official position and his leadership ability.

The principle had long been established in England that Parliament controlled taxation and thus the monarch and cabinet depended on a vote of Parliament for the funds necessary for the carrying out of the functions of government. It became necessary then for the cabinet to control Parliament and especially the House of Commons, where money bills originated, in order to gain power over finance.

The First Lord of the Treasury played a key role in ensuring this control. At that time the only really large department of government was the Treasury, and the First Lord of the Treasury had a large number of patronage positions at his disposal. It was advantageous for him to sit in the House of Commons and use this patronage to facilitate the passage of money and other bills, and patronage became an important means by which the House of Commons could be controlled by the cabinet. The individual who was First Lord of the Treasury would therefore appear to be the most important minister, and if such a minister also had a talent for administration and leadership he would be assured of the most important role in government. Walpole, who served as First Lord of the Treasury from 1721 to 1742, had these talents, and he became in effect the First or Prime Minister although the term "prime minister" was not yet in vogue. To this day British prime ministers also assume the title of First Lord of the Treasury on taking office. At any rate it would be expected that once the king stopped attending meetings, there would be a natural tendency for some minister to take his place as chairman and conciliator. Walpole's style was similar to that developed by later Canadian prime ministers; ". . . his record indicates that he always preferred peaceful accommodation to heroic defiance."[1]

The assumption of this role by Walpole had important implications for the future development of the cabinet, as well as for leading members. It is important to note, however, that the cabinet at this time was still the personal choice of the monarch, and the necessity of having some of the senior men of the cabinet in the House of Commons for purposes of management and to place before it the various proposals of the government was no great impediment to royal control. Various "rotten boroughs" controlled by the Crown could be used to enable the monarch's choices as ministers to enter the House of Commons if they were not already members on appointment to the cabinet. By the mid-18th century the king was coming to rely on the cabinet more and more, as the cabinet alone was able to secure supply from Parliament. Parliament, however, would only vote supply for specific purposes, as described by departmental policy; thus the control of departmental policy fell to the cabinet because it asked for supply in the king's name. Since it was possible to obtain supply regularly only be means of obtaining a majority in the House of Commons, a very close relationship grew up between the cabinet and the House of Commons. To the principle that the cabinet was responsible to the Crown (since it was appointed by

the monarch), there was added a second element of responsibility —
that of responsibility to the House of Commons — and it came to be
recognized that a cabinet that did not have the support of a majority in
the House of Commons could no longer remain in office. This principle
was clearly recognized in 1782 when Lord North resigned as First Lord
of the Treasury (in effect, Prime Minister) in anticipation of a certain
Parliamentary defeat.

When Lord North resigned in 1782, all his ministers, except one,
resigned as well. Pitt, who became Prime Minister in 1783 (and who was
the first person to find the title personally acceptable) was mainly responsible for the development of the convention that members of the
cabinet, whatever their private disagreements on policy were, should
always present a united front to the outside world. Thus a third level of
responsibility was added. The cabinet now found itself responsible to
the Crown, to the House of Commons, and to itself. Pitt, moreover, had
some very firm ideas about the nature of the office of Prime Minister. He
authorized one of his associates to outline his position to Mr. Adding-
ton. It was essential,

> . . . in the conduct and affairs of this country that there should be an
> avowed and real minister possessing the chief weight in the council and
> the principal place in the confidence of the King. In that respect, there
> can be no rivalry or division of power. That power must rest on the
> person generally called the Prime Minister and that person, he thinks,
> to be the person at the head of the finances . . . if it should come,
> unfortunately, to such a radical difference of opinion that no spirit of
> conciliation or conclusion can reconcile, the sentiments of the minister
> must be allowed and understood to prevail. . . .[2]

Thus it was that the Prime Minister became the dominant figure in the
cabinet, with his will prevailing in times of conflict in the cabinet.

The Reform Act of 1832 had important consequences for the development of the cabinet. It is true that by this time the power of the
monarch had diminished substantially in other areas, but he still held
the power to appoint the Prime Minister and the cabinet. The Reform
Act both eliminated a majority of the rotten boroughs and widened the
franchise, thus altering considerably the political conditions affecting
cabinet government. Now a cabinet could maintain itself in office only
so long as it either retained the confidence of a majority of the House of
Commons or could obtain a majority by appealing to the electorate after
having arranged for a dissolution of Parliament, rather than by retaining
the confidence of the sovereign. Either situation demanded a united
cabinet, and the only basis for such unity was through a political party.
The Crown could no longer choose and retain ministers; about all it
could do now was search for a prime minister who could command the

support of a majority in the House of Commons. Royal influence still existed, but it was a minor rather than a major one. The later Reform Acts broadened the franchise even further, increasing the power of the House of Commons and the cabinet, while the power of the House of Lords and the *personal* power of the monarch declined. After the Reform Acts government responsibilities widened to take into account growing industrialization and the welfare state. The power of the cabinet and the power of the Crown, since all cabinet powers are exercised in the name of the Crown, accelerated. The power of the House of Commons also increased, in that it exercised influence over a wider range of fields than it had done hitherto, but its control over the cabinet continued to decline.

Today the cabinet may be said to be the mainspring of government, even though all acts and decisions coming from it in theory emanate from the Crown. The existence of strict party discipline has assured that whatever disagreements government backbenchers may have with policy, they normally support the cabinet when it comes time to vote, and the cabinet has thus acquired almost complete control over the House of Commons. The increase in responsibilities that has necessitated cabinet control of the agenda of Parliament and the coincident increase in power delegated to the cabinet by Parliament have both contributed to making the cabinet the most powerful organ of government. The Prime Minister's power as leader of the party, which gives him both control of the party machinery and a source of popular support, and his power to appoint members of the cabinet, have made him far more than *primus inter pares* in the cabinet. As long as the party is convinced that the Prime Minister has the ability to win elections, his power remains unchallenged.

At the time of Canadian Confederation (1867) the cabinet in the United Kingdom had not attained the ascendancy it has today. Queen Victoria still retained a degree of control over the cabinet that was not really compatible with the provisions of the Reform Acts, so that involvement by the Crown in the business of the cabinet was not entirely unknown. Moreover, government responsibilities were not as extensive as now, and as a result the civil service was quite small and had little influence on policy. Thus cabinet ministers could supervise their departments and formulate departmental policy, and the cabinet collectively had time to consider all important policy questions. The cabinet as a body decided policy, defended it in the House, and saw to its execution. The Prime Minister's degree of authority varied with the individual, and he was not yet in the exceedingly strong position he is in today. It was in this context that Sir John A. Macdonald formed the first Canadian cabinet in 1867.

The Queen's Privy Council for Canada

Bagehot, in his famous book *The English Constitution*, described the cabinet as ". . . a combining committee — a hyphen which joins, a buckle which fastens the legislative part of the state to the executive part of the state."[3] Such a definition is inadequate, however, when one realizes the immense power of the cabinet; furthermore, it provides no indication of the source of the cabinet's power or of the manner in which this power is exercised.

There is no precise legal definition available of either the British or the Canadian cabinet in a written constitution or a definitive statute. In explaining the workings of the British government, Lord Melbourne told Queen Victoria that ". . . the Ministerial part of the working of executive government was determined largely by practical usage and understanding . . .",[4] and Gladstone said later that the cabinet ". . . lived and acted by understandings without a single line of written law or constitution to determine its relations to the Monarch, to Parliament or to the nation or the relations of its members to one another or to its head."[5] Custom, usage, practice, convention, and a large number of non-legal understandings are the basis for the operation of the cabinet, which even today is in a constant state of change.

There is no mention of the cabinet in the British North America Act of 1867, in any of its amendments, or in any Act of Parliament. The "administration" and the "ministry" and individual ministers are mentioned in various statutes, but never the cabinet itself.[6] There is, however, a firm legal basis for the Queen's Privy Council for Canada. Section II of the BNA Act (1867) provides that:

> There shall be a council to aid and advise in the Government of Canada, to be styled the Queen's Privy Council for Canada, and the Persons who are to be members of that Council shall be from Time to Time chosen and summoned by the Governor General and sworn in as Privy Councillors. . . .

Section 13 of the same Act further specifies that:

> The Provisions of this Act referring to the Governor General in Council shall be construed as referring to the Governor General acting by and with the Advice of the Queen's Privy for Canada.

The first members of the Queen's Privy Council for Canada were sworn in at Ottawa by the Governor General, Viscount Monck, on Monday, July 1, 1867. In addition to taking an oath as a Privy Councillor, each took an oath of office as head of the department of government to which he had been named; i.e., each member of the Privy Council also became a minister. Thus in the beginning membership in the Privy Council and in the cabinet were synonymous. An Act passed by the

Canadian Parliament in 1868 provided salaries for a specified list of ". . . Ministers, Members of the Queen's Privy Council for Canada".[7] It became automatic that new appointees to the thirteen existing portfolios were admitted to the Privy Council on being appointed to these positions. As the number of portfolios increased, this provision was extended to their occupants as well.

Evolution of the Queen's Privy Council for Canada

A problem arose, however, when Hon. A. Archibald of Nova Scotia, who was one of the original cabinet ministers, was defeated in the general election of 1867 and subsequently submitted his resignation as a member of the Privy Council and as a cabinet minister. The Governor General hesitated because he was determined that the Queen's Privy Council for Canada should acquire some of the prestige and distinction possessed by its British counterpart. He told Sir John A. Macdonald that, while he would accept Archibald's resignation as a minister, he would not accept his resignation as a member of the Privy Council unless he was overruled by the Colonial Office in London. Macdonald supported the Governor General and, as a result, Archibald remained a member of the Privy Council and retained the title of "Honourable" for life, although no longer in the cabinet or in Parliament. In this way the cabinet in Canada, as in Britain, became a committee of the Privy Council, consisting of those individuals invited by the Prime Minister to act with him as advisors to the Crown.

The cabinet, then, may be defined as a committee of Privy Councillors whose members have seats in Parliament. The members of the cabinet are appointed to their position by the leader of the political party that commands a majority in the House of Commons. ". . . The Privy Council and Cabinet are two aspects of the same constitutional organism and composed of the same individuals."[8] The Privy Council is a legal entity established for the purpose of tendering advice to the Crown. "The Governor-In-Council is therefore the Governor acting on the formal advice of a quorum of responsible Ministers of the Cabinet. . . ."[9] The cabinet, a non-legal body, concerns itself with making decisions on questions of policy. The implementation of such decisions may require the cabinet to convert itself into a committee of the Privy Council in order to make a submission to the Governor General, or implementation may be carried out via a statement of policy in Parliament. Once signed by the Governor General, the decisions of the cabinet can be described as Acts of the Governor-in-Council.

From 1867 to 1891 the Queen's Privy Council for Canada was made up entirely of cabinet ministers and former cabinet ministers. In May 1891, however, two former Speakers of the House of Commons and three former Speakers of the Senate were sworn in as members of the Privy Council, although they had not been members of the cabinet. Since that time a large number of honorary appointments have been made, and as of October 31, 1972, of the 129 members of the Privy Council, 23 had never been members of the federal cabinet.[10]

The Cabinet and the Crown

A literal interpretation of the BNA Act and of the Letters Patent and the Instructions of the Governor General (that is, the instruments by which he is appointed) would lead one to the conclusion that the Crown is by far the most influential element in the government of Canada. For example, Section 9 of the BNA Act vests all executive authority over Canada in the Queen. The Queen is also Commander-in-Chief of the Armed Forces, must assent to all bills through the Governor General (whom she appoints), and in theory appoints all members of the Privy Council. Legally the Crown and the Crown's representative in Canada have enormous power, but by custom, as in the United Kingdom, the power is exercised by the cabinet.

From the very beginning the Canadian cabinet was able to assume a degree of independence from the Crown far exceeding that enjoyed by its British counterpart and model. The prestige and mystique surrounding the throne in Great Britain enabled Queen Victoria to interfere in the affairs of her cabinets, and her influence and views had to be taken into account when the cabinet was determining policy. In Canada, however, the Governor General was never able to exercise the same amount of influence as the monarch in Great Britain, even though there was nothing in the BNA Act that required the Governor General to accept the advice offered by the cabinet, except in those sections that referred specifically to the Governor-in-Council. Moreover, Canadian politicians were unlikely to be impressed by a transitory governor who usually knew little about the country, and so the constitutional position of the Governor General at the summit of government did not unduly influence or restrain Canadian politicians.

There is, however, some evidence to indicate that in 1867 the British government did expect the Governor General to have a very active part in the governing of Canada, and that it assumed that cabinet government in Canada was to operate so that the Crown, through the Governor General, would take a far more active role than the monarch did in Great Britain. In the instructions given to the first Governor General, Lord Monck, and to his successor, the Earl of Dufferin, the Governor General was assigned responsibility that appeared to make him an active and integral element in the acutal executive of the government.

It was assumed, apparently, that the Governor General would

summon and preside over meetings of the Privy Council, and he was authorized in certain cases to act contrary to advice offered by the Privy Council. Lord Monck, however, wisely interpreted these instructions in the spirit of responsible government and, while frequently consulted by Macdonald, at no time attempted to exert undue influence or to participate in the proceedings of the Privy Council.

Monck's successor, the Earl of Dufferin, had more positive notions of his role. He seemed to be under the impression that he should preside over meetings of the Privy Council, but Macdonald discouraged this practice. According to one author, Dufferin attended meetings of the Privy Council ". . . only on formal or ceremonial occasions, except for one recorded case where Lord Dufferin attended on August 15, 1782."[11] The biographer of the Marquis of Lorne, Dufferin's successor, has a different impression of Dufferin. He notes, "Shortly after his arrival in Ottawa Lorne was astonished by an invitation to sit in Council . . . as public business was discussed. . . . Dufferin had sat like a Stuart monarch and sometimes summarily influenced debate."[12] Lorne refused the invitation and took a far more passive attitude than his precedessors.

Dufferin's high opinion of his office was reflected in a letter he wrote early in his term:

> The Governor-General's opportunities to supervise extend to the most minute matters of administration — about every act of the Government requiring an Order-in-Council, which only becomes valid on his signature being attached to it. The means therefore of checking whatever is going wrong is always ready to his hand.[13]

Dufferin was able to make such an interpretation of his responsibilities by referring to his Instructions. His interference became intolerable to Prime Minister Alexander Mackenzie and his Minister of Justice, Edward Blake, and they set out to effect a change in his Instructions. Blake argued that the Instructions appeared to give the Governor General of Canada a far more active and influential role in government than that enjoyed by the monarch in Great Britain, thus implying that there was a distinction to be made between cabinet government in Great Britain and cabinet government in Canada. As a result of Blake's arguments, almost every clause in the Instructions was removed that could allow the Governor General to hamper the operation of the cabinet. It thus was no longer possible for the Governor General to find anything in his Commission or Instructions that would enable him to take an active part in the conduct of the executive branch of government. The Governor General remains the titular head of the Canadian government, but it is the cabinet that exercises executive power.

Since the time of Dufferin, Governors General have tended to fulfill a ceremonial and social role. When as in the case of Lord Byng, they do become involved, their actions have been regarded as symbolic of inter-ference in the affairs of Canada by Great Britain, regardless of the merits of the constitutional issue involved. (In 1926 the Governor General, Lord Byng, refused to grant a dissolution to Prime Minister King.) What influence has been exerted has been discreet and secretive. An example of this influence is in the comments of Governor General Lord Gray to Prime Minister Borden in 1911, when he objected to the appointment of Colonel Sam Hughes to the cabinet. As a further example, Harold Mac-millan, who served as aide-de-camp to Governor General the Duke of Devonshire, describes in his memoirs how the Governor General ar-ranged a secret meeting between Sir Robert Borden and Sir Lormer Gouin, the Premier of Quebec, in 1919.[14]

Macmillan also noted that:

> In 1919 the functions and duties of a Governor-General were more than ceremonial. . . . He and his office were the chief, if not the only, method of communication between the Canadian and British Govern-ments. Everything of importance passed through him, and was re-ported by him to the Colonial Secretary. The Governor-General, espe-cially if he was a man of political experience, was freely consulted by Ministers and his advice was welcome.[15]

However gratifying the role of messenger and consultant might be, it cannot be regarded as a major constitutional or political one, and it is doubtful if in recent times any Governor General has had a great deal of influence on the cabinet. The role of counsellor still exists, as evidenced by remarks made by Prime Minister Trudeau when paying tribute to former Governor General Michener at the time of his retirement in 1973: ". . . I recall with personal gratitude the many Wednesday nights since 1968 when you have offered me your encouragement and counsel on the nation's business. . . ." In addition to specific changes being made in the position of the Governor General via alterations in the Letters Pa-tent, Instructions, etc., certain formal requirements of the office have been dispensed with over the years. It can be assumed, for example, that by virtue of Section 56 of the BNA Act, copies of all enacted statute law must be forwarded by the Governor General to the British govern-ment. This practice was discontinued many years ago, and it might well be argued that failure to observe this procedure is a technical violation of the BNA Act.

The Instructions to the Governor General are prepared on the ad-vice of the Canadian Prime Minister rather than his British counterpart. Since 1931 the Governor General has been appointed by the monarch on the recommendation of the Canadian Prime Minister, and since 1952 the office has been held by a Canadian. This second development, while being emotionally satisfying to Canadians, may have at the same time detracted from whatever mystique surrounded the position when it was held by a titled Britisher, and downgraded its political importance even more.

It should be noted that occasions for direct intervention in the affairs of the cabinet by the Governor General arise far less frequently in Canada than in Great Britain. The fact that Canadian government has been characterized by lengthy terms of office by one party and one prime minister has resulted in fewer constitutional crises than might have otherwise been the case had there been a frequent turnover of parties and prime ministers. The custom of selecting party leaders by national party conventions, which has been in vogue for the Liberal Party since 1919 and the Conservatives since 1927, has practically eliminated the option of the Governor General to select a particular individual to serve as Prime Minister. A situation similar to that which arose in Great Britain when Mr. Macmillan resigned as Prime Minister and the monarch had to appoint a successor has not arisen in Canada since 1920, and with the possible exception of the 1926 incident, the Governor General has not in fact had an option in selecting a prime minister for the last 75 years.

It is clear that at the present time the Governor General is not influential in the conduct of cabinet government in Canada, and that little attention is paid to him in the day-to-day operation of the government. The vagueness of his role is well illustrated by an exchange in 1970 between Mr. Trudeau and Mr. Diefenbaker in the House of Commons. Mr. Diefenbaker asked, "Has [there] been any change in the traditional policy under which the Queen and her representative in making speeches that in any way contain material that may be of a political nature . . . can only deliver them provided they have the consent and approval of the Prime Minister?" Mr. Trudeau replied, ". . . there has been no change in policy, *whatever it was*, in regard to the relations between the Queen and government."[16] The reply is indicative of the relative unimportance of the office in the operation of cabinet government in Canada at the present time. The position thus has not been of value in uniting the various subcultures of Canada or in serving to help integrate the country. This is in spite of the fact that the position of Governor General involves a great deal of travel and hard work. Mr. Trudeau noted this in saying farewell to Governor General Michener when he said, "In the past 6½ years it seems you have taken 203 official tours. You have delivered 522 formal speeches. You have entertained 109,207 people. And you have travelled . . . count them . . . 267,757 miles."

The Basis of Cabinet Membership
At the time of Confederation, British constitutional theory had reached the point where it was accepted doctrine that the House of Commons

could criticize and dismiss the cabinet by a vote of non-confidence. The monarch had the responsibility to select as Prime Minister someone who was likely to command a majority in the House of Commons; the Prime Minister in turn was free to appoint members of the House of Lords, as well as members of the House of Commons, to the Cabinet. Frequently the monarch had little real choice. If there was a clear majority in the House of Commons supporting an individual as leader, the Crown had no option but to appoint him Prime Minister.

The preamble to the British North America Act of 1867 had specified the desire of the original provinces to be united ". . . with a Constitution similar in principle to that of the United Kingdom". Viscount Monck was therefore following a well-established precedent when he called upon Sir John A. Macdonald to serve as Canada's first Prime Minister, since Macdonald appeared to be the one best able to command a majority of supporters in the House of Commons. Macdonald also followed precedent in retaining only Members of Parliament in his cabinet after the first dominion election. Although there is no legal requirement that a minister be a member of either House, it is understood that he must acquire a seat within a reasonable time. In an unpublished study, Dr. E.A. Forsey has noted that between 1867 and 1962 there have been 68 cases in which people without seats in either the Senate or the House of Commons were taken into the cabinet. Since 1962 there has been only one such case, that of the Hon. C.R. Granger, who was sworn in as a member of the Privy Council and appointed minister without portfolio on September 25, 1967, but was not elected to the House of Commons until November 6, 1967. The longest time any minister has held office without holding a seat was General A.G.L. MacNaughton's tenure as Minister of National Defence — nine-and-a-half months in 1944-1945.

The absence of any precise rule regarding whether or not members of the cabinet must be Members of Parliament illustrates one of the greatest virtues of the Canadian cabinet system — its flexibility. This makes it possible for a prime minister to go outside of Parliament for ministers if he feels it necessary, although it is understood that those selected will find seats as soon as possible. There have been several noteworthy additions to the cabinet from outside Parliament, people usually brought in to strengthen it or to provide representation for a particular group within the Canadian community. The earliest example was the appointment of Sir Francis Hincks as Minister of Finance on October 9, 1869. As far as Macdonald was concerned, there was no one in Parliament as capable of filling this position as was Sir Francis, even though in other respects he was a man of ordinary ability. Again in Laurier's first cabinet, five of the fifteen ministers he appointed were drawn from provincial politics and had had no prior parliamentary experience at the federal level.

The Authority and Power of the Cabinet

The fact that the cabinet consists of Members of Parliament does not necessarily mean that the authority of the cabinet is derived exclusively from Parliament or that it functions as a committee of Parliament. A survey of Hansard, however, would encourage such an idea. Former Prime Minister Bennett said on one occasion, ". . . the Governor-In-Council consists of the Cabinet of the country, a committee of the House of Commons. . . ."[17] Mr. King remarked in 1934, ". . . the government has proceeded in practically everything it has done, as if it were an executive wholly independent of the House of Commons rather than *an executive which derives its powers from and is responsible to the House of Commons.*"[18] Mr. Bracken, Leader of the Opposition, said in 1945, "Except in some *minor* matters where the King's prerogative has not been abridged, the executive or Cabinet act properly only when authority is delegated by the Parliament."[19]

Mr. J.L. Ilsley, the Minister of Finance, speaking in 1945 during a debate on the same subject, gave a more accurate assessment:

> The authority of the government is not delegated by the House. His Majesty's advisers are sworn in as advisers to the Crown. The government is responsible to Parliament but that is a different thing from the doctrine that the Government is a committee of the House of Commons or that it exercises authority delegated by the House of Commons.[20]

The British North America Act of 1867 supports Mr. Ilsley's argument. Section 9 is quite specific: "The Executive Government and Authority of and over Canada is hereby declared to continue and be vested in the Queen." The rights and powers of the executive include ". . . the determination of objectives, the initiation of policy, the manipulation of means, control over the instruments of action, and stimulation of co-ordinated action."[21] These rights and powers are exercised by the cabinet as advisers to the Crown; thus it is clear that the right to exercise these powers does not derive from Parliament, but from the Constitution. The legal existence of the government is derived from the Crown. The authority of the Queen is delegated to the Governor General through the Letters Patent, the Instruments, and the Commission; that is, the instruments by which the Governor General is appointed to office. Thus the Letters Patent of 1947 specifically provided that the Governor General, on the advice of the Privy Council of Canada, may exercise ". . . any or all of the Sovereign's power with respect to Canada". The cabinet in fact exercises these powers as a result of the fact that it is composed of those members of the Privy Council who have the responsibility of advising the Crown, advice which the Crown must accept. Authority then flows from the Crown via the Privy Council to the cabinet.

It has been argued that since all government departments in Canada are created by Act of Parliament, the power of a minister as a department head comes from Parliament; since the ministers, as a group, form the cabinet, the source of the cabinet's power must be Parliament. It should be noted, however, that on entering the cabinet each minister takes two oaths. One of these is as a Privy Councillor and it reads as follows:

> You will serve Her Majesty truly and faithfully in the place of her Counsel in this Her Majesty's Dominion of Canada, you will keep close and secret all such matters as shall be treated, debated and resolved on in Privy Council, without publishing or disclosing the same or any part thereof, by word, writing or any otherwise to any person out of the same Council, but to such only as be of the Council.

It is this oath that provides entré to the cabinet and enables the minister to act as an advisor to the Crown, not the oath taken as a departmental head.

The right to exercise executive power is derived from the constitution The actual executive powers of the Crown (exercised by the cabinet) can be divided under two headings — prerogative powers and powers delegated by Parliament (statutory powers). The prerogative powers are those powers of the sovereign that have never been formally delegated to any other government organ and which are exercised by the cabinet on behalf of the sovereign. These powers include:

i summoning, prorogation, and dissolution of Parliament, exercised in Canada solely on advice from the Prime Minister;

ii participation in international affairs, including the appointment of diplomats, negotiation and ratification of treaties, participation in international meetings, recognition of foreign governments (reference to Parliament is necessary only in those cases where legislation must be passed to give effect to provisions of treaties or to authorize expenditures agreed to under a treaty);

iii granting of clemency;

iv originating and recommending money bills to Parliament.

Secondly, the cabinet as executive exercises statutory powers delegated to it by Parliament. It is not possible for Parliament to take into account all circumstances and conditions when passing legislation, and thus it delegates to the executive the power to make additional rules and in some cases to act as a final court of appeal for administrative decisions. Almost every statute passed by Parliament grants to the executive the power to make additional rules. Mr. Robert McCleave, an opposition Member has noted: "I would point out that about three out of every four statutes that parliamentarians pass contain at least one section that enables regulations to be made."[22] A special study revealed ". . . that 303 of 416 statutes examined contained power to make subordinate laws . . . 6,892 regulations covering 19,972 pages were published during the period January 1, 1956 to December 31, 1968, average 520 regulations per year."[23]

In delegating power to make regulations, Parliament may have undermined its own position by relinquishing part of its legislative responsibility to the cabinet and in the process reducing its ability to control the cabinet. "It is obvious that the direct result of this increase of delegated legislation has been a gradual erosion of the power of Parliament in its role as guardian of the people of Canada."[24] It is difficult to see, however, how this could be avoided in the light of the volume of demands made on the government and the complexity of the matters for which it must assume responsibility. The result has been that Parliament has become an arena for debate and for the ventilation of grievances and is not the chief law-making body, which now consists of the cabinet and the civil service.

Prior to 1971, there was a requirement that all regulations issued by the Governor-in-Council, Treasury Board, a minister, or any official or agency of the government must be published in the *Canada Gazette* and be tabled in Parliament. There was also a provision that made it possible for the government to exempt certain regulations from these requirements, which in any case did not include regulations issued by certain government agencies such as crown corporations, and it was therefore possible for many administrative rules and regulations to be kept secret. No fundamental change was made with reference to the use of delegated power under the provisions of the Statutory Instruments Act of 1971.[25] The new Act provides that all statutory instruments will be referred to a parliamentary scrutiny committee, but the committee has no power to take action other than to criticize; its recommendations will have no compulsory effect and can be ignored by cabinet. It is unlikely then that the cabinet will be any more responsible to Parliament than it has been in the past, especially since it will be able to exempt the publication of certain regulations and thus there will be no guarantee of scrutiny.

Cabinet Responsibility

As in Great Britain, cabinet responsibility in Canada has three meanings. Appointed by and acting in the name of the Crown, the cabinet is responsible for acts performed in the name of the Crown on the ancient principle that the Crown can do no wrong. In reality, the cabinet is responsible to the Prime Minister. It is he, rather than the representative of the Crown, who effectively appoints and dismisses ministers. Thus in

1944 Mr. King, not the Governor General, accepted Mr. Ralston's resignation from the cabinet, and in 1962 Mr. Harkness addressed his letter of resignation to the Prime Minister. (Both Mr. Ralston and Mr. Harkness were Ministers of Defence.) In 1965 Mr. Pearson, not the Governor General, demanded the resignation of Mr. Dupuis, a minister without portfolio.

The members of the cabinet are also responsible to Parliament, both individually and collectively. The minister, as the political head of a department, is held responsible for everything that is done in that department, and thus he has the final word in all important decisions since he can be criticized by Parliament and in theory penalized for exercising powers delegated to him. Responsibility to Parliament then requires the cabinet to explain its actions to Parliament and to answer questions posed by the opposition and, in some cases, its own backbenchers.

The fact that the cabinet is responsible to Parliament does not mean that Parliament controls the cabinet. As Mr. Lapointe noted, "This House of Commons can dismiss the government after it has acted because the action of the government does not meet the approval of the House of Commons, but it cannot instruct the Governor in Council what should be done."[26] In fact this would seem to be true only in a minority government situation; very few cabinets in Canadian history have been defeated in the House of Commons. Parliament is in effect controlled by the cabinet rather than vice versa, and has become in most cases merely the institution through which policy already decided upon by the cabinet is passed in order to meet the prescribed procedural tests necessary for the enactment of legislation. It would seem that Lloyd George's comments to a Parliamentary Committee in Great Britain in 1931 are equally applicable to the Canadian situation. "Parliament has really no control over the executive, it is pure fiction."[27]

The influence of Parliament is by no means negligible, however, and government bills are sometimes amended after being introduced in Parliament, or the debate during the passage of a bill will introduce the issues presented to the electorate in a subsequent election. The pipeline debate of 1956, when Parliament finally passed a bill after much formal debate, provided the major issues fought in the 1957 election, which led to the defeat of the Liberal Party after 22 years in power. The electorate, then, is the body that makes or unmakes cabinets. The cabinet's responsibility to Parliament is thus usually a formal one, although when there is a minority government the House of Commons may have more influence than when the government has a majority. Even then, the fact that the majority in the House is divided among several parties which do not always combine in votes helps the cabinet to remain relatively secure. Usually, then, the House of Commons is the locale of "happenings", the arena for conflict between the cabinet and the opposition, rather than the locale of effective control. The results of this conflict are continually reported to the electorate and thus influence it in making its judgment during general elections.

The cabinet is able to dominate Parliament due to the nature of the party system, a system that effects a very great change in the theoretical pattern of government. Usually during Canadian history the same party has controlled both the cabinet and the House of Commons. The tradition of strict party discipline ensures the control of Parliament by the senior men of the governing party, the cabinet, and as long as the Prime Minister retains his mastery of the cabinet he controls Parliament.

There is a third aspect of cabinet responsibility that is significant. In addition to being responsible to the Crown and to Parliament, the members of the cabinet are responsible to one another. Possibly the best explanation of the principle of cabinet solidarity was given by Sir Wilfrid Laurier:

> The gentlemen who are assembled at the Council Board are not expected to be any more unanimous in their views because they sit at Council than would be expected from any other body of men . . . the Council acts for the purpose of examining the situation and, having examined it, then to come to a solution, which solution becomes a law to all those who choose to remain in the Cabinet . . . the necessity for solidarity between the members of the Cabinet is absolute, that the moment a policy has been determined upon then it becomes the duty of every member of that administration to support it and support it in its entirety.[28]

Laurier went on to say that even if a minister was convinced that an agreed-upon policy was not the best, he may remain in the cabinet only if ". . . he thinks that on the whole, it is better that his views on that subject should give way to the views of others." Moreover, if a cabinet member advocates reform of an existing policy ". . . the reform has to be advocated in the first place in the Cabinet of which he is a member."

For the first hundred years since Confederation this practice was interpreted to mean that ministers never disagreed publicly, either before or after a policy was settled upon. Actual examples of public disagreements are very rare. One of the most noteworthy was the attempt of Hon. Israel Tarte, Laurier's Minister of Public Works, to change the policy of the government on the matter of protection by making a series of public speeches advocating higher tariffs. Laurier, who was abroad when Tarte began his campaign, returned home and promptly fired the minister. In Laurier's view there was to be no questioning of the doctrine of cabinet solidarity in the Canadian system.

After Mr. Trudeau took office there was evidence to indicate that this practice of cabinet solidarity was being significantly altered. For several months cabinet ministers debated matters of government policy in public, and some sharp differences of opinion on significant matters were noted. When questioned on this matter in the House of Commons, Mr. Trudeau replied:

> A decision which has become government policy is not debatable by ministers. All of them are responsible for the decision and all of them must abide by it or else withdraw from the Cabinet. However, regarding policies that are in the formulative stage, regarding priorities that the government will have to decide upon in the future . . . ministers and all members of the government party are encouraged to discuss, not only in the House but in the country, all kinds of new ideas conducive to the progress and dynamic future of the country.[29]

This statement marked a new interpretation of the meaning of cabinet solidarity and it would have been interesting to see how it affected the cabinet once such policy decisions had been taken. The opposition party would be bound to make much of a minister's earlier stated opposition to a government policy, and his integrity could well have been questioned. Fear of such criticism, on the other hand, could seriously retard the formation of policy and leave the initiative for making change to anonymous civil servants. This, however, turned out to be a short-lived experiment because of the embarrassment caused to the government as ministers quarrelled publicly, and the old system of solidarity seems to have been restored.

Cabinet responsibility in the third sense, then, means that every member of the cabinet must accept and support decisions made by the cabinet, even if he is not present when the decision is taken or indeed even if he is unaware of it. Regardless of whether the decision-making process is fragmented or collegial, once the decision is taken it is binding on every cabinet member.

After policy has been decided upon and appropriate legislation passed, the policy may be put into effect in one of four ways:

1. The minister may take action himself; that is, under authority delegated by Parliament, the minister may make certain rules and regulations. It should be noted that up to the present time each department of government has been created by a statute which usually defines the functions of the department by specifying that the minister of the department is empowered to administer specific Acts of Parliament. As will be pointed out later, the collegial nature of the Canadian cabinet tends to discourage ministers from acting individually.

2. The cabinet acting collectively may take action. This is typically Canadian and provides some very important advantages. When the cabinet acts collectively each minister is provided with an opportunity to become informed on a wide range of important matters beyond the scope of his own department, and in the process every minister becomes more conscious of the implications of policy in all its aspects. The practice of

participating in cabinet decision making, however, has not been interpreted to mean that ministers are free to speak out in public on policy matters directly affecting other departments, as demonstrated by Mr. Kierans' experience in 1971 when he began to speak out on economic policy, a field in which he had no direct responsibility. If the new committee system of the cabinet reduces the scope for collective action the result may be that only the Prime Minister will be in a position to be well informed, and ministers may become specialists in particular fields, depending on their cabinet committee assignments.

3. Action may be taken through a special committee of the cabinet; an example is the special committee established for the purpose of passing routine Orders-in-Council, covering matters that do not involve major questions of policy or introduce subject matter not previously discussed by the cabinet.

4. Action may be taken through a statutory committee of the Privy Council — for example, the Treasury Board, which acts as a Board of Management for the cabinet in particular areas of responsibility such as the supervision of government spending, staff relations, and interdepartmental co-ordination.

It should be noted that there are times when the cabinet can take action that has the effect of altering or going beyond the original intention of Parliament. At times when Parliament has passed a law, the cabinet acting as Governor-in-Council has seen fit to proclaim only part of that law and to thus delay bringing other parts into effect. After Parliament had passed a law in 1969 relating to breathalyzer tests, the cabinet proclaimed only certain sections of the Act approved by Parliament, and in so doing altered the original intent. The original bill provided that a motorist requested to take a breathalyzer test had the right to have an independent analysis made of the alcoholic content of his breath. This section of the Act was not proclaimed when other sections were because it was impossible to develop a container that would preserve breath long enough for the independent analysis to be made. An opposition member of the House of Commons charged that such action was ". . . a form of selective delegation which warps the meaning and intent of Parliament."[30] The omission of parts of the Act from the proclamation had the effect of "removing the integral part of the section, a safeguard given to the subject in a matter of penal law and saying we, the Cabinet, are going to pass this law in a different form from that approved by Parliament."[31] The Supreme Court of Canada has ruled that the cabinet may legitimately do this when the Act makes the time and manner of the coming into force of the Act or any of its provisions conditional upon the exercise of discretion by the Governor-in-Council.[32] This places in the hands of the cabinet the ability to alter to some extent the already expressed will of Parliament. The fact that this may be justified by technical reasons or because of different circumstances does not change the fact that the cabinet can, even after Parliament has spoken, exert its will upon legislation.

Specific Responsibilities of Ministers

In addition to participating in the collective work of the cabinet, each minister has a variety of specific duties to perform. Most ministers are heads of government departments and are responsible for the administration of their departments and play a role in departmental policy formation. The minister must see the potential effect of policy proposals made by departmental officials not only on his own department but on the entire government as well. In doing so he must be careful not to be overawed by his advisors who are generally experts in their own particular field and who consequently may not have taken a broad view of policy implications. He must pay close attention to public opinion in order to avoid serious criticism of his department. This in turn requires him to appear frequently in public and to keep in touch with opinion throughout the country. In addition, the cabinet minister as a political leader and representative of a particular region or group must devote time to the responsibilities arising out of this position, and he must also look after the needs of the constituents he represents in Parliament. He must also find time to attend sessions of Parliament. Mr. Pearson remarked on the problem thus created for ministers of:

> . . . how to reconcile the political, parliamentary and governmental aspects of their responsibilities. Departmental management is now a complex and difficult task with the subjects to be dealt with going far beyond, in nature and in scope, those that faced ministers 50 years ago. A minister needs more than full time to deal with them. . . . Yet ministers are also politicians and parliamentarians and must spend time on these duties. The reconciliation of these three commitments to government, to politics and to parliament is difficult.[33]

The cabinet is then the supreme decision-making organ in our system of government. It is, as advisor to the Crown, and as a result of its control over the House of Commons, at the apex of the constitutional system. Because it assumes responsibility for the administration of government, it has become the highest administrative body. As will be described later the cabinet stands at the top of the party system; it is the object and centre of political struggle. Finally, it is an elite, a group of individuals whose personlaity, background, and temperament all affect the quality of the decisions of government. As an elite it has served as an integrating force in Canada, reconciling the various subcultures and thus ensuring effective and stable government.

NOTES

[1]A.S. Foord, *His Majesty's Opposition 1714-1830*. (London; Oxford University Press, 1964), p. 123.

[2]Quoted in John Ehrman, *The Younger Pitt*. (London; Constable, 1969) p. 281.

[3]W. Bagehot, *The English Constitution*. (London; Fontana Library edition, 1963), p. 68.

[4]*Letters of Queen Victoria*, First Series, Vol. 1. (London; J. Murray, 1908) p. 358.

[5]W.E. Gladstone, *Gleanings of Past Years, 1843-1878*, Vol. 1. (London; J. Murray, 1878), p. 241.

[6]See for example, *Revised Statutes of Canada*, 1970 Vol. III, Chapter F-14, Sections 4-5; Vol. VII, Chapter S-15, Sections 1-6.

[7]*Revised Statutes of Canada*, 1970 Vol. VI, Chapter S-2, Section 4.

[8]W.E.D. Halliday, "The Executive of the Government of Canada". *Canadian Public Administration*, Vol. II, No. 4 (December, 1959), p. 231.

[9]R. Mac G. Dawson, "The Cabinet-Position and Personnel". *Canadian Journal of Economics and Political Science*, Vol. XII, No. 3 (August, 1946) p. 264.

[10]*The Canadian Parliamentary Guide*, 1972.

[11]J.R. Mallory, "Cabinets and Councils in Canada". *Public Law*, Vol. II, No. 3 (Autumn, 1957), p. 233.

[12]W.S. McNutt, *Days of Lorne*. (Fredericton; Brunswick Press, 1955), pp. 127-128.

[13]Quoted in C. De Kiewiet and Frank Underhill, *Dufferin-Carnarvon Correspondence, 1874-1878*. (Toronto; Champlain Society, 1955), p. 240.

[14]Harold Macmillan, *Winds of Change, 1914-1939*. (London; Macmillan, 1966), p. 114.

[15]*Ibid.*, pp. 110-111.

[16]Canada, House of Commons, *Debates*. (April 29, 1970), p. 6409 (emphasis added).

[17]*Ibid.* (March 23, 1932), p. 1408.

[18]*Ibid.* (January 29, 1934), p. 42 (emphasis added).

[19]*Ibid.* (October 31, 1945), p. 1681 (emphasis added).

[20]*Ibid.* (November 12, 1945), p. 2022.

[21]Michael Curtis, *Comparative Government and Politics*. (New York; Harper & Row, 1968), p. 202.

[22]Canada, House of Commons, *Debates*. (January 25, 1971), p. 2738.

[23]*Ibid.*

[24]*Ibid.* (January 25, 1971), p. 2735.

[25]*Statutes of Canada*, Chapter 38, Third Session, 28th Parliament, 19-20 Elizabeth II, 1970-71.

[26]Canada, House of Commons, *Debates*. (May 30, 1938), p. 3372.

[27]Great Britain, Parliament. *Special Report from the Select Committee on Procedure in Public Business*. (London; H.M. Stationery Office, 1932), p. 125.

[28]Canada, House of Commons, *Debates*. (March 18, 1903), p. 132-3.

[29]*Ibid.* (February 4, 1969), p. 5110-5111.

[30]*Ibid.* (April 6, 1970), p. 5487.

[31]*Ibid.*

[32]*Reference re Proclamation of Section 16 of the Criminal Law Amendment Act, 1968-1969*. Dominion Law Reports, Vol. 10, 1970, p. 699.

[33]Rt. Hon. L.B. Pearson, *Politics and Participation*. Address, Dominion Chalmers United Church, Ottawa, Ontario, November 7, 1968.

Chapter II

The Cabinet as a Representative Body

Mechanism of Accommodation

The Canadian cabinet has been far more than "a buckle or a hyphen" fastening together the legislative and executive aspects of government. In addition to fulfilling legislative and executive functions of government, the cabinet has served to join together the political elites of the two major cultural groups, the various religious groups, and the major geographic areas. Thus the Canadian cabinet has reflected both the federal *and* pluralistic nature of Canadian society and has played an important role in counteracting the immobilizing and unstabilizing effects of Canadian pluralism. The Canadian cabinet, in addition to the functions normally expected of it in a parliamentary system, has also become a mechanism of accommodation, the truly federal body in Canada, fulfilling the forecast made by Christopher Dunkin at the Quebec Conference in 1865 that the cabinet in Canada would perform the same function as the Senate in the United States — i.e., be the significant federal institution. Consequently, the Canadian system of government seems to fit fairly well with the consociational model of democracy described by Lijphart, Daalder, Noel, and McRae.[1]

The Consociational Model

A consociational democracy may be defined as a democracy with subcultural cleavages tending towards immobilism and instability but which is deliberately turned into a stable system by the leaders of the major subcultures. In the specific context of Canada, it has been noted that ". . . the lack of a pan-Canadian identity combined with strong regional subcultures is not necessarily a dysfunctional feature in terms of the successful operation of a federal system, as long as within each subculture demands are effectively articulated through its political elite."[2]

The consociational model makes several important assumptions about political life in such a democracy. The key word in the definition is articulation and one Canadian writer has noted that since 1867 in Canada ". . . what has been sought, and to some degree achieved is not really unification, but the articulation of regional patterns in one trans-continental state."[3] It would appear essential that the demands of the various subcultures be articulated in a politically effective body — the cabinet. By having channels of articulation open to the subcultures and by providing a mechanism whereby the articulated demands of the sub-groups are accommodated satisfactorily, the Canadian political system has attempted to deal with the problems created by pluralism in Cana-dian society.

Effective articulation of demands made within a stable political sys-tem requires that the elites of the various subcultures have the ability to recognize the dangers inherent in fragmentation of the system — that is, to prefer the maintenance of the existing system to the alternative of several independent systems. In other words, the elites must have a strong commitment to the maintenance of the system. This does not require a strong sense of nationalism (in a pan-Canadian sense), but it does require that the elites value the system positively and that they be prepared to help preserve the system by deliberately working to check its continuing tendency to distintegrate. Articulation, commitment, and preservation are all key concepts in the consociational model.

The establishment and maintenance of a consociational democracy makes demands on the masses as well as on the elites. The masses must have confidence in the elites who participate in the process of accom-modation and be deferential to them. If the elites lose touch with the masses and are no longer considered representative of them, the deli-cate balance of the consociational state will be endangered.

The stability of a consociational democracy will also be helped if the important subcultures are isolated from one another, either geographi-cally or culturally, so that contacts among members of the subcultures are limited, thus minimizing stress on the system. A useful side effect of isolation among such groups is the greater likelihood of cohesion within them. A subculture that has a cohesive and tightly organized social structure, as was the case in Quebec prior to the Quiet Revolution, is more likely to provide support for, and deference to, its elites than a subculture that has sharp internal divisions. It may also happen that in a situation where there are two major subcultures, with one being not only linguistically and culturally distinct from the other but also severely outnumbered, stability will be assisted if the numerically superior group is spread over a large geographic area and lacks the cultural cohesion of the smaller group. In such cases regional, rather than cultural, issues may divide the larger group, thus preventing it from combining against the smaller one. The overwhelming importance of regional interests in English Canada then may be a factor in maintaining the operation of the Canadian system of government.

The First Cabinet

The necessity of accommodation was evident in Macdonald's first cabinet and was in a sense not really a new development. The practice of including representatives from various areas and interest groups within the country was a continuation of a practice followed in the formation of governments in the old Province of Canada. In that situation it had been the custom for the Executive Council of the Province of Canada to include a balanced representation of members from various regions and the French and British races, as well as French and non-French Roman Catholics. As Creighton has noted, ". . . there had to be in every self respecting administration two members from the District of Quebec and three from the District of Montreal. One of these had to be British, not a French Canadian." If there were two British, then one ". . . might be usefully an Irish Roman Catholic."[4]

After Confederation the task of cabinet building was not unlike that which Macdonald had faced in the Province of Canada, with the additional complication that membership in his cabinet had to be limited to supporters of Confederation from both political parties in each of the provinces. Macdonald found the task of forming his first cabinet under these circumstances extremely difficult; indeed at one point he considered giving up the attempt and advising Lord Monck to ask George Brown to assume the responsibility. He persevered, however, and eventually succeeded in forming a cabinet containing representatives of all four provinces, both major language groups, and the significant religious groups, with important subsequent effects on the operation of the cabinet system in Canada.

The first Canadian cabinet consisted of thirteen members. This number ". . . was not determined by consideration for an efficient and economical departmental division of the executive authority, but was the result of the provincial, racial and religious representation of the first federal administration formed by Sir John A. Macdonald."[5]

Macdonald took for himself the portfolio of Minister of Justice and created the following additional posts: Militia, Marine, Agriculture, Postmaster-General, Secretary of State for Canada, Secretary of State for the Provinces, Public Works, Customs, Inland Revenue, Receiver-General, Finance, and President of the Privy Council. These were distributed among five representatives from Ontario (including Macdonald himself), four representatives from Quebec, and two each from Nova Scotia and New Brunswick. There were three French Canadians and one English Canadian from Quebec, and a total of nine Protestants and four Roman Catholics, including one Irish Catholic. Of the positions created by Macdonald, the two positions of Secretary of State could have been combined, the portfolios of Customs, Inland Revenue, Receiver-General and Finance could have been combined into one and the position of President of the Pricy Council involved no departmental responsibilities at all, so that the cabinet could have quite easily consisted of only nine members had efficiency been the only criterion employed. The representation principle triumphed however for, as Macdonald told Parliament on April 3, 1868, his objective was ". . . to have such a large full Cabinet as would secure a proper representation of all parts of the Dominion."[6] Macdonald's cabinet was also designed to win votes and Macdonald was pleased with the outcome. Races and creeds as well as geography were represented and a precedent well-established.

The Establishment of Precedents

When Mackenzie succeeded Macdonald as Prime Minister in 1873, he followed the precedent established by his predecessor, although he complained that the exigencies of sectional representation deprived him of needed executive ability. Mackenzie was nevertheless pleased with his creation; especially satisfying was the religious balance. The cabinet included four Catholics, three Presbyterians, three Anglicans, two Methodists, one Congregationalist, and one Baptist (himself). Mackenzie was to suffer for emphasizing these qualities over ability, for the cabinet turned out to be inept and nondescript.

When Macdonald became Prime Minister for a second time in 1878, he continued the custom he established in 1867, and in his cabinet there were an equal number of ministers from Ontario and Quebec, two each from Nova Scotia and New Brunswick, and one from Prince Edward Island. Macdonald himself sat for a constituency in British Columbia and hence acted as western representative. He kept an eye on religious representation as well. It was noted that Macdonald appointed Sir George Foster as Minister of Marine and Fisheries in 1885 because Foster was a Baptist, an influential denomination that had not hitherto been represented in the cabinet. The leading candidate for the position was a Roman Catholic, and to have given him the appointment would have given that religion disproportionate representation.

In 1896 Laurier managed to construct a cabinet balanced in terms of geography, religion, and race. Borden, his successor, attempted to adhere to the same principle in 1911, with cabinet membership broadly representative of the whole country, although some of his ministers were of questionable ability. Meighen, Borden's successor, in order to give Quebec representation in his cabinet during 1920-1921, took in four ministers from that province, all of whom lacked seats in Parliament. King attached great importance to the representation principle, going so far in 1921 as to arrange for the election of a former premier of Alberta,

TABLE 2-I

Summary of Cabinet Representation After Cabinet Formation by Language Group, Religion and Province

Year	Prime Min.	Language Group		Religion			Province										Total
		Engl.	Fr.	Prot.	Cath.	Other	Ont.	P.Q.	N.S.	N.B.	Man.	B.C.	PEI.	Sask.	Alta.	Nfld.	
1867	Macdonald	10	3	9	4		5	4	2	2							13
1873	Mackenzie	11	3	10	4		6	3	2	2			1				14
1878	Macdonald	11	3	10	4		4	4	2	2		1	1				14
1896	Laurier	11	3	11	3		4	5	2	1	1		1				14
1911	Borden	15	3	14	4		7	5	1	1	2	1			1		18
1917	Borden	20	2	19	3		9	4	2	1	2	1		1	2		22
1920	Meighen	16	1	15	2		6	3	2	1	2	1		1	1		17
1921	King	14	5	12	7		6	6	1	1	1	2	1	1			19
1930	Bennett	16	3	14	5		7	5	1	1	1	1	1	1	1		19
1935	King	11	5	10	6		4	5	1	1	1	1		3			16
1948	St. Laurent	14	6	13	7		7	6	2	1	1	1		1	1		20
1957	Diefenbaker	19	2	16	4	1*	6	3	1	1	2	3	1	2	1	1	21
1963	Pearson	16	9	13	12		10	7	1	1	1	2		1	1	1	25
1968	Trudeau	20	9	15	14		10	10	1	1	1	3		1	1	1	29
1974	Trudeau (October 1974)	20	9	11	17	1**	10	11	1	1	1	2	1		1	1	29

* Ukrainian Catholic
**Jewish

Sources: *Guide to Canadian Ministries since Confederation*
Who's Who in Canada
Directory of Members of Parliament
Parliamentary Guide

Charles Stewart, in a Quebec constituency, so that Stewart could represent Alberta in the cabinet. This confirmed his statement in the House of Commons after forming his first cabinet: "There can be nothing more unfortunate for this Dominion than that any part of it should have come to feel it is not to have its voice in the councils of the country."[7]

Bennett had difficulty in forming a balanced cabinet in 1930. Out of a total of nineteen men whom he named to office, only three were French Canadians and five were Roman Catholics. Each province had at least one representative, while Ontario had seven and Quebec five, but the claims of Ontario were difficult to ignore in favour of Quebec, since it had elected 59 members from the Conservative Party compared with Quebec's 24 in the 1930 general elections.

King also adhered to the representation principle in forming the 1935 cabinet, giving every province except Alberta a cabinet member, with Quebec getting five and Ontario four out of a total of sixteen. There were five French Canadians and six Roman Catholics. Mr. St. Laurent adhered to the pattern developed over the years, in spite of the fact that he hoped it would be established" . . . that it is not a matter of one's religion or race, that it is solely one's position as a Canadian citizen that determines whether one will be fitted for the highest offices in the land."[8] Mr. Diefenbaker, as noted later, was criticized for not giving French Canadians sufficient places in the cabinet, but his selections followed the familiar representation pattern and he made one important innovation, appointing the first woman to the Canadian cabinet, the Hon. Ellen Fairclough. Mr. Pearson's cabinet included representatives from all provinces with Liberal representation in the House of Commons, including Manitoba and Alberta, which had each elected only one Liberal in the 1963 election. The first Trudeau cabinet included members from Nova Scotia, Newfoundland, and Saskatchewan, each of which had only one Liberal member in the House of Commons. An analysis of representation in the cabinet after the formation of most Canadian cabinets is provided in Table 2-I.

It is now impossible for a prime minister to disregard these precedents in the formation of a cabinet. The practice of ensuring representation from provinces and groups has now broadened into a rigid convention of the Canadian constitution and has had several important effects on the conduct of Canadian government.

The Position of the Prime Minister

The first effect of the representation principle has been to enhance the role of the Prime Minister, for he, and he alone, becomes the only truly national figure in the cabinet. His colleagues are limited in importance because of their narrower constituencies; they are delegates. Thus, when Mr. Trudeau was asked in the House of Commons who was filling in for the then Minister of Energy, Mr. Greene, during his illness, he replied quite correctly, "The Minister without Portfolio from Saskatchewan, Mr. Lang."[9] To the public mind the Prime Minister becomes the leading light, far more than *primus inter pares*. This can be a source of great personal power for the Prime Minister, for in difficult times he may appear to go over the heads of his colleagues and opponents and appeal to the masses for support. It has been noted that in times of exceptional stress leaders ". . . rely on a particularly intense dramatization of the function of leadership in order to perform their difficult roles".[10] The national status of the Prime Minister automatically draws attention to him and makes such dramatization easier, as he can assume a symbolic role and derive support from the masses. The October crisis of 1970 and the attention focused on Mr. Trudeau possibly exemplifies this, providing the Prime Minister with power independent of Parliament and the cabinet.

It is also important to note that by permitting ministers to be spokesmen for various groups, the Prime Minister helps to prevent ministers from achieving national prominence and thus becoming potential rivals, while at the same time enhancing his own role as conciliator and peacemaker.

The Style of Government

A second effect of the representation principle is that a Prime Minister, in order to be successful and to keep together a cabinet composed of representatives of so many diverse groups, must adopt a style of operation that often appears unattractive and uninspiring to the public. Precisely because the cabinet must be representative of diverse groups, it is essential to have a leader who, having brought the cabinet together, can keep it together. If the Prime Minister is able to manipulate men who are leaders of strong interests in their own right, then one can expect strong government. If, however, the Prime Minister is not able to bring into his cabinet the effective leaders of important groups or cannot neutralize differences of opinion among cabinet members through his own skill and personality, or cannot guide the cabinet to a program on which all can unite, ineffective government will likely be the consequence. It is not an accident that the three prime ministers who have had the greatest success in holding onto the office — Macdonald, Laurier, and King — had tremendous ability to keep divergent interests together. A prime minister who can do this becomes indispensable, and his importance, relative to that of his colleagues, is enhanced even more.

This style of leadership, however, is usually unattractive and undramatic. Macdonald's tendency to procrastinate was reflected in the sobriquet "Old Tommorow". Laurier was said to have had a talent for inaction and King seemed to believe that the things he did not do were as important as the things he did do. Such an approach is neither dramatic nor exciting, nor is it likely to stimulate the enthusiasm of the population. Mr. Pearson has said:

> No strong man in the emotionally satisfying sense has ever ruled this country — none will if it is to survive. Attempting to reconcile what appears to be the irreconcilable will continue to be the task of Prime Ministers and in this task Prime Ministers tend to look uninspiring.[11]

The resultant style is typical of consociational democracies. In such democracies compromise is essential in resolving issues. If a mutually acceptable compromise is not possible, the solution least offensive to all is frequently the one settled upon. This readiness to compromise requires that the leaders not only be flexible, but that they be keenly sensitive to what political and social reality will allow, as well as have the trust of the rank and file who probably do not have this sensitivity. The continual need to compromise leads to a prudent style of politics, a style unlikely to be exciting or glamorous.

The Level of Competence

A third result of the representation principle is that the level of competence in the Canadian cabinet is not generally as high as one might like. A cabinet of *"all the talents"* is probably impossible in Canada, although Laurier came close to one in 1896 when he imported from the provinces a large number of premiers to serve under him. Very often political considerations, rather than the needs of the country, determine who gets into the cabinet. In this way, Sir Charles Tupper was excluded from Macdonald's first cabinet so that the inconsequential Kenny from Nova Scotia could be appointed to represent the Irish Catholics. Laurier was left out of Mackenzie's cabinet in favour of Cauchon, who had little talent but good connections in Quebec City and good relationships with the Quebec clergy. Peter Heenan was appointed Minister of Labour in 1926 by Mr. King, even though King had reservations about his ability for this position. Heenan, however, was a locomotive engineer (popular with labour), a Roman Catholic (a group under-represented in the cabinet), and was from northern Ontario, which had been demanding a representative in the federal cabinet for some time.

It would seem, then, that every cabinet must contain at least a few dullards or nonentities to represent some important interest. Adherence to the representation principle has had the effect of severely limiting the ability of the Prime Minister to pick the most desirable cabinet ministers, and consequently also probably discourages able Members of Parliament from remaining in office for a long period of time. In Mr. Pearson's cabinet, Mr. Hays and Mr. Teillet were the only Liberal members of the House of Commons from Alberta and Manitoba and could have been excluded from the cabinet only with great difficulty and at serious political risk, regardless of their competence. Mr. Jamieson, Mr. MacEachen, and Mr. Lang, ministers from Newfoundland, Nova Scotia, and Saskatchewan respectively in the first Trudeau cabinet, were in a similar position. The pre-eminence of the representation principle illustrates very clearly the lack of ideological commitment of the two main Canadian political parties. The fact that it is possible to have a Howe and a Pearson, a McCutcheon and an Alvin Hamilton, a Walter Gordon and a Robert Winters, a Jean Marchand and a Mitchell Sharp serving together in the same cabinet in spite of obviously different ideological viewpoints indicates that ideological agreement is hardly significant in the selection of a minister for the Canadian cabinet. This is consistent with the situation in other countries that conform to the consociational model, in which the political elite is oriented more toward achieving practical results than to attaining ideological objectives.

The Sharing of Responsibility

Another result of the representation principle has been the necessity for the cabinet collectively to consider a large number of matters that would never reach as high a level in a well-organized business. The Canadian cabinet seems to be characterized by the limited capacity of ministers to act on their own authority rather than that of the cabinet as a body. It would seem that almost every important act of a minister is covered by the authority of an Order-in-Council (i.e. a cabinet decision formally recorded — see page 80), for it would be politically dangerous to give a minister unrestricted authority over the policy of his department. It would appear that very often each minister tends at times to have a veto over executive action that affects his group or his part of the country. In 1904 the Commander-in-Chief of the Militia appointed political enemies of the Minister of Agriculture (and Acting Minister of Militia, Sydney Fisher) to be officers in the militia unit located in the minister's home territory. The minister vetoed the appointments. The Commander-in-Chief complained in public about political interference with the militia and was promptly fired by the cabinet. The Order-in-Council that gave effect to the decision highlighted the importance of sharing responsibility very clearly:

> In the case of members of the Cabinet, while all have an equal degree of responsibility in a constitutional sense, yet in the practical working out of responsible government in a country of such vast extent as Canada, it is found necessary to attach a special responsibility to each Minister for the public affairs of the province or district with which he has close political connection.[12]

Thus it is clear that responsibility is shared in the cabinet, and no minister must assume *entire responsibility* for what he does. Consequently it has been more usual in Canada for Parliament to delegate power to the Governor-in-Council, rather than to the minister, unlike the United Kingdom. This assures the use of Orders-in-Council and helps to protect the minister from personal criticism. As one minister remarked, ". . . it is a comfortable position for any minister to be able to refer matters to the Governor-in-Council."[13]

This procedure helps to assure that the points of view of the various groups in Canada are brought to bear before decisions are taken. This does not necessarily give any bloc a veto, however, but it does insure that an individual group's wish will be taken into account. Thus in the conscription crisis of World War II, the decision to impose conscription was finally taken only after careful consideration of the views of Quebec and after some concessions had been made, such as offering to those conscripted the opportunity to volunteer for domestic rather than overseas service. The Foreign Takeovers Review Bill introduced by the Trudeau government in 1972 is another example. This bill gave some comfort to those concerned about American investment in Canada but did not unduly offend those areas of the country which were prepared to welcome investment from any foreign source. Again, this is consistent with the consociational model, wherein questions vital to any politically significant segments can be resolved only with their concurrence or after concessions have been made to them.

The Size of the Cabinet

Traditionally Canada has had very large cabinets and frequently new portfolios have been created, not for functional reasons, but to accommodate an additional cabinet minister from a politically significant group. This was true of the first cabinet, as noted earlier, and the practice of creating additional posts to provide representation has continued. There was, for example, under Mr. Diefenbaker an Associate Minister of Defence who had few responsibilities, but the position did provide a place for an additional minister from Quebec, and there has been for many years a Minister of National Revenue whose functions could easily be performed by another minister. Table 2-II illustrates the growth of the cabinet since 1867.

TABLE 2-II

Cabinet Membership at Beginning and End of Ministries, 1867-1974

Prime Minister	Date	Number of Ministers
Macdonald	1867	13
	1873	13
Mackenzie	1873	14
	1878	13
Macdonald	1878	14
	1891	16
Laurier	1896	14
	1911	18
Borden	1911	18
	1917	22
	1920	21
Meighen	1920	17
	1921	21
King	1922	19
	1930	19
Bennett	1930	19
	1935	21
King	1935	16
	1948	19
St. Laurent	1948	20
	1957	22
Diefenbaker	1957	21
	1963	24
Pearson	1963	25
	1968	28
Trudeau	1968	29
(Oct. 30)	1974	29

The Allocation of Portfolios

A concomitant development of the principle of representation has been the notion that certain portfolios must be held by representatives of certain areas. It has been generally agreed that a member from western Canada should hold the Agriculture portfolio and that a member of the cabinet from the Atlantic provinces or British Columbia should be responsible for Fisheries. This notion tends to compound the problem of cabinet building and places further limitation on the Prime Minister's ability to choose capable men for cabinet positions. In the case of the two portfolios mentioned above, economic and scientific expertise are probably as necessary as any other requirement, and such knowledge is not necessarily confined to the residents of a particular area of Canada. If there is a necessary connection between a minister's point of origin and the department he heads it is a political connection, in the sense that his presence in a particular cabinet position reassures an important segment of the population.

The Effect of the Representation Principle on the Efficiency of the Cabinet

The representation principle tends to prevent the Canadian cabinet from being an efficient body, as decisions normally cannot be made in a minimum of time and take maximum advantage of practical experience. Because ministers are not selected solely on the basis of ability and are not assigned responsibilities in accordance with their particular knowledge, because many decisions must be taken collectively by a large, cumbersome group, and because decisions must be based on political priorities, the decision-making process at the federal level is often inefficient, slow, and frustrating. Mr. Pearson remarked, "It is futile to believe that the Cabinet . . . can be run as efficiently as a business corporation."[14] A former minister, recalling his frustration said:

> We had to spend too much time convincing one another of the wisdom of our projects. Every one had the right to comment and criticize, even if they were uninformed. As a result, decisions were made after a long slow process and very seldom did a minister get a decision exactly to his liking.[15]

Consociationalism is of necessity an inefficient form of government and becomes increasingly so as demands placed on the political system increase. "The price to be paid for a system of participation by all elites, mutual veto, autonomy and proportionality is inevitably a certain amount of inefficiency, slowness and lack of decisiveness."[16]

Quebec and the Representation Principle

Over the years prime ministers have been especially concerned with securing adequate representation in the cabinet from Quebec, adequate not only in terms of numerical representation but also in terms of political satisfaction; that is, it has been considered important that Quebec be satisfied with the degree to which it has had recognition in the cabinet by virtue of the portfolios held by its representatives. This helps to ensure that the outputs of the political system are substantially in accord with the expectations of the people of Quebec.

The Quebec Lieutenant Theory

The way in which English-speaking prime ministers have dealt with the problem of providing satisfactory French-Canadian representation in the cabinet is of particular interest. Their problem has been made more difficult by the fact that, with one exception (J.J. Abbott), no English-speaking prime minister has come from Quebec or has been bilingual, and as a result each one has suffered from an inability to directly establish firm rapport with French Canada. In these cases the English-speaking prime minister has often selected one French-Canadian minister and accorded him special status, with a particular responsibility for Quebec. Thus ". . . this bi-racial coalition has always been kept together through trials and troubles by the close co-operation of a pair of leaders, one English and one French, who have found each other intellectually and temperamentally congenial and whose personal partnership has held their followers in line. Without this kind of leadership the coalition is unstable."[17] This procedure emphasizes one of the most persistent patterns of politics in a consociational democracy — the pre-eminent role of the political leaders in finding solutions to political problems without reference to the rank and file. The ability to ignore the rank and file rests on the trust and deference accorded to the leaders by the masses, so that while the masses are ignored in the actual decision-making process, each leader is able to co-operate and compromise with others in such a way that he does not lose the allegiance and support of his own group.

Prior to Confederation, it had been found necessary in the Province of Canada to provide for duplicate ministries in many policy areas, symbolizing the bicultural character of the population and that leadership of the government was shared by a French Canadian and an English Canadian. It was to be expected, then, that some special recognition would be given to French Canadians in the new federation, although there was no thought of providing for a dual prime ministership. Macdonald, however, relied heavily on Cartier, for in their relationship there was evidence of an equal partnership between French Canada and English Canada that made the task of dealing with Quebec much easier. Other Prime Ministers — notably Mackenzie, Borden, Meighen, Bennett, and Diefenbaker — were to find that the lack of such a colleague made their careers as Prime Minister very difficult. After Cartier's death, Macdonald relied on Sir Hector Langevin as his lieutenant in Quebec, although he did not accord him the trust he had given Cartier. Mackenzie was not able to find a suitable lieutenant in Quebec during his term as Prime Minister. The strong opposition of the Quebec bishops to liberalism and the continuing rapid turnover of ministers from Quebec in his cabinet (eight French Canadians served in Mackenzie's cabinet; only one served as long as three years and four of the eight received appointments as judges or as lieutenant governors after a short time in office) gave him little opportunity to win the confidence of the French Canadians or to select a lieutenant.

While Laurier was Prime Minister there was no need for a lieutenant in Quebec. Borden, who succeeded Laurier as Prime Minister, had come to an understanding with a French-Canadian Conservative, Monk, to whom he delegated responsibility for selecting cabinet ministers from Quebec. Monk and Borden soon disagreed, Monk resigned from the cabinet, and none of the other French-Canadian ministers had sufficient status with Borden or in Quebec to succeed him. Meighen experienced similar difficulties in Quebec. His French-Canadian ministers were relatively weak, and the leading minister from Quebec was Hon. C.C. Ballantyne (an English Canadian), a former Liberal who had broken with Laurier over the conscription issue in 1917 and who was very unpopular among French Canadians. Under Mr. King, Lapointe, who acted as his Quebec lieutenant, became ". . . the most powerful French Canadian in Federal politics, a national figure second only to Mackenzie King in the structure of Liberal leadership."[18] St. Laurent succeeded Lapointe as King's lieutenant in Quebec, but he did not seem to be as respected among French Canadians as Lapointe had been. This was probably because he was ". . . *un peu trop anglifié* for most Québécois."[19] Certainly St. Laurent and King were never personally as close as Lapointe and King. Diefenbaker refused to give any of his French-Canadian ministers any special recognition as lieutenant, although there was an obvious candidate for the role in Balcer. Mr. Pearson experienced great difficulty in finding an effective French-Canadian lieutenant. Mr. Favreau had special responsibilities for the province of Quebec and was succeeded in this role by Mr. Marchand, but the role seems to have altered so that it now involves mainly party organization and it appears to have lost much of its symbolic significance.

A recent study[20] has conclusively shown that no prime minister has ever really shared power with any of his colleagues to the point where there has ever been anyone fulfilling a function resembling that of a co-prime minister or a deputy prime minister. At the same time, however, it is obvious that in many cases an English-speaking prime minister has delegated to one French-Canadian minister special responsibilities, affecting the province of Quebec. By delegating special status to one minister, these individuals are assisted in acquiring a measure of pan-Canadian identification, while at the same time retaining their special relationship with Quebec; that is, the special status of one minister from Quebec has given him prestige both inside and outside of his own province. A man who is able to inspire trust and confidence in each of he major language groups can be most useful to the Prime Minister. Cartier, Lapointe and St. Laurent, to some extent, are examples of such men but it is important to note that at no time did any of these individuals pose a threat to the Prime Minister of the day, but while they were active in politics, their party was successful in Quebec.

Langevin, who succeeded Cartier, and Monk, who acted for a time as Borden's lieutenant, were never able to obtain such status and in the course of their careers in Ottawa appear to have lost touch with events in their own province and eventually lost influence, with important political consequences. It is also clear that if an English-speaking prime minister is unwilling to delegate responsibility or is not prepared to share publicity and prestige with a French Canadian, as seems to have been the case with Mr. Diefenbaker and Mr. Balcer, then he can expect great dissatisfaction to arise in Quebec. It would seem politically essential for one minister from Quebec to acquire some form of special status in the eyes of his compatriots when the Prime Minister himself is not a French Canadian.

The Changing Position of the Quebec Lieutenant

Since the beginning of the Quiet Revolution, changes in the province of Quebec have brought about a change in the position of the Quebec lieutenant. During the period 1896-1957, the Liberal Party won a majority in Quebec in every federal election, and during this 61-year period the Liberals were in power 46 years. During this time the party was either led by a French Canadian (Laurier and St. Laurent) or by King, who made sure that he had a lieutenant in Quebec. In terms of votes in Parliament, this majority was always a large one, reflecting the ability of the Liberals to appear as the party most representative of both French and non-French, since representatives of both occupied conspicuously important positions in the party. As a consequence, there were no real rivals from other political groups to the Liberal lieutenant as the federal spokesman for Quebec; whatever conflict there was for the position of leading spokesman for Quebec at the federal level was an inter-party one. This greatly strengthened the hand of the leader in Quebec, for he had control over the party and could check the rise of rivals. Thus Cartier, Lapointe, and St. Laurent were never challenged as spokesmen for Quebec at the federal level.

As long as the Quebec lieutenant had a commitment to the maintenance of the Canadian political system as it then existed, the chances of stability were enhanced. Prior to the Quiet Revolution, nationalism was an important force in Quebec, but it had not become as explicitly political as it has today. While it could not be said that there was a high degree of political consensus in Canada there seemed to be, both in Quebec and in the other provinces, a consensus on preserving the Canadian federal system. This is consistent with the consociational model wherein conflict among groups is conducted within the confines of the system, with no group threatening to separate or engage in civil war. This consensus was true among both the elite and masses, for both favoured the maintenance of the federal system, and the masses were also inclined to be deferential to those in authority, including Quebec's representatives in the Canadian cabinet. This again corresponds to another aspect of the consociational model in which, "The people must have an inherently strong tendency to be obedient and allegiant — regardless of particular circumstances. This tendency will be referred to as *deference* . . . used in its broadest meaning; an individual's acceptance of his position both in the social hierarchy and in the scale of political authority. . . . For the masses this entails respect for and submission to their superiors."[21]

The support received by the federal Liberal Party in Quebec during the period 1896-1957 can be taken as an indicator of support for the maintenance of the federal system and of deference to Quebec's political leaders at the federal level. This was by no means enthusiastic support; the political strength of the Quebec provincial premiers of the day indicates this and shows also that great efforts had to be made to maintain the system. It is true that from time to time splinter parties arose as a challenge to the elite, but these parties served more to indicate to the elite the degree of political dissatisfaction within the province and to highlight a grievance rather than to act as a threat. In federal elections, even when Quebec had a grievance, it would tend to massively support the party (usually the Liberal) least offensive to it in this regard. What Quebec appeared to be most interested in was maintaining the *status quo* and thus preserving its way of life. Those who assisted in achieving this goal, including the federal elite, were rewarded by the voters, not for bringing about changes, but for adhering to old ways.

Since 1959, however, many changes have taken place in Quebec, with profound effects on the style of politics. The masses are no longer deferential and there now may be a substantial gap between the old elites and the Quebec masses; i.e., the authority patterns are no longer congruent and the masses are no longer prepared to accept the accommodations made for them at the federal level by the elite. It may well be that federal cabinet ministers from Quebec are no longer considered to be the authentic spokesmen for Quebec; there are rival elites in the provincial government and in other political parties. This is reflected in the disaffiliation of the Quebec Liberal Party from the National Liberal Federation and the emergence of new and relatively powerful political parties such as the Creditistes and the Parti Québécois. One prominent French Canadian, Claude Morin, formerly Deputy Minister of Intergovernmental Affairs for the province of Quebec, resigned his position and joined the separatist Parti Québécois commenting:

After several years, after four Premiers and after having explored every conceivable type of federalism — co-operative, decentralized, profitable and God knows what — I believe I can identify one fact: never under this political regime can Quebec really free itself. [22]

There is then no longer a widespread consensus on the importance of maintaining the federal system, and consequently there has developed a wide gap between the federal elites and the masses. The Liberal Party in Quebec does not appear to be as representative of those elites involved in the Quiet Revolution as of the older, more conservative ones. Yet for many years the older elites dominated the party at the federal level in Quebec and gave the impression that they were representative of prevailing views, when in fact new attitudes, requiring new action, had developed. Thus the party elite lost influence in Quebec while still remaining prominent and influential in Ottawa.

Influence at the federal level, without influence at the provincial level, indicates a breakdown in the system of consociational democracy. The role of the Quebec lieutenant has consequently changed. He has rivals as spokesman for Quebec, because he cannot speak with the authority he once did (since he is no longer representative), and thus he may lose influence at the federal level as well as at the provincial. His rivals are not dealt with within the usual pattern of accommodation politics, and as a result his position has further weakened. It is difficult for him to make concessions on behalf of Quebec without alienating the people there.

The Selection of Cabinet Ministers from Quebec

There has been a tendency for English-Canadian Prime Ministers to leave the selection of ministers from Quebec to their lieutenant there. Macdonald allowed Cartier to pick the Quebec ministers in his first cabinet, and in later years, Langevin fulfilled a similar function, although with not as much freedom as Cartier. Mackenzie was never able to secure an able lieutenant in Quebec and left the direction of political affairs to his Quebec ministers as a group. They could rarely agree on anything. When Borden was forming his first cabinet in 1911, Monk named the Quebec ministers. Borden, however, had little confidence in Monk and was not sufficiently sensitive about Quebec, and it soon became clear that French-Canadian ministers had little influence on policy. When both Conservatives and Liberals entered the Union government of 1917 under Borden in order to enforce the Conscription Act, it was almost impossible for ministers to be recruited in Quebec and consequently there were no strong ministers from that province in the cabinet. This deficiency continued into Meighen's cabinet. King used Lapointe and later St. Laurent as his lieutenants in Quebec. Both were able to influence the party at both the federal and provincial levels. Mr. Diefenbaker did not delegate responsibility to the senior French Canadian in his cabinet, Mr. Balcer, and as a result Balcer's prestige in Quebec soon declined. Under Mr. Pearson, Mr. Favreau and Mr. Marchand served as leaders of the Quebec wing of the federal Liberal Party. According to Newman, at one point in 1966 Marchand threatened to resign unless he was kept fully informed on matters affecting Quebec. When he was assured that in future he would be consulted on major policy proposals, he withdrew his resignation.

It is important to point out that French-Canadian Prime Ministers have not found it necessary to have a lieutenant either in Quebec or in English Canada. The three French-Canadian Prime Ministers have been fluently bilingual and as a result have had no problems in communicating with either linguistic group. English-Canadian Prime Ministers have not been bilingual — a reflection in miniature of the whole problem of bilingualism in Canada. It is true that Mr. Howe was very powerful in Mr. St. Laurent's cabinet, but this was more due to his exceptional competence rather than because he was an English-Canadian minister. If Mr. Howe was a delegate of any area or group he was representative of Ontario or big business, but never English Canada as a whole. Regional diversity among English Canadians would seem to negate the possibility that any one English Canadian would be acceptable as a lieutenant for all of English Canada.

Quebec Ministers and Their Portfolios

It has been argued that while Prime Ministers have been careful to include representatives from Quebec in their cabinets, they have not allocated the more important portfolios to French Canadians, except in the case of the Justice Department. Thus it is argued that French Canadians have by and large had responsibility only for the relatively minor functions of government. To some extent this criticism is justified, in that since Confederation there has never been a French-Canadian Minister of Finance, and only one French Canadian, Mr. Pépin, has served as Minister of Trade and Commerce, although French Canadians have served in almost every other department of government.

Eleven French Canadians out of a total of 37 individuals have been President of the Privy Council. If one eliminates those occupants who have served simultaneously as Prime Minister, French Canadians have served in this minor post for 20.3 per cent of the time. Eleven French Canadians have been Ministers of Justice for 25.8 per cent of the number of years the department has existed, hardly verifying the frequently heard comment that this portfolio is a monopoly of French Canadians. Nine French Canadians (out of 25) have served as Solicitor-General for

44.2 per cent of the time this relatively unimportant position has existed, including those times when it was not of the cabinet (see page 66). Only five French Canadians have served as Minister of Defence or Militia, out of a total of 38 ministers, for 19.9 per cent of the time the position has existed. This fact is possibly partially explained by the wide-scale opposition in Quebec to Canadian participation in foreign wars, dating back to 1899. No French Canadians served in this position from 1896 to 1967, although of six Associate Ministers of Defence, three have been French Canadian and have served for 57.9 per cent of the time this unimportant portfolio has existed. In the very important Transport Department (and including its prececessor department, Railways and Canals), six French Canadians have been ministers for 23.2 per cent of the time. In the 107-year period covered by this study, 21 of 41 Postmasters-General have been French Canadians, serving for 46.3 per cent of the time. Sixteen of the 44 Secretaries of State have been French Canadians and they have served a total of 39.8 per cent of the time. In the Department of Public Works, which, like the Postmaster-General's Department was for many years an important source of patronage, ten out of 35 ministers have been French Canadians, but they have held the position for 47.9 per cent of the period. In one other relatively minor portfolio, the Department of National Revenue (but one with, for many years, considerable patronage at its disposal), there have been seventeen French Canadian ministers out of a total of 45, serving for 29.2 per cent of the time.

It is clear then that some departments in the past have been more likely than others to have French Canadian ministers, although the situation has not been as discriminatory as has been alleged. The explanation provided for the fact that French Canadians have not filled the key economic portfolios such as Finance and Trade and Commerce has usually been that in the past French Canadians have not been business oriented; another explanation offered is that the educational system in Quebec did not provide adequate training for these positions. When, however, it was pointed out that of the 26 Ministers of Finance Canada has had, thirteen have been lawyers (10 serving in the last 50 years) and also that of all the French Canadians who have served in the cabinet since 1867, almost 75 per cent have been lawyers, it was argued that the legal training provided in Quebec did not sufficiently emphasize corporate law and thus lawyers trained in Quebec were not prepared for the position of Minister of Finance. The correct explanation is probably somewhat simpler; that is, the occupants of these positions had to maintain close relationships with the Canadian business community, a community dominated by non-French Canadians and one unlikely to welcome or approve the appointment of an "outsider" to these important and prestigious positions.

Some people argue, however, that within the cabinet no one position is more important than another. One former minister under Mr. Diefenbaker remarked in this connection that while some portfolios are, in the eyes of the public and the press, more prestigious than others, and while some departments carry heavier responsibilities than others, it does not necessarily follow that the minister with a "prestigious" portfolio is more influential in the cabinet than others, since influence is more the result of judgment and ability than the particular portfolio for which a minister is responsible. It is claimed then when matters are discussed in cabinet all members are equal, and thus the fact that a particular group has not been well represented in a particular portfolio does not mean that that group has been denied influence in the cabinet. This has probably been true in the past, since nearly every major matter was discussed by the full cabinet. There has, however, been a tendency, in almost every cabinet for a small group of ministers to be closer to the Prime Minister. The reasons for this closeness may be personal, but certain departments are functionally so important (Finance, Justice, Trade and Commerce, External Affairs) that of necessity these ministers have very close relationships with the Prime Minister. When one recognizes, however, that Macdonald, King, and Pearson, who were prime ministers collectively for 45 years and had French Canadian lieutenants in whom they constantly confided, and one notes that Laurier, St. Laurent, and Trudeau have served as prime minister collectively for 31 years, the argument that French Canada has not had proper influence in the cabinet is somewhat diluted. What does seem to be true, however, is that in the 20th century, when the Conservative Party has been in power, Quebec representation and influence have been very weak. While it could be truthfully said that there were no strong French-Canadian representatives in the Union cabinet of 1917, it should also be remembered that there were only three non-Liberal members elected from Quebec in 1917 and available for cabinet positions. Under Bennett, French Canadians served only in the portfolios of Marine, Fisheries, Solicitor-General, and Postmaster-General, but most of the Conservatives from Quebec in the House of Commons were not French Canadians. The comment was made of Mr. Diefenbaker's cabinet that the French Canadians ". . . were a sad sextet who easily earned their reputation as the Conservative Cabinet's least effective ministers."[23] The nature of Conservative Party support then, rather than outright discrimination, explains to a considerable extent why French Canadians have been under-represented in Conservative cabinets, except in Mr. Diefenbaker's cabinet from 1958-1962, when he had a large contingent of French-Canadian members in the House of Commons.

A final argument against the suggestion that Quebec has suffered from discrimination is that, as far as French Canadians were concerned, the cabinet positions they have traditionally occupied, such as Post Office and Public Works, were the ones they desired most. Some confirmation of this argument can be found in a statement made in the House of Commons by an indignant member from Quebec commenting on the replacement of a French-Canadian Minister of Public Works by an English Canadian: ". . . it is important to that province (Quebec) . . . that it should have its fair share of the administration and patronage in the government of Canada. . . . I wish to enter my protest against the removal of Public Works from the province of Quebec to another province."[24] Bourassa, in an article on the formation of Borden's Cabinet in 1911 ". . . mentioned the desire of some of the politicians that Quebec receive two 'good' — that is, large patronage-dispensing departments and the desire was fulfilled."[25] It is argued that French Canadians, due to the political climate and particular social conditions of Quebec, were more interested in positions that would enable them to dispense patronage more freely than in positions such as the Ministry of Finance or Trade and Commerce, which have involved relatively little patronage. One writer noted in 1943 that "French Canadian society is strongly familial, as well as being a minority. On both counts one would expect personal claims to position to be pushed strongly. Every family acts as a lobby for its members. The French Canadian in public life feels this pressure to provide for friends, relatives and French Canadians."[26] One must be cautious, however, and not assume that the desire for patronage in Quebec was any stronger than elsewhere in Canada, but it may well be true that Fench-Canadian politicians were more secure in those positions where there was an obvious amount of patronage for them to dispense, and it is probably true that because French Canadians held these portfolios their compatriots were reassured that they would indeed receive their fair share.

A study made for the Royal Commission on Bilingualism and Biculturalism tends to support the contention that the French-Canadian attitude towards Members of Parliament is quite different from that of non-French Canadians. An analysis of the subject matter of letters received by Members of Parliament indicated that ". . . Quebec M.P.'s are overwhelmingly confronted with job seeking letters while letters of disinterested opinion are relatively light."[27] Although not only Quebec members receive such letters, the volume received by them is far in excess of that received by other members. When backbenchers were asked if their constituents were more interested in the services an M.P. could perform than in his views on legislation, 79 per cent of French-Canadian backbenchers agreed, while only 52 per cent of English-speaking backbenchers did.[28] This would tend to support the argument that patronage-dispensing portfolios are of great importance to French Canadians.

The problem of keeping French Canada satisfied with its cabinet representation will in future be more difficult. The decision-making process has changed; some cabinet positions are obviously more important than others. French Canadians must not only take part in the decision-making process at the highest level, as they have done in the past, but they must appear to be taking part and Prime Ministers, for obvious political reasons, will probably be careful to appoint French Canadians to those cabinet positions that seem to the public mind to be most prestigious and significant.

The Representation Principle — An Established Convention

In spite of the disadvantages, the representation principle seems to be firmly entrenched in the Canadian cabinet system, justifying Prime Minister Mackenzie's remarks to Governor General Lord Dufferin:

> . . . Canada is a difficult country to govern. While there are no class interests to consult there are more difficult interests always cropping up in those of Race and Creed. It is difficult to do anything for an English speaking Canadian without giving a corresponding benefit to a French Canadian. A preponderance of Catholic or Protestant appointments or honours is instantly detected. Sectional interests are also pretty strong and must be consulted by the government no matter how desirable it may be to avoid doing so as a matter of principle.[29]

It is clear that the representation principle has some serious limitations, yet all persons interviewed felt that it was an essential aspect of Canadian government and could not be done away with. Mr. Pearson remarked, "I do not see how these limitations can be removed in a federal society, especially one such as ours, at least without consequences which would far outweigh any advantages in efficiency that might come from it."[30] Mr. Diefenbaker said, "Experience cannot be changed, it is essential for national unity."[31]

It is clear then that in the formation of a cabinet a prime minister must take into account various manifestations of the principle of representation; if he ignores them he will find himself in serious political difficulties. Hansard and other journals are replete with complaints from various groups that have felt excluded from the cabinet.

Probably the most important aspect of the representation principle is that of providing for representation from the various provinces. As early as 1884, Sir John A. Macdonald was asked in the House of Commons: ". . . whether it is the intention of the Government to make provision to have British Columbia represented at an early date?"[32] A few years later another Member from British Columbia argued that many of the difficulties that had arisen between the federal government and the provincial government ". . . would not have occurred had there been sitting in the Cabinet a gentleman who was thoroughly well acquainted with the wants and requirements of the people of that province."[33]

However, it is not sufficient only to provide for provincial representation. Various regions in some provinces must have representation as well. One of the reasons advanced for the defeat of the Liberal government in 1957 was the fact that Toronto had been largely ignored in the selection of cabinet members. Hon. Paul Hellyer was appointed Associate Minister of Defence on April 26, 1957, but in the June election of that year the Liberals were routed in the Toronto area.

The demands of ethnic and linguistic groups must also be met in the matter of representation in the cabinet. Mr. Diefenbaker was bitterly criticized for ignoring French Canadians when selecting members of his cabinet after his 1958 victory. At the time of the next election in 1962, Mr. Diefenbaker's party fared badly in Quebec.

It is also necessary to balance religious representation in the cabinet and to take account of various segments of certain religious groups as well. Mention has been made of the importance of having Irish Catholics in the cabinet in the early days, and the increase in the number of Roman Catholics in recent cabinets is, in part, a reflection of the increased size of that denomination in Canada.

It is also necessary to take into account economic interests in cabinet formation. In 1941 Mr. King appointed Humphrey Mitchell as Minister of Labour because he believed the cabinet would be greatly strengthened by the presence of a man identified with the labour movement. When Mr. Diefenbaker appointed Mr. McCutcheon a senator and Minister of Trade and Commerce, he was recognized as the representative of the business community, and it was hoped that his presence in the cabinet would moderate the antagonism shown by this group towards the Diefenbaker government. In 1965 Mr. Pearson, in a great coup, was able to convince both Robert Winters, a right-wing business tycoon and Jean Marchand, a left-wing union leader from Quebec, to join his cabinet.

Recent Prime Ministers have also given consideration to representation by non-French and non-English groups in making cabinet appointments. Mr. Diefenbaker for example, appointed Hon. Michael Starr, a Ukrainian-Canadian, as Minister of Labour, and Mr. Trudeau appointed Hon. Herb Gray, a Jewish-Canadian, as Minister of National Revenue, and it is likely that this practice will be continued.

An additional consideration which prime ministers will likely have to take into account in the future is a demand for representation by women. There has already been some evidence of this. Mr. Diefenbaker, for example, appointed Mrs. Ellen Fairclough, the only female Progressive Conservative in the House of Commons, to the cabinet. Mr. Pearson appointed Miss LaMarsh, at that time the only female Liberal elected in 1963, to his Cabinet, and shortly after Mrs. Margaret Ridout was elected as a Liberal M.P. in a by-election, Mr. Pearson appointed her parliamentary secretary to the Minister of National Health and Welfare. Mr. Trudeau appointed Mme. Jeanne Sauvé to the cabinet after her election in 1972 when she was the only female member of the Liberal caucus after the 1972 election.

It is clear, then, that in the selection of a cabinet, competence and the ability to work well as an administrator are not necessarily the prime considerations. The maintenance of national unity is of the utmost importance, even though this may have some unfortunate side effects on the Canadian system of government. Mr. King's words regarding this objective would probably be endorsed by almost every Prime Minister. "In the formation of this government I have aimed above all else at national unity."[34] The Canadian cabinet may thus have played a major role in maintaining Canadian unity. The question now arises if it is capable of continuing to do so.

NOTES

[1]See for example Arend Lijphart, "Typologies of Democratic Systems". *Comparative Political Studies*, Vol. 1, No. 1 (April, 1968), p. 3.

Hans Daalder, "On Building Consociational Nations: The Cases of the Netherlands and Switzerland". *International Social Science Journal*, Volume XXIII, No. 3 (1971), p. 355.

S.J.R. Noel, "Political Parties and Elite Accommodation", in Peter Meekison ed., *Canadian Federalism, Myth or Reality?* Second edition. (Toronto; Methuen, 1971), p. 121, and K.D. McRae ed., *Consociational Democracy: Political Accommodation in Segmented Societies*. (Toronto; McClelland and Stewart, 1974).

[2]S.J.R. Noel, *op. cit.*, p. 135.

[3]J.M.S. Careless, "Limited Identities in Canada". *Canadian Historical Review*, Vol. 1 No. 1, March 1969, p. 9.

[4]Donald Creighton, *John A. Macdonald, The Young Politician*. (Toronto; Macmillan, 1952), p. 256.

[5]Norman MacL. Rogers, "Evolution and Reform of the Canadian Cabinet". *Canadian Bar Review*, Vol. XI. No. 4 (April, 1933), pp. 227-8.

[6]Canada, House of Commons, *Debates*. (April 3, 1868), p. 453.

[7]*Ibid*. (March 13, 1922), p. 48.

[8]Quoted in *Ottawa Citizen*. (October 11, 1948), p. 1.

[9]Canada, House of Commons, *Debates*. (February 24, 1969), p. 5846.

[10]Leon Dion, "The Concept of Political Leadership". *Canadian Journal of Political Science*, Volume 1., No. 1 (March, 1968), p. 9.

[11]Rt. Hon. L.B. Pearson, *Politics and Participation*.

[12]Sessional Papers of the Dominion of Canada, Session 1904: 3-4 Edward VII, Volume XXXVIII, No. 13, *Paper 113*, p. 2.

[13]Canada, House of Commons, *Debates*. (June 18, 1956), p. 5126.

[14]*Interview*. (May 21, 1969).

[15]*Interview*. (October 3, 1971).

[16]Arend Lijphart, "Cultural Diversity and Theories of Political Integration". *Canadian Journal of Political Science*, Vol. IV, No. 1 (March, 1971), p. 14.

[17]Frank Underhill, "The Canadian Party System in Transition", in Frank Underhill ed., *In Search of Canadian Liberalism*. (Toronto; Macmillan, 1961), p. 201.

[18]F.W. Gibson, "The Cabinet of 1935", in F.W. Gibson ed., *Cabinet Formation and Bicultural Relations*. (Ottawa; Queen's Printer, 1970), p. 114.

[19]J.L. Granatstein, "Strictly on its Merits: The Conscription Issue in Canada After 1945". *Queen's Quarterly*, Volume LXXIX, No. 2 (Summer, 1972), p. 203.

[20]F.W. Gibson ed., *Cabinet Formation and Bicultural Relations, Seven Case Studies*, 1970, Chapter VIII.

[21]Arend Lijphart, *The Politics of Accommodation*. (Berkeley; University of California Press, 1968), pp. 144-145.

[22]Quoted in Anthony Westell, *Paradox, Trudeau as Prime Minister*. (Scarborough; Prentice-Hall, 1972), p. 51.

[23]Peter Newman, *Renegade in Power*. (Toronto; McClelland and Stewart, 1963), p. 283.

[24]Canada, House of Commons, *Debates*. (March 18, 1903), p. 192.

[25]Roger Graham, "The Cabinet of 1911," in F.W. Gibson ed., *Cabinet Formation and Bicultural Relations*, p. 60.

[26]E.C. Hughes, "French and English Canadians in the Industrial Hierarchy of Quebec" in B. Blishen et al., *Canadian Society*, 3rd ed. (Toronto; Macmillan, 1968) p. 679.

[27]David Hoffman and Norman Ward, *Bilingualism and Biculturalism in the Canadian House of Commons*. (Ottawa; Queen's Printer, 1970), p. 95.

[28]*Ibid.*, p. 94.

[29]Mackenzie to Dufferin, May 28, 1877. In DeKiewiet and Underhill (eds.) *Dufferin-Carnarvon Correspondence 1874-77*, p. 355.

[30]*Interview*. (August 18, 1969).

[31]*Interview*. (May 25, 1970).

[32]Canada, House of Commons, *Debates*. (February 25, 1884), p. 505.

[33]*Ibid.* (July 19, 1895), p. 4786-7.

[34]*Canadian Annual Review*, 1922, p. 522.

Chapter III

Cabinet Making in Canada

It is the prerogative of the Prime Minister to appoint members of the cabinet, and it is also his prerogative to determine its organization and procedure. Consequently, the organization and procedure of the cabinet will depend to a large extent on the personality of the Prime Minister. His ability to appoint, transfer, and demote ministers, his status as party leader and as a national figure make him extremely powerful and far more than *primus inter pares* in the cabinet. The informal nature of the cabinet has enabled the Prime Minister to innovate at will, to dispose of rivals, and to downgrade the importance of ministers who occupy important functional ministries. In this process, of course, he must take care not to antagonize various groups or their leaders; that is, he must maintain among his ministers a sense of commitment to the party and to the national political system. If he is unable or unwilling to perform an elite-accommodation role, he is not likely to remain Prime Minister for very long. When differences exist among ministers he must ". . . resolve them eventually, in the end the Prime Minister decides and this is his ultimate responsibility. He exercises that responsbility with due regard for the fact that he has to have a Cabinet with him to govern effectively."[1] This does not mean that he must act as an autocrat, but it illustrates the critical importance of the skills of the leader (i.e., the Prime Minister) in maintaining the stability of the system. It does mean that he must be the master of his cabinet, "first minister" in fact as well as in form. The all important role of the Prime Minister in this respect reflects the fact that in a consociational democracy: "The crucial factor in the establishment and preservation of norms and democratic stability is the quality of leadership."[2]

The Mechanics of Appointment

The procedure followed prior to 1957 required the Governor General to designate an individual as Prime Minister who would then sign an Order-in-Council recommending his own appointment to the portfolio he would hold in addition to being Prime Minister. If, as in the case of Macdonald, Mackenzie, and Diefenbaker, the Prime Minister was not already a Privy Councillor, it would first be necessary for him as Prime

Minister to recommend his own appointment to the Council. Other ministers would then be appointed via an Order-in-Council signed by the Prime Minister only, if this was at the time when a new ministry was being formed.[3] It would seem that the traditional notion that Orders-in-Council must be passed by a quorum of four Privy Councillors is incorrect, in spite of statements to the contrary such as the one made in 1963 by a parliamentary secretary: "It has been the custom for many years that the committee of the council does not advise the Governor General to approve an Order-in-Council without the presence or concurrence of at least four ministers. This practice originated in the Queen's Instructions to the Governor General at the time of Confederation."[4] It would appear that for some purposes at least the Prime Minister himself has constituted a quorum. Subsequent appointments to an already existing cabinet would be made via an Order-in-Council with more than the Prime Minister's signature; that is, at least four Privy Councillors would approve the Order.

The use of Orders-in-Council for this purpose illustrated very clearly the special relationship between the Governor General and the Prime Minister, but it was irregular. In September 1953 a new procedure was devised to more clearly ". . . indicate the constitutional position of the Prime Minister and the Governor General with regard to the appointment of Ministers and Privy Councillors."[5] Since advising the Governor General to make appointments to the Privy Council and the cabinet is the sole prerogative of the Prime Minister, it was decided that the use of an Order-in-Council was inappropriate. Since 1953 an Instrument of Advice has been used — that is, a letter to the Governor General from the Prime Minister advising that certain appointments be made. The Governor General writes "approved" on the Instrument, signs it, and the appointment takes effect.

On taking office, each minister designate takes an oath of office as well as the Privy Councillor's oath, which includes the oath of allegiance and an oath of secrecy. Prior to 1930, ministers without portfolio took an oath only as Privy Councillors; now, however, they take both oaths. The new cabinet comes into existence after the persons selected by the Prime Minister have taken the oaths of office.

Because the appointment of the cabinet is the prerogative of the Prime Minister rather than the Governor General, ministers need not be reappointed when a new Governor General assumes office, even though the Governor General does the actual appointing. On the appointment of a new Governor General a proclamation is issued, announcing the new appointment and commanding all officers and ministers to continue with their duties. If the Prime Minister dies, however, then the cabinet is automatically dissolved. Although ministers retain their appointments as ministers and as Privy Councillors, the collectivity, the cabinet, no longer exists. Thus the cabinet as a collectivity depends on the fact that there is a Prime Minister so that when a Prime Minister dies, while a ministry still exists, there is no cabinet. In 1926, when Mr. King resigned as Prime Minister, all his ministers resigned as well. They "had not followed the customary practice of holding office till their successors were appointed. They had left the Crown without a Ministry, the country without a Government."[6] Although a minister is appointed in theory by the Governor General, when he resigns he submits his resignation to the Prime Minister who indeed may request the resignation. It is perhaps illustrative of the informality of the cabinet to point out that no procedure has yet been devised to deal with the situation where the Prime Minister wants a minister to resign and he refuses to do so. During Mr. Pearson's term of office, it was necessary for him to request the resignation of Mr. Dupuis and he is quoted as having said to Mr. Dupuis: "I'm asking for your resignation. I am the Prime Minister. I name my ministers. I'm demanding your resignation. I have the right to do so."[7] These words fittingly describe the relationship between the Prime Minister and members of the cabinet.

Rules Governing Incoming Cabinets

There are certain important precedents that an incoming cabinet must adhere to. There is, for example, the understanding that a new cabinet will not examine cabinet minutes from earlier administrations or interrogate members of the civil service on matters discussed previously in secret. One of Mr. Diefenbaker's ministers stated that the Prime Minister had directed that ". . . we would not look back at the conclusions of the earlier administration, but follow the well-established practice of parliamentary government, by putting aside those conclusions. . . ."[8] It should be noted, however, that Mr. Diefenbaker did read and release a secret report prepared for the previous government and he did admit to reading the minutes of the defence committee of the St. Laurent Cabinet. This tradition of not referring back to the papers of previous cabinets is not necessarily a good one, in that the new cabinet may be handicapped in dealing with problems it has inherited, since the tradition makes it highly dependent on civil servants and whatever information they see fit to provide. If the civil service is biased or politically suspect, this would complicate the decision-making process for an incoming cabinet by preventing it from obtaining all of the relevant information.

The Appointment of Ministers

As noted earlier, various conventions limit the Prime Minister in his choice of cabinet colleagues, but the responsibility is his to make the final selection. An incoming Prime Minister will consult with associates in the party, but even if he has appointed a powerful lieutenant, he retains the prerogative of making the actual selection himself. The Prime Minister is usually placed under pressure to appoint certain individuals, and it has happened that supporters of such people have organized campaigns to have their candidate appointed.

The entries in the diary of Sir George Foster written at the time Sir Robert Borden was forming his cabinet in 1911 indicate the anxieties and pressures of aspirants to cabinet positions. At one point Foster feared he would be left out, and so he took action to apply pressure. "I have advised my friends and they are at work."[9] When Mr. Pearson was forming his cabinet in 1963, it was reported that a great deal of pressure was applied on behalf of various candidates, including a telegram signed from 700 residents of one particular constituency urging that their member be appointed to the cabinet. Mr. Pearson noted:

> It is true that a Prime Minister is subjected to pressure in appointments to the Cabinet. This pressure comes from ambitious Members themselves . . . from friends of such Members including organizational friends who would like to have a spokesman of their particular organization or association in the Cabinet; or from local or provincial bodies which are anxious for their locality or their province to be represented by a chosen candidate.[10]

Occasionally a prime minister will have difficulty in persuading an individual to enter the cabinet and may have to make concessions to him. When in 1935 King invited the then premier of Saskatchewan, Mr. Gardiner, to enter his cabinet, Gardiner would accept the appointment only if the responsibility for wheat sales was transferred from the Department of Trade and Commerce to the Department of Agriculture. King refused to do this, but he did promise to set up a cabinet committee to be responsible for all matters having to do with grain, and he agreed to put Gardiner on the committee. It can also happen that a prime minister will have to make concessions to a minister already in the cabinet in order to persuade him to take on a new portfolio. When King persuaded Mr. Howe to take on the new Department of Reconstruction in 1944, Howe agreed to do so very reluctantly and only after King promised that he would accept his resignation if Howe became dissatisfied. This agreement was made only after the then Minister of National Defence for Air, Hon. C.G. Power, had declined the position absolutely and King had embarrassed Howe at a cabinet meeting on Sept. 7, 1944, when he ". . . then and there asked Howe to take on Reconstruction. Howe objected very strongly."[11] King then attempted again to induce Power to accept the position. He declined, and once again King asked Howe to assume the responsibility. When in 1953 Mr. St. Laurent asked Hon.

Robert Winters, then Minister of Resources and Development, to become Minister of Public Works and clean it out, eliminating graft and patronage, he agreed only on the condition that he be permitted to take the Deputy Minister of Resources and Development with him to Public Works.

It is likely that, in the process of selecting a cabinet, the Prime Minister consults with various individuals but the decision is his personally. The necessity of balancing appointees and portfolios requires that the decision to appoint an individual to the cabinet often takes place before the decision is made as to which portfolio the individual will receive. Mr. King stated, ". . . in the formation of any Cabinet no positions are finally determined until the last minute. All sides and possible relations are carefully canvassed. Until a ministry is formed, it is impossible to say what the final decision is going to be."[12] This also applies to the situation where a prime minister is making new appointments to an already existing ministry. Interviews with former ministers indicated that it seems to be the custom, although not an inflexible rule, for Prime Ministers to consult their cabinet colleagues regarding new appointments, but frequently this is a formality and is done after the Prime Minister's mind is made up. "When new ministers were appointed by Mr. Diefenbaker, the members of the Cabinet were informed, several may have been consulted privately, but the decision was not dependent upon a Cabinet conclusion."[13] It would, however, be folly for a prime minister to appoint a person to his cabinet who was unacceptable to many members in it; the need for harmony within the cabinet calls for some form of approval from it before the appointment is made. It is also true, however, that it would be a very bold minister who would strongly oppose the Prime Minister's choice. Laurier wrote to Hon. David Mills on September 23, 1897, regarding Mills' appointment: "I have consulted the Cabinet as to who should be his successor [to Oliver Mowat] as member of the administration and leader in the Senate. It was the unanimous wish of all my colleagues that you should be asked to enter the Cabinet."[14] Mr. King sometimes discussed new appointments with his cabinet and also the transferring of a minister from one department to another. Thus, before Dunning became Minister of Finance in 1929 after having served as Minister of Railways and Canals, King ". . . took up with my colleagues in council the question of a successor to be appointed to fill the position of Minister of Finance. With the warm and hearty co-operation of members of the government, I advised His Excellency to call on the Hon. Mr. Dunning. . . ."[15] This is probably an example of Mr. King's insistence on piously going through the motion of consulting the cabinet even when his decision had already been made. In most cases, however, it is likely that prime ministers do not consult the cabinet *en bloc* but merely advise its members of the decision. Mr.

Diefenbaker stated that he would seek advice from individual ministers, and ministers who served in his cabinet stated that he would sometimes mention the names of various candidates in order to get a reaction. Mr. Pearson stated that he would not consult with the cabinet as a whole. "Often, however, a Prime Minister will wish to consult one or two close colleagues in their individual capacities before an appointment is made; especially a senior minister from the province where the appointment is made, whose judgement he has learned to value."[16]

Cabinet ministers, however, are only one source of advice. Other people are consulted as well. Two former national directors of each major party stated that they were consulted at times, but neither one felt that he had an especially influential voice in the matter. They seemed to feel, however, that it was a vital part of their responsibility to provide advice, and one had the impression that prime ministers receive advice and suggestions from this source without ever asking for it.[17] Party treasurers denied that they were ever consulted or ever provided advice on such matters.

The Allocation of Portfolios

The allocation of particular portfolios is also the prerogative of the Prime Minister. If the party has spent time in opposition and certain members have specialized as critics of particular departments, they will likely become the ministers of these departments. Thus, in the case of Mr. Pearson's cabinet, "The senior appointments were almost automatic since they merely involved moving his associates into the portfolios they had held in the 'shadow cabinet'."[18] Occasionally those members of the party whose prominence makes their inclusion in the cabinet inevitable will be asked which portfolio they prefer. At the time Mr. Diefenbaker was making his cabinet selections, ". . . Hees, Churchill and one or two other M.P.'s close to Diefenbaker were asked to submit lists of Cabinet choices, [and] the Toronto member placed Trade beside his name."[19] Mr. Hees was not appointed to this portfolio immediately although one of his colleagues, Mr. Fulton, who had advised Mr. Diefenbaker that he wished the Justice portfolio, did receive this appointment.[20] More often it is the case that the Prime Minister decides on his own which portfolio a cabinet member will receive. At the time of Miss LaMarsh's appointment, Mr. Pearson called her into his office and after ". . . we chatted for a moment or two about the election he told me that he wanted me to serve in the Cabinet as Minister of National Health and Welfare."[21]

It is clear, then, that while there are constraints on a Prime Minister in appointing members of the cabinet and allocating portfolios, he has the final responsibility, which provides him with immense personal power.

Prime Ministers and Cabinet Portfolios

Prior to 1957, every Prime Minister also held a cabinet portfolio. Macdonald served at various times as Minister of Justice, Minister of the Interior, President of the Privy Council, Minister of Railways and Canals, and Postmaster-General. Mackenzie served as Minister of Public Works, and Laurier acted as President of the Privy Council. Borden was also President of the Privy Council for the first part of his ministry, and then acted as Secretary of State for External Affairs; Meighen also held the External Affairs portfolio while he was Prime Minister. Mr. King served as President of the Privy Council for his entire term of office and was also Secretary of State for External Affairs for almost all that time. Mr. Bennett was also President of the Privy Council during his term of office and filled other positions as well. When Mr. St. Laurent became Prime Minister he also became President of the Privy Council but resigned this position on April 24, 1957, thus becoming the first Prime Minister to hold that office exclusively. Mr. Diefenbaker while Prime Minister also acted as President of the Privy Council and as Secretary of State for External Affairs for brief periods. Neither Mr. Pearson nor Mr. Trudeau have held any other position while serving as Prime Minister, indicating that the burden of responsibility now resting on the Prime Minister makes it impossible to assume additional duties.

Prestigious Positions in the Cabinet

It would seem that over the years certain cabinet positions have appeared to be more prestigious than others; that is, they have had a higher standing or reputation in the public's mind. Cabinet positions acquire prestige for one of three possible reasons. Some departments, such as the Department of Finance, have more functional importance than others, and the incumbent acquires greater influence and thus greater prestige. Some portfolios gain prestige because of the conduct of the incumbent; that is, a minister who is particularly colourful or aggressive can draw attention to his portfolio and thus enhance its importance in the public mind. One minister remarked that in the Trudeau cabinet the Labour portfolio seemed far more important than it was under earlier Prime Ministers because of the attention that Mr. Mackasey, the minister from 1968 to 1972, drew to himself.[22] A third reason why a particular cabinet position can be regarded as being prestigious is because of the personal relationship between the minister and the Prime Minister. It may be that when it is clear to the public that a particular minister enjoys an unusually close relationship with the Prime Minister, it may also feel that the position is especially important. This could be true in the case of Mr. Trudeau's cabinet with Mr. Marchand, or in the case of Mr. St. Laurent's cabinet with Mr. Howe.

An examination of the names and occupants of the various portfolios is of considerable interest. It is clear that those portfolios generally considered to be of lesser importance have a far higher turnover of ministers than the more prestigious ones such as Finance or External Affairs. Since Confederation there have been 41 Postmasters-General and 44 Secretaries of State, compared with 26 Ministers of Finance and 35 Ministers of Public Works. There have been 45 Ministers of National Revenue (or the equivalent position), and there were eight Ministers of Manpower and Immigration in the period 1963 to 1974. In many cases the less prestigious portfolios have served as stepping stones to other more important positions, and in other cases they have provided positions for ministers whose performance in more demanding ones has been unsatisfactory and/or embarrassing.

The most important departments in 1867 were those of Justice and Finance. Macdonald assumed the Justice portfolio himself. The position derived much of its importance from the fact that it was the responsibility of the minister to review provincial legislation and to recommend disallowance in certain cases. In addition, the Minister of Justice had some extremely important patronage positions to dispense. Moreover, since the position of Attorney-General was combined with that of the Minister of Justice, most of the prestige which went with the Attorney-Generalship in the old province of Canada attached itself to the office of the Minister of Justice. The fact that the first occupant was the Prime Minister also contributed to the prestige of this particular department.

Recently the Ministry of Justice has been stripped of some of its responsibilities, which have been allocated to the Department of the Solicitor-General and the Department of Consumer and Corporate Affairs. The department has remained important, however, because that is where legislation giving effect to government policies is drafted. Thus the department has been inevitably a source of input for such policies, in that the wording of the actual legislation can affect the intention of the policy. In addition, the Department of Justice must ensure that bills presented to Parliament are consistent with the Bill of Rights, and alterations in proposed legislation to make this possible may also affect the actual policy. A second reason for the importance of the department is that the impact of the department's activities with respect to law and order fall heavily upon the public. Legislation regarding abortion, divorce, the Criminal Code, etc. all come within the purview of the Department of Justice and help to focus public attention on it.

The Ministry of Finance was especially important for two reasons. The responsibility for raising the money necessary to fill the extensive developmental plans of Macdonald's government fell upon the Minister of Finance, a responsibility requiring a great deal of ability. It would appear that in addition to being capable, the occupant had to be acceptable to the business community of Canada, which has traditionally been the preserve of the English-Canadian community. In 1869 the Treasury Board was created with the Minister of Finance as chairman, which meant that almost every item of government expenditure had to come before the minister, and as a result he became even more important in the eyes of his colleagues and the country in general. The advent of Keynesian economics increased the importance of the Finance portfolio as the federal government became deeply involved in the regulation of the economy through the use of fiscal and monetary policy. Thus, although some of the functions performed by the Minister of Finance, such as acting as chairman of Treasury Board and as Receiver-General have been transferred to other ministries, the Department remains one of the most important government departments, because of ". . . its key position as the major source of advice on fiscal policy and on the economic consequences of government action".[23] The occupant draws to himself a great deal of public criticism so that in spite of its high status, the post is not regarded as a stepping stone to the prime ministership. Only two Ministers of Finance have ever become Prime Minister — Tupper, who served for sixteen months in 1887-1888, and Bennett, who served for four months in 1926.

As noted above, the Minister of Finance is no longer chairman of the Treasury Board, although still *ex officio* a member of it. As a result of the recommendation of the Royal Commission on Government Organization, a separate cabinet position was created in 1966 for the president of Treasury Board. Treasury Board has three broad areas of responsibility; it is responsible for expenditure control and co-ordination in the Canadian government, for the establishment of personnel policy and supervision of personnel relations; that is, in a sense the Treasury Board is the employer of the federal civil service since it bargains with employee unions on behalf of the government. It is also responsible for ". . . the establishment of administrative regulations and the promotion of improvements in administration practices".[24] The Treasury Board thus has a key role in indicating the financial and administrative implications of government policy — existing and proposed — and thus the president of the Board has an overview of government activities that makes him one of the most important ministers in the cabinet. As minister responsible for the body that has been described by its secretary as ". . . the Cabinet's committee on the Expenditure Budget and the Cabinet's committee on Management,"[25] the president of Treasury Board occupies one of the most influential positions in the cabinet and thus can have a great effect on cabinet decisions.

There is one other department which, because of its functional importance, has been regarded as very prestigious over the years, the Department of External Affairs. The creation of a Department of External Affairs in 1909 was to some extent a reflection of Canada's increasing independence from Great Britain, but the manner of its establishment and its early years of operation indicated that Canada was taking a very cautious attitude towards participation in world affairs. In the beginning the department was placed under the Secretary of State, although Laurier assumed effective control of the department. In 1912 it was brought under the Prime Minister's direct authority, where it remained until 1946, when it became a separate ministry. During the early years of this century the cabinet as a body participated in decisions having to do with foreign affairs. This was partly the result of the temperaments of Laurier and Borden, partly the result of the intensely political aspects of the problems confronting the country in this particular area; questions such as reciprocity, immigration, and Canada's relationship with the United Kingdom insofar as defence was concerned. "In addition, lack of diplomatic representatives abroad meant that negotiations were frequently entrusted to ministers of departments. . . . Such functional division of labour in external affairs naturally imparted a collegial character to consideration of foreign policy matters."[26] Over time, however, foreign affairs became more complex and required quick decisions; the procedure of placing problems before the cabinet for leisurely discussion became impossible. As a result, from the time of World War I the Prime Minister assumed more and more personal responsibility for such matters, with a consequent increase in his importance and prestige. Borden was prepared to share his authority and had ministers accompany him on his visits to Europe. Mr. King, however, had no intention of sharing power with anyone. ". . . he appears to have made many foreign policy decisions himself and to have consulted Cabinet colleagues and departmental officials only when he thought it necessary."[27]

World War II had the effect of greatly increasing the work load and importance of the Department of External Affairs. Parliament tended to leave the important matters arising out of the revolutionary changes in foreign relations brought on by World War II to the cabinet, thus greatly enhancing its power. This is consistent with the British tradition, in which the conduct of foreign affairs has been left to the executive.

Mr. St. Laurent became Canada's first full-time Secretary of State for External Affairs in 1946, and when he became leader of the Liberal Party he was succeeded in that position by Mr. Pearson, who also in time became leader of the Liberal Party. The position came to be regarded as second in importance to that of the Prime Minister.

Subsequent events, however, have indicated that the position is not nearly as prestigious as it once was, and the change in its status is illustrative of how the Prime Minister can dominate the cabinet and, on his own, downgrade the status of a department and thus the importance of the minister responsible for it. Mr. Trudeau has tended to assume responsibility for foreign policy himself, and has sent his own representatives, rather than officials of the Department of External Affairs, on important foreign-policy missions. Consequently, the department and its minister have not occupied the limelight, and the position has thus lost prestige.

It has been noted that several of the cabinet positions created by Macdonald in 1867 were mere sinecures with little or no responsibility attached to them. One such position was that of the President of the Privy Council. The office of President of the Council had been created in the Province of Canada in 1841 by Lord Sydenham as the result of recommendations of another pre-Confederation institution that has survived to the present day, a Royal Commission. The Royal Commission on the Public Departments proposed in 1839 that a President of the Executive Council be appointed ". . . whose first and principal duty it should be to attend to details of the Council office, in all their branches and who should have it peculiarly in charge to examine and report all matters submitted to the Board".[28] When Lord Sydenham appointed in 1841 a committee of his Executive Council to advise him on applications or claims for lands, he also appointed a president to preside over the committee. When the Governor ceased to attend meetings of the Council, the president assumed the chair. Since, however, the Governor remained the most important figure in government, the president of the Council never outranked him in prestige and status. As the power of the Governor declined, it tended to drift not to the president, who was always very much equal in status to his fellows in the Council, but to the heads of the party factions making up the Council. As it happened, these men usually occupied the position of Attorney-General.

Section V of the Instructions to the first Governor General specified that the Governor General was responsible for appointing a member of the Privy Council to preside as president in his absence. In fact, Macdonald could have appointed himself as president but, because of the need for a large cabinet, did not do so, using the position as a place in which to satisfy another claim to office. It would seem that, in fact, the Privy Council as such never met, hence the president had no responsibilities. The instruction to the Governor General regarding the appointment of a president was omitted from the revised Instructions issued in 1878, but the position was maintained, although it had no responsibilities attached to it and only rarely did the occupant have an opportunity to act as chairman of cabinet meetings. Tupper, however, who was President of the Privy Council from 1870 to 1872, did preside in Sir John A. Macdonald's absence. Once when Macdonald was in Washington, he wrote Tupper: "Let me ask you to submit this letter in the strictest confidence to the Council and let me have some general expression of opinion for my guidance. . ."[29]

In 1883, Macdonald combined the offices of President of the Privy Council and Prime Minister and the practice was followed with some interruptions until 1957. In those cases where the two offices were held separately, there is no evidence that there were any serious responsibilities connected with the Presidency of the Privy Council, although occasionally some special duty might be assigned, such as in 1873, when the President of the Privy Council assumed responsibility for the R.C.M.P. In 1917 Mr. N.W. Rowell, leader of the Unionist Liberal wing of the wartime coalition government, was appointed President of the Privy Council and the post acquired considerable symbolic significance. When Mr. King came to power in 1921 he saw to it that he became President of the Privy Council so that there would be no possibility of his sharing power with anyone.

The anomalous position of the President of the Privy Council illustrates the importance (or lack of it) of the distinction between the cabinet and the Privy Council. The cabinet is chaired by the Prime Minister, both when it functions as cabinet and as Privy Council; thus the title President of the Privy Council is a complete misnomer. Over the years there have been four categories of use of the office of President of the Privy Council. It has, on many occasions, been held by the Prime Minister of the day; only Mackenzie, Pearson and Trudeau have not held this position at one time during their tenure as Prime Minister. It has also been used as a prestigious title for politically important ministers who, for one reason or another, have not been given departments. An example here would be the appointment of Edward Blake, the volatile rival of Alexander Mackenzie, in 1878, or the appointment of Rowell in 1917. There have also been times when the office has been used merely as a title for a comparatively insignificant minister, who was appointed in order to satisfy some sectional or group need. This would possibly be true in the case of Dorion in the Diefenbaker government. "As President of the Privy Council Dorion presided over exactly three Privy Council meetings."[30] In recent times the position has been used for ministers who have been given special responsibilities by the Prime Minister.

The recent practice of assigning special responsibilities to the President of the Privy Council began during the Pearson administration. In 1963 Hon. Maurice Lamontagne was appointed President of the Privy Council with special responsibility for the problem of French-English relations and for cultural matters that were later assigned to the Department of the Secretary of State. Mr. Lamontagne was succeeded by Hon. George McIlraith, who became Leader of the Government in the House, who was in turn succeeded by Hon. Guy Favreau, who was given special responsibilities for dominion-provincial relations and special responsibility for corporate law, which eventually led to the creation of the Department of Consumer and Corporate Affairs. Hon. Walter

Gordon, who succeeded Mr. Favreau, had special responsibilities for a study of American ownership of industry in Canada, which led to the Watkins Report.

Under the Trudeau government the President of the Privy Council has been assigned very specific responsibilities, but these responsibilities, have little to do with the Privy Council *per se*. The President of the Privy Council under the Trudeau government has acted on a full-time basis as Leader of the Government in the House of Commons. "The responsibilities of the House Leader are not confined to setting up the House but extend to the preparation of legislation in Cabinet, the administration of the House establishment and relations with the government back bench."[31] It was also announced at the time of the appointment of the first person to assume these responsibilities, Hon. Donald Macdonald, that he would ". . . have the task of recommending to the Government an appropriate procedure for the review of administrative action and of delegated legislation."[32]

As an indication of the importance of this position, it should be noted that the President of the Privy Council now has a personal staff as large as that of ministers who have departments to administer. In 1972 the President of the Privy Council had a private secretary, an associate private secretary, an executive assistant, an executive secretary, an administrative assistant, and two special assistants. His representatives attend parliamentary committee meetings, many interdepartmental committee meetings, as well as meetings of committees of the Privy Council Office. A staff under the minister studies parliamentary procedure with a view to expediting the passage of government legislation. An attempt is made to anticipate as closely as possible all likely reactions by Parliament, and especially the opposition, to proposed government legislation and to develop procedures to ensure reasonably smooth passage of government bills. In effect an effort is being made to program Parliament by anticipating future developments in the House of Commons. Legislation drafted by the Department of Justice is examined to ensure that, as far as possible, political factors are taken into account and to eliminate loopholes that might be seized on by the opposition. The President of the Privy Council is kept aware of all government planning and is informed continuously of proposed legislation in order to plan the government's tactics in the House of Commons. He also acts as Chairman of the Cabinet Committee on Legislation and House Planning.

A "Parliamentary Enquiries and Co-ordination Division" has been established under the President of the Privy Council to expedite the provision of information for Members of Parliament. This involves seeing to it that the various departments provide responses to questions and co-ordinating returns when more than one department or agency are involved. In addition,

The Parliamentary Enquiries and Co-ordination Division provides guidance and advice to Ministers' staffs and to officials of departments, Crown corporations and agencies with regard to relevant practices and procedures in Parliament; provides guidance and leadership to the departments, Crown corporations and agencies to ensure effective assistance in the conduct of their work; advises parliamentary returns sections on the sense of a Parliament Enquiry by obtaining, through direct contact with the Member or by reference to experience, the interpretation of a Question or Notice of Motion for the Production of Papers and by issuing directives to promote the more orderly and prompt preparation of replies and returns to Questions and to Notices of Motions for the Production of Papers; advises on the acceptability by the Government of a Notice of Motion for the Production of Papers in accordance with established guidelines; advises Ministers' staffs and officials of departments, Crown corporations and agencies on the tabling of Statutory Reports in the House of Commons and in the Senate; carries out liaison with the House of Commons staffs, Ministers' staffs, and officials of departments, Crown corporations and agencies on issues of a general nature; and provides guidance to Ministers' staffs and officials of departments, Crown corporations and agencies on the approach to several parliamentary exercises, including writing and style of Parliamentary Enquiries.[33]

All of the foregoing enable the President of the Privy Council to be completely informed and thus influence government activities. Thus this position must be counted as one of the more influential ones in the cabinet.

Evolution of the Cabinet

Of the thirteen original cabinet positions filled by Macdonald in 1867, eight remain. These are the offices of Postmaster-General, President of the Privy Council, Secretary of State, and the Ministers of Agriculture, Finance, Justice, Militia and Defence (renamed National Defence in 1923), and Public Works. The others have either been abolished or absorbed into new departments. The office of Secretary of State for the Provinces was abolished in 1873, and the offices of Minister of Customs and Minister of Inland Revenue were finally combined into the office of Minister of Customs and National Excise in 1921, which in turn was supplanted by the office of Minister of National Revenue in 1928. This office still exists.

The office of Receiver-General was combined in 1879 with the office of Minister of Finance and remained so until 1969, when it became part of the office of Minister of Supply and Services.

The office of Minister of Marine and Fisheries remained in existence until 1930 when it was divided into two offices, Minister of Marine and Minister of Fisheries. The office of Minister of Marine was abolished in 1936, and its responsibilities assumed by the newly created office of

Minister of Transport. Fisheries remained a separate portfolio until 1969, when it was combined with the Department of Forestry into the office of Minister of Fisheries and Forestry. As a result of the Government Organization Act of 1971, Fisheries became part of the office of Minister of the Environment and Minister of Fisheries. In 1974 Fisheries became the sole responsibility of a minister once again.

The first new office to be added was that of Minister of the Interior, which was created in 1873 as a result of the responsibilities acquired by the federal government when Manitoba and British Columbia entered Confederation. This department was responsible, among other things, for immigration and the settlement of the west. For western Canada the department was very important, and from 1888 to 1930 every Minister of the Interior represented a western constituency. Laurier, after considerable difficulty, persuaded Clifford Sifton to serve in his cabinet as Minister of the Interior, and ". . . Mr. Sifton said in accepting office he had stipulated for a free hand in politics designed to settle the West."[34] When Mr. Meighen was invited to enter the Union government in 1917, he ". . . demanded that he be made Minister of the Interior, an office which then signified Western leadership."[35] This ministry was abolished in 1935 and its functions distributed among various other departments. From 1911 to 1972 the Minister of Agriculture had always been from one of the western provinces (except for the period 1965-1968 when the minister, Mr. Greene, was from Ontario), and he has usually been regarded as the chief western spokesman, replacing the Minister of the Interior. The assigning of responsibility for the Canadian Wheat Board to a minister other than the Minister of Agriculture may have diluted the latter's status, and one notes that when the Hon. Otto Lang, who represented a Saskatchewan constituency, was appointed Minister of Justice in 1972, he continued to have responsibility for the Wheat Board, as he had when he was Minister of Manpower and Immigration. This unlikely combination of responsibilities indicates the continuing importance of the representation principle and the awkward results it can produce.

In 1879 the office of Minister of Railways and Canals was created, emphasizing the importance of railways, both economically and politically, at that time. The first Minister of Railways was Sir Charles Tupper, whose appointment created certain difficulties. The resolution of these difficulties illustrates the flexibility of the cabinet system. Sir Charles Tupper was appointed High Commissioner to the United Kingdom in 1883, but as Macdonald was unwilling to permit him to resign either his cabinet position or his seat, Tupper served as High Commissioner without salary. An Order-in-Council was passed that enabled Tupper to draw his salary as a minister even though he was in London, while an acting minister was appointed to fulfil his responsibilities as minister.

This did not involve additional expense, as Pope, who acted for Tupper, was also Minister of Agriculture. Several years prior to this, when Tupper, then a member of the cabinet, had gone to the United Kingdom for an extended period of time, an Order-in-Council was passed appointing Pope as acting minister. The procedure was formalized by P.C. 2153, December 3, 1886, as follows: ". . . in any case in which there is a vacancy in the office of a Minister of the Crown another Minister shall be specially named by Order-in-Council during such vacancy."

The unusual practice of having a cabinet minister located outside the country was discontinued in 1884 but was revived in 1916 when the portfolio of Minister of Overseas Military Forces from Canada in the United Kingdom was created by Order-in-Council through the War Measures Act. The minister was responsible for the administration of the armed forces in Great Britain and in Europe and for acting as a watchdog for Sir Robert Borden, who was anxious to ensure that Canada's interests were not overlooked by the British government. The Ministry of Overseas Military Forces was abolished in 1920.

The creation of the offices of Minister of Trade and Commerce in 1892, Mines in 1907, and Labour in 1909 reflected the growth of industrialization of Canada and the need for government action in these areas of activity. The office of Minister of Mines was abolished in 1935 and a new office, that of Minister of Mines and Resources, created. This in turn was abolished in 1950 and two new offices created; the Minister of Mines and Technical Surveys and the Minister of Northern Affairs and National Resources. The Department of Mines and Technical Surveys was abolished in 1965 and a new office was created, that of Minister of Energy, Mines and Resources. The office of Minister of Northern Affairs and Natural Resources became the office of Minister of Resources and Development in 1953 and in 1966 became the office of Minister of Indian Affairs and Northern Development.

The creation of a separate Department of Immigration and Colonization in 1917 reflected the government's expectation that there would be a resumption of the large-scale immigration that had taken place prior to World War I. This department was abolished in 1935 and its functions were taken over by the Department of Mines and Resources. In 1949 the office of Minister of Citizenship and Immigration was created and remained in existence until it was replaced in 1965 by the present office of Minister of Manpower and Immigration.

It was felt necessary at the end of World War I to create the office of Minister of Soldier's Re-Establishment (in 1918). In 1919 the office of Minister of Health was created, and in 1921 these two offices were placed under one minister. The two offices were formally merged into the office of Minister of Pensions and National Health in 1928. This arrangement continued until 1944, when two new offices were created, the Minister of National Health and Welfare and the Minister of Veterans' Affairs, both of which are still in existence.

World War II required the creation of several new offices. These included the office of Minister of National Defence for Air, the Minister of National Defence for Naval Services, the Minister of Munitions and Supply, the Minister of National War Services (all created in 1940) and the office of Minister of Reconstruction in 1944. These offices were abolished after the war, except for Reconstruction, which became the office of Minister of Reconstruction and Supply in 1946. This in turn was abolished in 1950 and replaced by the office of Minister of Defence Production. This office was abolished in 1969 and its functions absorbed by the office of Minister of Supply and Services, created in the same year.

Under Mr. St. Laurent, the office of Associate Minister of National Defence was established and continues to exist, although at the present time it is vacant. The only innovation made by Mr. Diefenbaker with respect to the creation of new offices was the creation of the office of Minister of Forestries in 1960, which was merged with Fisheries in 1969 and which was eventually abolished as a separate office in 1971.

In 1967 the office of Registrar-General of Canada was created, and in 1969 this office was made part of the responsibilities assumed by the newly created office of Minister of Consumer and Corporate Affairs. Also in 1969 the office of Minister of Regional Economic Expansion was created and the office of Minister of Communications was established as well.

The result of all these changes is that the cabinet has increased in size from thirteen to thirty members (in 1975). The increase in size reflects the increased complexity of government and the additional demands on it. In addition, the entry of new provinces into Confederation and the demand for cabinet representation by various groups also required an increase in the number of cabinet ministers.

There were some attempts made over the years to reorganize the cabinet on a more efficient basis. Thus in 1878 the cabinet post of Receiver-General was abolished and a second legal portfolio, a Solicitor-Generalship, was created in order to divide the responsibilities of the Minister of Justice. The notion of providing assistance to the Minister of Justice through a Solicitor-General proved to be unworkable for several reasons. The fact is that Ministers of Justice, although frequently overworked, were reluctant to share any of their authority and responsibility with anyone else. Moreover, as an additional expedient to make the cabinet more efficient, the Solicitor-General was often sworn into the ministry but not made part of the cabinet. As a result, the position over the years came to be regarded as relatively insignificant and a source of neither power nor prestige, even when the incumbent was in the cabinet. Thus it could be said that in 1958 "Balcer was literally insulted by being appointed to the least regarded position in the Cabinet — the non-departmental post as Solicitor-General — the glider who is towed insignificantly in the wake of the powerful and prestige laden Minister of Justice."[36] In 1966 the Government Organization Act created a new Department of the Solicitor-General, giving the minister responsibility for the R.C.M.P., the National Parole Board, and the Canadian Penitentiary Service.

Ministers Without Portfolio

In addition to appointing ministers as heads of government departments or to occupy sinecure positions, prime ministers have from time to time appointed ministers without portfolio, either to provide some form of sectional or group representation, to provide a link with the Senate, to perform special duties that might require cabinet rank but not a departmental organization or to permit entry into the cabinet for an individual who does not wish departmental responsibilities. An example here would be the appointment by Prime Minister Alexander Mackenzie in 1873 of Edward Blake as a minister without portfolio. Blake would not at that time ". . . undertake any administrative tasks and became a minister without portfolio, an expedient then unprecedented in Canadian practice."[37] In fact, Skelton was incorrect since Senator James Aitkins served as minister without portfolio for a brief period in Macdonald's first Cabinet, but since 1873 every cabinet has generally included one minister without portfolio.

Under the Trudeau administration there have been several important developments regarding ministers without portfolio. One such development was to assign specific responsibilities, such as for Housing, the Wheat Board, and the government's new information agency, Information Canada, to ministers without portfolio. Prior to 1969 the position of minister without portfolio indicated a minister free from specific responsibility in connection with the executive of the government of Canada, although such a minister might be assigned specific responsibilities for a very brief period of time. The new procedure was followed to enable the government to deal with the problems of a temporary nature that might not require the creation of a separate department. It was also suggested that filling such responsibilities would provide useful experience for ministers who would eventually be placed in charge of departments.

A further development took place in January 1971 when the Trudeau government introduced a Government Organization Bill which, among other things, established two new types of ministers in addition to those already in existence — i.e., departmental ministers,

ministers without portfolio and without particular administrative responsibilities and ministers without portfolio but with administrative duties. It should be noted that it has been possible in the past to assign to ministers specific duties under the *Public Service Rearrangement and Transfer of Duties Act.*

Section two of this Act provides:

> The Governor in Council may (a) transfer any powers, duties or functions or the control or supervision of any part of the public service from one Minister of the Crown to any other Minister of the Crown, or from one department or portion of the public service or (b) amalgamate and combine any two or more departments under one Minister of the Crown and under one Deputy Minister.

The earlier Trudeau appointments had apparently created confusion. One minister told the House of Commons that ". . . we thus arrived at a situation where ministers without portfolio in fact had portfolios. A complicated situation became further confused."[38]

The new legislation provided for ministers without portfolio but with responsibilities, giving them the rank and status of departmental ministers. Such ministers are referred to as ministers of state for designated purposes (such as for Urban Affairs or for Science and Technology) and are ". . . charged with a particular mission, usually of a policy nature, generally of short or at least not necessarily of permanent duration."[39]

There was to be a second type of minister of state, a ". . . minister who is assigned primarily to assist another minister . . . able to receive powers, duties and functions from other ministers and . . . responsible to Parliament in accounting for the manner in which they exercise them".[40] These ministers receive the same salary as ministers without portfolio, which is less than that of ministers with portfolios (ministers of state for designated purposes receive the same salaries as ministers with portfolio), and these salaries will be provided for in the estimates of the minister with whom they are to be associated. There may also be ministers without portfolio and without responsibility as in the past. It should be pointed out that the experiment involving having ministers of state assist departmental ministers did not work well and appears to have been abandoned by the Trudeau administration. This is likely because of the unwillingness of departmental ministers to share duties and publicity and the desire of some of the appointees to these positions to attract as much publicity as possible.

Inner and Outer Cabinets — Cabinet and Ministry

The size of Canada's cabinet has brought forth from time to time complaints that the cabinet is too large to be efficient. There have been suggestions that the Canadian cabinet should be divided into an inner and outer cabinet as in Great Britain. It should be pointed out that it is not necessarily true that the political head of a department is automatically a member of the cabinet. Acts of Parliament are the legal basis for departments and individual cabinet positions, but it is custom only that permits ministers to be members of the cabinet. There is, thus, a difference between the cabinet and the ministry. The cabinet may be said to consist of those ministers who have become Privy Councillors and who, on the invitation of the Prime Minister, have become members of the cabinet. The ministry *per se* consists of those individuals who are the political heads of government departments and any ministers who do not have specific departmental responsibilities. At the present time in Canada, indeed since 1945, the membership of the ministry and the cabinet have been identical.

Under Prime Minister Thompson there were three ministers outside the cabinet: the Controller of Customs, the Controller of Inland Revenue, and the Solicitor-General. These ministers were not members of the Privy Council, although they were accorded the title of "honourable" during their incumbency. They were, however, paid less than members of the cabinet ($5000 per annum versus $7000).[41]

Laurier brought the two controllers into his first cabinet as Ministers of Customs and Inland Revenue, respectively. The occupant of the position of Solicitor-General was not a member of the cabinet until the Rt. Hon. Arthur Meighen, who served as Solicitor-General from June 26, 1913, was elevated to the cabinet on October 2, 1915. When Meighen was transferred to another portfolio in 1917, his successor as Solicitor-General, Guthrie, remained outside the cabinet until July 5, 1919. After that the position was frequently left vacant, and in 1936 the Minister of Justice assumed the responsibilities of the Solicitor-General. The position was revived in 1945, and its occupant has been in the cabinet and Privy Council ever since. The position in the cabinet, however, was less secure than other positions until 1966, when legislation was passed requiring that the Solicitor-General be sworn in as a member of the Privy Council.

The idea of non-cabinet ministers, however, was not popular because it ran contrary to the representation principle. Provinces and groups objected to lack of representation in the cabinet and to exclusion from the patronage such representation assured. There was obviously no political advantage in the idea, and the small number of ministers left outside of the cabinet made no appreciable difference to the cabinet's efficiency; in any event one would expect representation to triumph over efficiency.

While Canada has really not had an official inner cabinet, there is considerable evidence that there has usually been an informal inner cabinet — that is, a group of individuals who are close to the Prime Minister and who influence him more than others. ". . . There usually arises within the Cabinet a small group of four or five Ministers who, because of ability of various kinds, exceptional local or sectional confidence, personal qualities or character, will be consulted by him on all matters of importance."[42] In Laurier's cabinet, for example, Clifford Sifton ". . . was recognized as one of the inner group which develops naturally in every government . . . [who] take the lead in council in facing difficulties and shaping policies."[43] According to Mr. King's biographers, "At the middle of 1944 the most prominent members of the government were Ralston, the Minister of National Defence, Power, the Associate Minister of National Defence and Minister of National Defence for Air, Ilsley, the Minister of Finance, Howe, the Minister of Munitions and Supply, and St. Laurent, the Minister of Justice."[44] There was, however, a more informal group on whom King relied. This group included men such as Lapointe; O.D. Skelton, Under Secretary of State for External Affairs; Norman Rogers, Minister of Labour; T.A. Crerar, Minister of Mines and Resources; and Senator Raoul Dandurand, Government Leader in the Senate.[45]

Some observers have alleged that no such group existed under Mr. Diefenbaker. "Government by small select circle truly disappeared from the Canadian scene after the 1957 election and from then on each minister was consulted on every question, however unimportant his portfolio or knowledge of the matter. This process was highly flattering and a boost to the egos of many Cabinet members but it has led to confusion and a considerable waste of time."[46] There is no doubt, however, that in political matters at least Mr. Diefenbaker had a circle of advisors — Hon. David Walker, a Member of Parliament from Toronto who became Minister of Public Works; Senator Blunt, an old friend; and Mr. Grosart (now Senator), National Director of the Progressive Conservative party, but only Mr. Walker was a member of the cabinet. Similarly, there was under Mr. Pearson an inner group; it has been alleged that this group consisted of the Minister of Finance, Mr. Gordon; the Minister of Transport, Mr. Pickersgill; the Minister of Justice, Mr. Favreau; and Mr. Kent, a member of Mr. Pearson's personal staff.[47] Under Mr. Trudeau there have been references to a "Super Group", consisting of cabinet ministers, civil servants, and personal advisors. "The Super Group is an informal, loosely organized ring of advisors, some of them on Trudeau's staff, some in the public service, some elected, some appointed. . . ."[48]

It would seem inevitable that some ministers would have more influence than others. Influence arises because of various factors. The Minister of Finance, for example, has had almost a veto power over the spending plans of the other departments, and there are few issues that are not relevant to his position in one way or another. He thus has more opportunity to intervene than his colleagues. Sifton was close to Laurier because of his influence in the west. Those noted as being close to King were in important wartime portfolios and the fact that some, such as Ilsely, were personally unpopular with King did not detract from their key role. Under Mr. Trudeau there is a cabinet committee on Priorities and Planning that the Prime Minister has described as being close to the British system of an inner cabinet. Mr. Marchand and Mr. Pelletier were considered to be close confidants and constant advisors to Mr. Trudeau, and it would seem inevitable that there would be a few ministers who, because of their portfolios or personal congeniality with the Prime Minister, will form an informal inner circle advising the Prime Minister on problems as they arise.

The informal nature of such groups is very important. The membership of such groups can vary as different problems arise, but the most important point is that in the past the advice they gave was provided in secret and so their influence did not detract from the representation principle. The appearance of all ministers taking part was maintained and the absence of an obviously structured inner group preserved the illusion of all groups being represented in the decision-making process.

Parliamentary Secretaries and Parliamentary Assistants

Several proposals were made over the years regarding the possibility of relieving ministers of some of their duties while at the same time providing training for potential cabinet ministers. In 1912 Richard Cartwright, who served as a minister under both Mackenzie and Laurier, suggested that "What we need very much is to have a few posts like the English Parliamentary Under Secretary, to which young politicians would be appointed without giving them Cabinet rank."[49] Nothing was done, however, until World War I, when Sir Robert Borden appointed a Parliamentary Secretary of Militia and Defence and a Parliamentary Undersecretary of State for External Affairs. Both, by law, were to be Members of Parliament. The former was to assist the Minister of Militia and Defence and act for him within carefully defined limits if the Minister was away from Ottawa, but he could make no changes in the policy of the department without the approval of the cabinet, and under such circumstances any recommendations for change were to be made by the Prime Minister; in other words, the parliamentary secretary was definitely not a member of the cabinet (nor of the Privy Council). The Parliamentary Undersecretary of State for External Affairs was to assist the Prime Minister in administering the Department of External Affairs, and he was also not to be of the cabinet. In February 1918 the office of Parliamentary Secretary, Soldiers Civil Re-establishment was created, and the appointee was also not of the cabinet. The statute authorizing the payment of salaries for these positions provided that they be terminated at the end of the session of Parliament in which the war ended, and this was done. Of the three men who served as parliamentary secretary, one eventually became a member of the cabinet — Hon. F.B. McCurdy who served as Minister of Public Works under Prime Minister Meighen from July to December 1921.

When Mr. King became Prime Minister in 1921 he was very anxious to appoint parliamentary undersecretaries but was unable to convince the cabinet of the merits of the idea. He did appoint one Member of Parliament informally to assist him as Parliamentary Undersecretary for External Affairs, but this person served without remuneration, and when he resigned to take up a diplomatic position no successor was named. Nothing more was done until 1943, although a suggestion was made by Mr. Woodsworth in 1930 that parliamentary secretaries be appointed. The Speech from the Throne in 1936 indicated that the government was considering developing a system of parliamentary secretaries. Mr. King, however, apparently found the task of cabinet building in 1935 so exhausting that he was not prepared to go through a similar process with regard to parliamentary secretaries.

In 1943, Mr. King appointed seven "parliamentary assistants" via Order-in-Council. In the debate on the bill to provide salaries for them, Mr. King, who referred to the appointees as assistants to the minister, said they would ". . . be expected to help the minister in any way the minister may think his services are likely to be most advantageous."[50] It was clear, however, that he did not see parliamentary assistants becoming deeply involved in actual administration or policy making, pointing out that the duties of the parliamentary assistant would ". . . be of a character which will make it necessary for him to be *persona grata* to the deputy minister as well as the minister."[51] This remark is indicative of the strong position of the senior civil service at this time.

Of the seven appointed, six were to assist ministers who were also members of the war cabinet, including a Parliamentary Assistant to the President of the Privy Council (Brooke Claxton), a position Mr. King combined with that of Prime Minister. Claxton received special responsibilities in connection with the Liberal Party, acting as a link between the Prime Minister and the party and also developing a postwar program for the party. Mr. King probably felt that some of the burden would be lifted off the ministers by such appointments, especially political burdens. These appointments also gave Mr. King a chance to evaluate the ability of younger Members of Parliament, and it is important to note that, of the seven appointed in 1943, five — Abbott, Chevrier, Claxton, Jean, and Martin — subsequently became members of the cabinet.

The fact that King created these positions via Order-in-Council in

1943 rather than by statute indicates his great caution about change. He felt that a statute would be useful only after the country had become accustomed to having parliamentary assistants and after any possible flaws in the idea were discovered and removed. As a result, while the practice of appointing parliamentary assistants became standard and the number to be appointed at any time increased under Mr. St. Laurent, the procedure was not formalized until 1959, when the Diefenbaker government produced legislation that defined the position more clearly and at the same time changed the title of the position to parliamentary secretary.

In introducing the legislation in 1959, Mr. Diefenbaker stated that the purpose of establishing the position of parliamentary secretary was ". . . to make parliament more effective, to make provision for assistance in many of the phases of a minister's life and thereby lighten the load of responsibility which rests on those who occupy the treasury benches."[52] He also suggested that these positions would provide useful training for potential ministers. Possibly Mr. Diefenbaker was anxious also to find something to do for the large number of government backbenchers in the Parliament of 1958-1962. Parliamentary assistants, as a result of this legislation, were to be Members of the House of Commons, were appointed for a term of one year, which could be renewed, and received an additional $4000 per annum. They were appointed by the Governor-in-Council (actually by the Prime Minister) and according to the statute were ". . . to assist the Minister in such a way as the minister directs." As a result of the Government Organizational Act of 1971, the authorized number of parliamentary secretaries to hold office at any one time is to correspond with the number of ministers receiving salaries under the Salary Act. The term of office has been extended to two years, which is renewable. In 1975 the remuneration was increased to $5300 per annum.

It would seem that the idea of providing assistance to cabinet ministers through parliamentary secretaries has not worked well insofar as relieving ministers of some of their burdens is concerned. To make good use of a parliamentary secretary would require a minister to share the political limelight, and this has tended to discourage ministers from making effective use of them. One former minister has commented that parliamentary secretaries are ". . . far from being junior ministers as they are sometimes called and they are rarely privy to the secrets of a minister's work. The posts are only as important as the scope of the work a minister assigns to his parliamentary secretary."[53]

The fact that parliamentary secretaries are not in the cabinet and hence do not take an oath of secrecy also probably limits their effectiveness, because it will often not be possible for the ministers to confide in them. It has also been argued that the brief term of office is an inhibiting factor, but a study of the time spent as parliamentary secretary in individual departments (Table 3-I below) indicates an average time of 1.8 years, which would give a person ample time to become quite familiar with the working of the department to which he has been assigned. The present term of two years also provides ample time, and may have the effect, by locating an individual for a fairly lengthy time period in a department, of making him more useful to the minister.

Another reason why the position has not proved useful is that parliamentary secretaries do not receive a great deal of remuneration for the position. One parliament secretary replied, "I gross $440.00 a month, as a parliamentary secretary; after taxes that amounts to about $275.00. Consequently my priorities are my constituency responsibilities, my House work and my position as parliamentary secretary, in that order." Under these circumstances parliamentary secretaries who are not especially anxious to obtain further promotions are unlikely to exert themselves very much in assisting ministers.

The increasing use of executive and special assistants by ministers has also tended to downgrade the work of parliamentary secretaries. Such assistants can do many of the tasks that might be otherwise assigned to parliamentary secretaries without attracting publicity and thus protect a minister from the effects of his own incompetence. The fact that the executive assistant is the personal appointee of the minister and is thus congenial to him, while the parliamentary secretary is the appointee of the Prime Minister and may not be congenial to a particular minister, can also affect the effectiveness of the position. The possibility that unfriendly relations may develop between a minister and his parliamentary secretary when the minister is incompetent and is being

TABLE 3-I

Time Spent by Parliamentary Secretaries in Individual Departments, 1943-1974

Prime Minister	Time Period	No. of Parliamentary Secretaries Appointed	Avg. Time
King	1943-1948	20	1.5 yrs.
St. Laurent	1948-1957	28	2.5 yrs.
Diefenbaker	1957-1963	36	1.1 yrs.
Pearson	1963-1968	30	1.5 yrs.
Trudeau*	1968-1974 (June)	44	1.2 yrs.
Total		158	1.8 yrs.

*Covers only those no longer parliamentary secretaries.

assisted by an ambitious and bright parliamentary secretary is always present and is best dealt with by such a minister by giving the parliamentary secretary little to do, while the executive assistant quietly covers up for his minister. This exposes one of the weaknesses in the system, in that the position is what the minister decides to make of it. If an appointee is not in the good graces of the minister, as was apparently the case with Miss LaMarsh and one of her parliamentary secretaries, the position will be of benefit to no one. This could be compensated for by providing a more precise definition for the responsibilities of parliamentary secretaries and giving them special duties so that a minister would be obliged to keep them informed of developments within the department.

The position of parliamentary secretary has often served as the first step on the ladder leading to the cabinet. Table 3-II shows the number of parliamentary secretaries originally appointed by each prime minister and the number who subsequently were appointed to the cabinet, either by the prime minister who originally appointed them, or by subsequent prime ministers.

TABLE 3-II

Promotions of Parliamentary Secretaries to the Cabinet
(as of Jan. 31, 1975)

Prime Minister	Parliamentary Secretaries Appointed	Subsequent Cabinet Members
King	20	11
St. Laurent	18	8
Diefenbaker	36	9
Pearson	30	14
Trudeau*	44	11
Total	148	53

*Includes only those who are no longer parliamentary secretaries.

This table shows that 53 out of a total of 148 parliamentary secretaries have eventually been appointed cabinet ministers, representing 35.8 per cent of the total appointed.

It would appear that an appointment as parliamentary secretary to certain ministers is almost a guarantee of promotion to the cabinet. Table 3-III indicates the number of parliamentary secretaries appointed in

TABLE 3-III

Parliamentary Secretaries Subsequently Appointed to Cabinet

Department	Total Number of Parliamentary Secretaries Appointed (as of June 30, 1974)	Subsequently Appointed to Cabinet
Agriculture	10	0
External Affairs	17	9 (53%)
Finance	15	12 (80%)
Justice	8	3 (38%)
Labour	11	3 (27%)
Defence	14	5 (36%)
Health and Welfare	16	4 (25%)
Prime Minister	15	8 (53%)
Trade and Commerce	11	3 (27%)
Transport	11	2 (18%)
Public Works	9	0

selected departments and the number who eventually became members of the cabinet.

It is noteworthy that of the fifteen men who have served as parliamentary secretary to the Prime Minister, eight have entered the cabinet, thus refuting Miss LaMarsh's claim that as far as Parliamentary Secretaries to the Prime Minister are concerned ". . . the post is mostly a dead end."[54]

Possibly one of the reasons why the position of Parliamentary Secretary to the Minister of Finance has been so important is that until recently Treasury Board was part of the Department of Finance, and the position gave its occupant an excellent overall view of the operation of the government. Even after the creation of Treasury Board as a separate department, "The Department of Finance remains so important and gives the Parliamentary Secretary such an excellent overview of government that his experience there is a valuable asset as a minister later on."[55] Similarly, the position of Secretary of State for External Affairs was held at one time by both Mr. St. Laurent and Mr. Pearson, and it may well be that competent men who served them as parliamentary secretary were remembered when they had the responsibility for making cabinet appointments. Of the 28 ministers appointed by Mr. Trudeau, 16 have served as parliamentary secretaries (as of December 31, 1974.)

The position of parliamentary secretary has been used at times as a means of rewarding faithful and experienced party members, rather than for the express purpose of providing help for a minister. However, the average age of ministers on appointment in the period 1949 to 1974 is 48.5 years, that of parliamentary secretaries 44.8 years, and it would thus be wrong to conclude that appointments are merely rewards for past services. Appointments to the position of parliamentary secretary have also tended to follow the representation principle, with no particular area or group favoured.

Mr. Trudeau has stated that he expects to rotate the position of parliamentary secretary more frequently than has been the case — that is, parliamentary secretaries appointed to a two-year term will be replaced after that term is up, rather than having the appointment renewed. This will serve to provide more responsibilities for backbenchers and will also provide opportunities for ambitious backbenchers to attract attention to themselves. It would seem, however, that parliamentary secretaries in future are not likely to be of great help in relieving ministers of some of their responsibilities.

The Financial Remuneration of Cabinet Ministers

While it is true that the salaries of cabinet ministers have always been substantially above the income of the average Canadian (see Table 3-IV), it is questionable if the remuneration has been adequate in terms of the demands made upon them and the expenses involved in the position. There is evidence that some ministers, after having faithfully served for many years in the cabinet, have found themselves in serious financial difficulties in later years. Borden noted somewhat bitterly that since there were no pensions for cabinet ministers, ". . . the House of Commons in later years was asked to provide and did provide a pension of $1,000 per annum for Mr. Fielding while Sir George Foster, somebody in need and having had even longer service, was not provided for".[56] The pension for Fielding, who had served under Laurier, was provided for by a Liberal-dominated House, which may explain why Foster was not looked after in the same way.

A more recent case was that of the Hon. Michael Starr, who served as Minister of Labour under Mr. Diefenbaker. After his defeat in 1968, Mr. Starr was unable to find employment for quite some time and found himself in financial difficulties until he was appointed a Citizenship Court Judge by the Liberal government. The recent pension plan developed for Members of the House of Commons may help overcome this problem to some extent, but it is important to note that cabinet ministers do not receive any special consideration as such — that is, their pensions are identical to those of ordinary Members of Parliament.

There remains still, however, the problem of inadequate remuneration, which tends to have certain undesirable effects on the Canadian political system. The fact that Canadian cabinet ministers have in most

TABLE 3-IV

Salaries of Cabinet Ministers, 1867-1975

Year	Indemnity	Cabinet Salary	Allowances	Total
1867	600	5 000		5600
1873	1 000	7 000		8 000
1901	1 500	7 000		8 500
1905	2 500	7 000		9 500
1920	4 000	10 000		14 000
1945	4 000	10 000	2 000	16 000
1954	8 000	15 000	4 000	27 000
1963	12 000	15 000	8 000	35 000
1971	18 000	15 000	10 000	43 000
1975	24 000	20 000	10 600	54 600

Prime Minister's Salary, 1867-1974

Year	Indemnity	Cabinet Salary	Allowances	Total
1867	600	5 000		5 600
1873	1 000	8 000		9 000
1901	1 500	8 000		9 500
1905	2 500	12 000		14 500
1920	4 000	15 000		19 000
1931	4 000	15 000	2 000	21 000
1945	4 000	15 000	4 000	23 000
1954	8 000	25 000	4 000	37 000
1963	12 000	25 000	8 000	45 000
1971	18 000	25 000	10 000	53 000
1975	24 000	33 300	10 600	67 900

cases a tremendous amount of responsibility, are subject to a great deal of public scrutiny and criticism while at the same time are not remunerated at a rate competitive with positions outside of government service may well cause a cabinet minister to look upon a political career as an interlude. "The path to the judiciary or the board room of a large corporation must be considerably shortened by the route through the Privy Council chamber."[57] This attitude promotes a high turnover among cabinet ministers and prevents many from acquiring a great deal of expertise that would be useful to them in fulfilling their duties. It can also be argued of course that it is not desirable for ministers to have a long tenure in the cabinet, in that under such conditions ministers may become unimaginative, too settled in their ways, and too prone to rely on civil servants. It will probably always be true that capable ministers will be able to obtain much more lucrative positions outside of politics and that the financial rewards in themselves will never provide a rationale for men to enter politics. If this were the case, a party when turned out of office and thus deprived of power might well find its leading figures leaving politics for other careers rather than working for the indemnity of an ordinary Member of Parliament. As one commentator has remarked, "When the party can no longer provide the payoff with a Cabinet post or a judicial appointment, the political outsider drifts away and the ambitious younger man is not attracted."[58] However, the fact that former cabinet ministers do remain in politics after a governmental defeat indicates that neither financial reward nor the acquisition of power is the sole motivation for their involvement.

It would nevertheless seem sensible to provide ministers with an income commensurate with their responsibilities. One method of solving the problem would be to assign to a non-political board the responsibility for recommending to the government what cabinet ministers' salaries ought to be, providing an analysis by portfolio so that those ministers with especially onerous responsibilities could at least receive a salary in excess of their less-burdened colleagues. The burden of the Minister of Finance, for example, far exceeds that of the Minister of Veterans' Affairs and it would seem reasonable that salary differentials reflect this difference in responsibilities. The dominant role the cabinet plays in our political system requires that those involved be paid fairly for their efforts and responsibility.

The ultimate responsibility for cabinet making in Canada, then, rests with the Prime Minister. While he has power to appoint, promote, and dismiss ministers and to allocate portfolios, he exercises this power under various important constraints. The representation principle is one such constraint. In addition, certain experienced party leaders can be left out of the cabinet only with great difficulty, and it may be even more difficult to remove such ministers once they have been appointed. The claim of certain areas and groups to particular portfolios is another constraint. The remuneration of ministers, insofar as it is not competitive with that paid in the private sector, may also act as a constraint. Even after he has made his appointments, the Prime Minister is inhibited by certain rules of the game that restrict his freedom of action regarding decisions taken by previous cabinets. In spite of all these constraints, the role of Prime Minister is crucial in cabinet making and in cabinet operations. In addition to having the power to appoint, promote, and demote, the Prime Minister decides the agenda and determines the organization of the cabinet, has a monopoly of the most important patronage positions, appoints all deptuy ministers, and controls his political party. These all assist the Prime Minister in dominating his cabinet, in determining how it is to function, and in setting the tone of government during his term of office.

NOTES

[1]Canada, House of Commons, Standing Committee on Finance, Trade and Economic Affairs, *Minutes and Proceedings*, (April 24, 1969), p. 2136. (Testimony of Robert Bryce, former Clerk of the Privy Council, Secretary of the Cabinet and Deputy Minister of Finance).

[2]Arend Lijphart, *The Politics of Accommodation*, p. 211.

[3]Public Archives of Canada, *Guide to Canadian Ministers*. (Ottawa; Queen's Printer, 1957), p. 27.

[4]Canada, House of Commons, *Debates*. (June 17, 1963), p. 1234.

[5]Public Archives of Canada, *Guide to Canadian Ministries*, p. 62.

[6]E.A. Forsey, *The Royal Power of Dissolution of Parliament in the British Commonwealth*. (Toronto; Oxford University Press, 1943), p. 135.

[7]Quoted in Peter Newman, *The Distemper of our Times*, (Toronto; McClelland and Stewart, 1968), p. 283.

[8]Canada, House of Commons, *Debates*. (October 28, 1963), p. 4096.

[9]W.S. Wallace, *The Memoirs of the Rt. Hon. Sir George Foster*. (Toronto; Macmillan, 1933), p. 155.

[10]*Interview*. (August 18, 1969).

[11]Norman Ward, ed., *A Party Politician: The Memoirs of Chubby Power*. (Toronto; Macmillan, 1966), p. 255.

[12]Canada, House of Commons, *Debates*. (February 11, 1936), p. 78.

[13]*Interview*. (May 29, 1971).

[14]Fred Landon, "A Canadian Cabinet Episode of 1897". *Transactions of the Royal Society of Canada*, 1938, Section II, Vol. 32, Third Series, p. 54-5.

[15]Canada, House of Commons, *Debates*. (February 24, 1930), p. 31.

[16]*Interview*. (May 25, 1970).

[17]*Interviews*. (April 10, 1969; June 2, 1969; July 9, 1969).

[18]Peter Newman, "Portrait of a New Regime Taking Power". *Maclean's*, Vol. 76, No. 12 (June 15, 1963), p. 42.

[19]Peter Dempson, *Assignment Ottawa*. (Toronto; General Publishing Co., 1968), p. 162.

[20]Peter Newman, *Renegade in Power*, p. 109.

[21]Judy LaMarsh, *Memoirs of a Bird in a Gilded Cage*. (Toronto; McClelland & Stewart, 1968), p. 47.

[22]*Interview*. (August 12, 1969).

[23]Bruce Doern, "The Development of Policy Organizations in the Executive Arena", in Bruce Doern and Peter Aucoin eds., *The Structures of Policy Making in Canada*. (Toronto; Macmillan, 1971), p. 51.

[24]W.L. White and J.C. Strick, *Policy, Politics and the Treasury Board in Canadian Government*. (Don Mills; Science Research Associates, 1970), p. 3.

[25]A.W. Johnson, "The Treasury Board of Canada and the Machinery of Government of the 1970s". *Canadian Journal of Political Science*, Vol. IV, No. 3. (September, 1971), p. 346.

[26]James Eayrs, *The Art of the Possible*. (Toronto; University of Toronto Press, 1961), p. 5.

[27]Barry Farrell, *The Making of Canadian Foreign Policy*. (Scarborough; Prentice-Hall, 1969), p. 10.

[28]Quoted in J.E. Hodgetts, *The Pioneer Public Service*. (Toronto; University of Toronto Press, 1955), p. 87.

[29]E.M. Saunders, ed., *The Life and Letters of the Rt. Hon. Sir Charles Tupper*, Vol. I. (New York; Stokes, 1916), p. 207.

[30]Newman, *Renegade in Power*, p. 287.

[31]*Interview*. (May 25, 1970).

[32]Office of the Prime Minister, press release. (July 6, 1968).

[33]*Ibid.*

[34]J.W. Dafoe, *Clifford Sifton in Relation to His Times*. (Toronto; Macmillan, 1931), p. 96.

[35]Roger Graham, *Arthur Meighen*, Volume I. (Toronto; Clarke Irwin, 1960), p. 175.

[36]Patrick Nicholson, *Vision and Indecision*. (Don Mills; Longmans Canada, 1968), p. 99.

[37]O.D. Skelton, *The Life and Letters of Sir Wilfrid Laurier*, Vol. I. (New York; Century, 1922), p. 174.

[38]Canada, House of Commons, *Debates*. (January 26, 1971), p. 2771.

[39]*Ibid.*, p. 2772.

[40]*Ibid.*

[41]Margaret A. Banks, "Privy Council, Cabinet and Ministry, in Britain and Canada: A Story of Confusion". *Canadian Journal of Economics and Political Science*, Vol. XXXI, No. 2 (May, 1965), p. 199.

[42]R. MacG. Dawson, "The Cabinet — Position and Personnel". *Canadian Journal of Economics and Political Science*, Vol. XII, No. 3 (August, 1946), p. 278.

[43]John W. Dafoe, *Clifford Sifton in Relation to His Times*, p. 195.

[44]J.W. Pickersgill and D.F. Forster, *The Mackenzie King Record*, Volume II. (Toronto; University of Toronto Press, 1968), p. 6.

[45]J.W. Pickersgill, *The Mackenzie King Record*, Vol. I. (Toronto; University of Toronto Press, 1960), p. 7-8.

[46]Pierre Sevigny, *This Game of Politics*. (Toronto; McClelland & Stewart, 1965), p. 157.

[47]Richard Gwyn, *The Shape of Scandal*. (Toronto; Clarke Irwin, 1965), p. 51-52.

[48]Walter Stewart, *Shrug, Trudeau in Power*. (Toronto; New Press, 1971), p. 175.

[49]Richard J. Cartwright, *Reminiscences*. (Toronto; W. Briggs, 1912), p. 288.

[50]Canada, House of Commons, *Debates*. (April 20, 1943), p. 2344.

[51]*Ibid.*

[52]Canada, House of Commons, *Debates*. (May 24, 1959), p. 2187.

[53]Judy LaMarsh, *Memoirs of a Bird in a Gilded Cage*, p. 143.

[54]*Ibid.*

[55]*Interview*. (January 12, 1972).

[56]Henry Borden, ed., *Robert Laird Borden*, Vol. I. (Toronto; Macmillan, 1938), p. 168 (fn.).

[57]John Porter, "Political Parties and the Political Career". *Canadian Forum*, Vol. XXXVIII, No. 1 (June, 1958), p. 51.

[58]*Ibid.* p. 55.

Chapter IV

The Cabinet at Work

The Dominance of the Cabinet

Since 1867 there have been many changes in the responsibilities and organization of the cabinet. The acceptance in Canada of the mixed economy, of a government-regulated economy, and of the "welfare state" have all entailed a great expansion of governmental activity that has greatly increased the influence of the cabinet and of the civil service, with a decrease in the effectiveness and influence of the private Member of Parliament.

This is not to suggest, however, that any time since 1867 the Canadian House of Commons exceeded the Canadian cabinet in influence. It is true that in the early days, before party lines had formed and there were many "loose fish" floating about the House of Commons, the cabinet had to keep a constant watch on the House and pay particular attention to the views of individual members in order to maintain a majority and thus avoid being voted out of office. The representative nature of the cabinet and the judicious use of patronage assisted in enabling the Prime Minister and the cabinet to force their will on Parliament.

One reason for the early dominance of the cabinet has already been noted (see page 8) — the lack of influence of the Governor General. A second reason why the Canadian cabinet was predominant in the beginning was that the Canadian government immediately took on responsibilities that were unusually extensive for its time, when the spirit of *laissez faire* dominated political philosophy and it was generally agreed that governments should operate in the smallest possible sphere. The Canadian cabinet, faced with the challenge and responsibility of developing a new nation, began immediately to formulate plans for expanding the economy, plans that involved considerable government expense and participation. Aggressive government activities had to be planned and directed by the cabinet, and so railway construction, immigration schemes, Macdonald's National Policy, meant that the activities of the Canadian cabinet from the beginning differed substantially from that of its British model.

It is significant to note that the first Canadian budget earmarked 48 per cent of its total expenditures for 'developmental' expenses and this emphasis continued for many years, so that by 1913 the proportion had risen to 50 per cent.

The Mechanics of Formal Decision Making

The difference between cabinet and Privy Council has already been noted: it is the cabinet that makes decisions, it is the Privy Council that advises the Crown. Thus if a cabinet decision requires advice to the Crown the cabinet in effect converts itself into the Privy Council and tenders advice which for the most part emerges as "acts of the Governor-in-Council, (the Order-in-Council), that entity beloved of the Canadian statutes".[1] Frequently, however, cabinet decisions do not require formal advice but are manifested as policy pronouncements in Parliament, ministerial directives, etc. A cabinet decision may also take the form of a minute, which ". . . covers a much wider field in which the Governor-in-Council gives approval to ministerial action."[2] A minute would read that:

> The Committee of the Privy Council on the recommendation of the Minister of ——————— advise that (authority be granted etc.)

A dated report of the 'Proceedings of a Meeting of the Committee of the Privy Council' is then forwarded to the Governor General, who indicates his approval by signing it.

The Order-in-Council is worded:

> His Excellency the Governor General in Council on the recommendation of the Minister of ——————— and under authority of (Statute) is pleased to order and doth hereby order as follows:

The Order would then be signed by the senior Privy Councillor present and three others, the normal quorum for a meeting of the Privy Council being four members. In some cases, however, as when a Prime Minister recommends appointments to a new Ministry or when a Prime Minister recommends that Parliament be dissolved, the Prime Minister himself seems to constitute a quorum.

Frequently Orders-in-Council are passed in batches, in which case all the Orders passed at a particular time are numbered, beginning at number one for each year, and are then forwarded to the Governor General with a covering fact sheet listing the Orders passed. The Governor General personally signs the covering sheet; his signature is rubber-stamped on the actual copies of the Orders, and then appropriate copies are distributed to those concerned. The cabinet itself rarely takes time to formally pass an Order-in-Council; this is left to a committee which meets after the regular meeting. Mr. Pickersgill has said ". . .

in practice it is a very rare thing for the whole Cabinet to spend much time considering any Order-in-Council. . . ."[3]

It should be noted that Parliament passes many Acts containing a provision that the Act shall come into force on a day to be fixed by proclamation. It is the cabinet that decides when an Act is to be proclaimed in these cases, so that the cabinet can delay the actual implementation of an Act of Parliament. When it is decided to issue a proclamation, the cabinet issues an Order-in-Council instructing the Department of Justice to prepare the proclamation, which is signed by the Governor General and then filed in the Privy Council Office which arranges to have it published in the *Canada Gazette*.

If there is no specified date or requirement for a proclamation, an Act of Parliament comes into force on the day on which it is given Royal Assent. The giving of assent, however, is not necessarily immediate, but it is unlikely that the cabinet could delay Royal Assent for very long. "It would of course be unconstitutional, though there is no hard law, for the Royal Assent to be unduly delayed or for any bill that has passed both Houses not to be included in the first available list of bills for Royal Assent."[4]

Methods of Decision

Cabinet deliberations are conducted in secret, and the actual method of deliberation varies with the Prime Minister. The cabinet does not normally vote but rather a consensus is reached, determined by the Prime Minister. There is, however, evidence that in the early years the cabinet actually did vote on the matter of the route of the Intercolonial Railway.[5] The practice has usually been to permit all ministers to voice their opinions on any matters brought before cabinet before taking a decision. Mr. St. Laurent remarked, "The tradition that has been built up is that everybody is invited, a free discussion takes place and then it is the responsibility of the Prime Minister to advise the Crown."[6] It was not uncommon for Mr. King to force all ministers to speak out on a particular matter; at other times no one would speak. At one cabinet meeting Mr. King spoke ". . . on the desirability of having Old Age Pension age reduced from 70 to 65. I gave reasons very fully. They were accepted without comment."[7] During a discussion on family allowances, however, King ". . . went around the table and made each Minister express his views".[8] During the Conscription Crisis of 1944 King wrote in his diary that at a cabinet meeting he ". . . wanted every member of the Cabinet present when the matter was discussed and settled and that each member would have to show exactly where he stood. . . . The responsibility would have to rest on each one individually."[9] It would seem that on controversial matters Mr. King demanded the vocal approval of his cabinet. At cabinet meetings usually the final opinion heard was that of the Prime Minister. Policy decisions were taken after a consensus was arrived at by the whole cabinet and the consensus was determined by the Prime Minister. As responsibilities increased and more and more matters had to be decided upon, this method of policy formation became very inefficient. Even prior to World War II it became impossible for the cabinet to deal adequately with policy proposals or to co-ordinate governmental activities, which inevitably led to the acquisition of power by senior bureaucrats.

But such inefficiency in the decision-making process is characteristic of a consociational democracy. Policy making tends to be incremental — "the result of attempts to alleviate disruptions in the socio-political system by any means facilitating some change."[10] Under such a method the emphasis is on maintaining the system and frequently is a reaction to a problem, rather than a rational decision formulated through a series of neat and orderly stages. Thus the reciprocity policy devised by Laurier and his cabinet in 1911 appeared ". . . as a pacifying arrangement which might forestall critics and quiet unrest . . . "[11] in the west and in Quebec. In 1926 King persuaded his cabinet to adopt an Old Age Pension scheme after J.S. Woodsworth had offered the support of the two Labour members in the House of Commons if the federal government would adopt such a scheme.

> . . . King called a Cabinet meeting and had Woodsworth attend and repeat his offer. King then used Woodsworth's promise to persuade the French Canadian Ministers that the old age pension scheme should be introduced. Thus King, who had always favoured old age pensions in theory, adopted them as government policy when it seemed politically possible.[12]

The post-World War II immigration policy developed by the King cabinet encouraged only ". . . selective immigration, the flow related to the economy's absorbtive capacity . . . the government had no intention of fundamentally altering the character of the Canadian population."[13] In more recent times:

> The contracting out legislation for Quebec in 1965 was a response to immediate Quebec demands; few federal decision makers at the time perceived the consequences this *de facto* special status would have for the future. . . . Despite many officials' wishes to the contrary, the decision makers commonly react to immediate interests and immediate problems. . . .[14]

Over the years, however, attempts have been made to overcome inefficiency in the decision-making process and to increase co-ordination within the government (in addition to the device of inner and outer cabinets). One device that has been resorted to is a system of cabinet committees.

Cabinet Committees

Ever since Confederation, the cabinet has made extensive use of committees to facilitate its work; indeed, committees were used in the cabinet of Canada prior to 1867 in dealing with public works and control over government appropriations. The latter led to the formation of Treasury Board on July 2, 1867, established originally by Order-in-Council and then in 1869 by statute. There is one other statutory committee, the Committee on Scientific and Industrial Research established by the National Research Council Act of 1966. Since these two committees are established by statute, they are more properly referred to as committees of the Privy Council rather than of the cabinet.

Cabinet committees have several important advantages. They can make it possible for various matters to be investigated more fully than by the entire cabinet; they can involve various ministers whose departments each have a specific interest in a policy matter, thus promoting co-ordination; they can spread the work load more evenly among ministers; and they can also serve to sidetrack difficult problems. Macdonald made dubious use of one cabinet committee to cover up a special Secret Service Fund. A sum of money had been deposited in the name of a four-man cabinet sub-committee while Macdonald actually controlled the funds himself. After he had resigned as Prime Minister, Macdonald personally had written two cheques on the bank account set up to hold these funds, one of these cheques being made out to himself.

Before 1914 the procedure had been to set up an *ad hoc* committee to consider a particular problem, and then dissolve the committee after the problem had been solved. World War I led not only to an increase in the use of *ad hoc* committees, but also to several standing committees. One was to deal with marketing of grain, one to deal with price controls, and one to deal with the question of extending the franchise. After the formation of the Union government in 1917, more permanent committees were established. "Upon the formation of the Union Government, Sir Robert Borden had divided his Cabinet into a War Committee and a Reconstruction and Development Commitee."[15]

Between World War I and World War II, cabinet committees were rarely used and the pre-World War I pattern was followed, but World War II brought about an increase in the use of cabinet committees. As early as 1936 a Defence Committee was set up, consisting of the Prime Minister (who was also at that time Secretary of State for External Affairs) and the Ministers of National Defence, Justice, and Finance; the committee met only twice before the outbreak of World War II. The Defence Committee was briefly superseded by an Emergency Council and then, in December 1939, by Order-in-Council nine sub-committees were established: War, War Finance and Supply, Food Production and Marketing, Fuel and Power, Shipping and Transportation, Price Control and Labour, Internal Security, Legislative and Public Information Committees. Later a committee on Demobilization was established, also by Order-in-Council.

The decision to form these committees and the appointment of the ministers to them was made by the Prime Minister. The effectiveness of these committees was disputed. "In actual fact, of these ten only the War Committee of the Cabinet had any continuing and active existence early in the war."[16] The War Committee was very active, co-ordinating all Canadian war activity, and it became the chief policy-making body with respect to the war. The committee originally consisted of the Prime Minister, the Ministers of Finance, Defence, Justice, and Mines and Resources. These latter two (Lapointe of Quebec and Crerar of Manitoba) were members, not because of the functional importance of their ministries with regard to the war effort, but because of their seniority and experience. It should be pointed out that this committee contained representatives of the major geographical areas in Canada, the Minister of Finance, Ralston, being a Nova Scotian who was a Member for a Quebec constituency; Rogers, the Minister of Defence was from Ontario; Lapointe was King's Quebec lieutenant; and Crerar was the senior cabinet minister from western Canada. Later other ministers were added, including the three Associate Ministers of Defence and the Minister of National War Services, and Mr. Howe, Minister of Munitions and Supply. Some of the changes in membership were made via Order-in-Council, but others were made simply as a result of instructions from Mr. King, again illustrating the flexibility of the cabinet system and its capacity for change. The importance of the War Committee is illustrated by the fact that it met 343 times between December 8, 1939, and the end of the war.[17]

The War Committee that functioned under Mr. King is important for various reasons. It frequently had permanent officials attend its meetings, illustrating one of the virtues of committees — that meetings can be conducted informally and greater use can be made of outside experts. A second important feature was the fact that the committee had a secretary, who prepared an agenda for it and kept a record of its deliberations, a new procedure in Canada. A third feature was the fact that the War Committee made decisions that were in effect executive decisions — that is, it acted much like a cabinet. Mr. Heeney, the secretary, remarked that while it " . . . was never an executive body but was in fact as in form purely advisory in character, its prestige was such that its decisions were for practical purposes the decisions of the government."[18]

Following the war, every government made extensive use of cabinet committees. Some of them were standing committees; others were *ad hoc* set up regularly to deal with special problems as they arose. None of these other committees, however, made executive decisions and normally matters discussed in committees were discussed again by the full cabinet.

The absence of executive authority for cabinet committees and the necessity of the entire cabinet considering almost every item of business tended at times to impede the work of the government and its representatives. During the Reparations Conference in Paris in 1945, the British representatives had a great deal of freedom in determining policy and only infrequently had to seek cabinet approval. An *ad hoc* cabinet committee had been established, and it was able to give approval in the name of the full cabinet. In contrast, the Canadian delegation had to ask for instructions from the full cabinet on almost every matter and the procedure was slow and cumbersome.

Under Mr. St. Laurent the use of committees was continued. Mr. St. Laurent apparently gave committees slightly more independence than his predecessor. An effort was made to streamline the work of the cabinet through the creation of a Cabinet Legislation Committee, which prepared:

> . . . legislation well in advance of the Session so as to ensure a year round work load. When a Minister decides upon a change of policy or an improvement in existing policy, a short statement of the principle involved is prepared which, after notice to all other Departments likely to be affected, is considered by the Committee . . . the Committee passes the papers, suitably altered where necessary to the Cabinet. After approval in principle a bill is drafted in the Department of Justice and goes to the Committee for a review before going on to Cabinet.[19]

The final decision, of course, was still taken by the full cabinet.

Under Mr. Diefenbaker cabinet committees were used less frequently than under Mr. St. Laurent. For example, the Cabinet Defence Committee " . . . which had sat at least once a month under the previous Liberal government met only seventeen times between June 21, 1957, and April 22, 1963."[20] Mr. Diefenbaker was very anxious to have unanimity among the members of his cabinet, which tended to discourage the use of committees, since anything considered in committee had to undergo discussion by the full cabinet anyway.

Mr. Pearson revamped the cabinet committee system extensively, setting up ten standing committees and a large number of special committees. These committees were: External Affairs and Defence; Legislation, which reviewed the drafting of bills; Sessional, concerned with determining the order of government business in Parliament and the priorities of the government; Finance and Economic Policy; Resources and Trade; Communications and Works; Manpower, Social Development and Labour; Agriculture; Forestry and Fisheries; Cultural and

Other Matters; and Federal-Provincial Relations. The noteworthy aspect of these committees was that the representation principle was not adhered to. There were no members from western Canada, for example, on the important External Affairs and Defence Committee or on the Communication and Works Committee, and Treasury Board did not have any ministers from the provinces east of Quebec. Another important point about the committees was that they were designed to cover specific functional areas of governmental responsibility. In most cases membership on the committee was related to each minister's departmental responsibilities; functional rather than group representation was the normal criterion, although there were a few aberrations. The presence of the Associate Minister of National Defence on the Agriculture, Forestry and Fisheries Committee is difficult to explain, as is that of the Minister of Defence on the Committee for Cultural and Other Matters, except that personal interests may have been also a factor. Mr. Pearson also altered procedure so that matters requiring a cabinet decision were referred first to the appropriate committee and then the committee decision was referred to the full cabinet. Prior to the time of the Pearson cabinet matters had normally gone to the full cabinet first and had then been referred to a committee, which reported back. In January 1968 a Cabinet Committee on Priorities and Planning was set up because the government " . . . found itself in recurring financial difficulties and crises and it became apparent there was serious need of a systematic assessment of overall priorities of expenditure with a view to better long term planning."[21]

The committee system under Mr. Pearson during this period was less than successful. Ministers were reluctant to spend a great deal of time discussing another minister's proposed legislation when they knew that it would be discussed again at a meeting of the full cabinet. In addition to the eleven standing committees and two statutory committees (Treasury Board and Science), there were eleven *ad hoc* committees. Of these 24 committees, the Prime Minister acted as chairman of six and each minister served on from three to eleven. Mr. Drury, Minister of Industry, was chairman of two committees and a member of nine others, while Mr. Benson, Mr. Nicholson, and Mr. Winters each served on nine. The average number of committees on which a minister served was seven, and if these met regularly only to have their subject matter discussed again at a full cabinet meeting, one should not be surprised that attendance at committee meetings was not good. The minority government situation also affected the operation of the committee system in that there was constant political pressure on the ministers; the political implications of every proposal had to be taken into account carefully and the logical place to do this was in the full cabinet.

Up to the time of the Trudeau administration, then, cabinet committees were quite common but, with the possible exception of the War Committee under Mr. King, ministers in committees discussed the end result of policy development rather than participating in actual policy formation. Policies were devised by civil servants and the Minister within the department. There were also interdepartmental committees of civil servants, but ministers were infrequently involved in their activities, so that frequently policies were developed and submitted to the cabinet without having had an input from most ministers, who were, however, expected to support the policy. When committees did exist, they were lacking in staff and so the departments involved provided the expertise in advising ministers, usually the same officials who had played important roles in determining the policy proposed.

Thus it was that while the cabinet was the place in which final decisions on policy were taken, participation in policy formation sometimes meant little more than putting the stamp of approval on an already developed program. Meaningful participation, however, requires that before approving a policy, a minister be clear on what is involved in the decisions — which in turn requires some participation in the decision-making process.

The procedure followed prior to the Trudeau administration not only made policy making a difficult process, it also concentrated a great deal of power in the civil service and made co-ordination of government activities very difficult. Under such conditions civil servants could sometimes choose whatever policy alternatives would be presented to the cabinet, or indeed provide only one policy suggestion. Often only the minister who was directly responsible for the policy would be informed on the matter under consideration. Under such circumstances other ministers could not offer useful suggestions, and policy proposals were often rubber-stamped with approval, rather than being approved after informed discussion.

The Trudeau administration has attempted to change the policy-making procedure in order to involve members of the cabinet more and at the same time provide for greater co-ordination of government activities.

Cabinet Committees in the Trudeau Cabinet

The committee system established during the first Trudeau government was an extension of the earlier system but with some very important changes. In his own words, Mr. Trudeau undertook " . . . a restructuring of the Cabinet committee system which enables the Cabinet to function more effectively."[22] Nearly all matters that would previously have come before the full cabinet were sent first to a cabinet committee, which was in effect a cabinet in its own right with power to make decisons. At these cabinet-committee meetings, which departmental and other officials attended on invitation (which has always been the custom with regard to committees of the Canadian cabinet), either a decision was reached or a recommendation to cabinet was made. Those ministers not on the committee were advised in advance of the matter to be discussed, and any minister who wished might attend and had access to all relevant documents. When a decision or recommendation was made, all ministers were immediately informed. If a minister disagreed with the decision he could, after advising the Prime Minister, raise the matter before the full cabinet at the appropriate time. Thus, the Prime Minister did not have absolute control over the cabinet agenda. The recommendations of cabinet committees, were, of course, discussed by the full cabinet and a decision taken.

Normal procedure was for the Prime Minister to begin a cabinet meeting by the reading of a list of decisions which had been taken by the cabinet committees since the last full cabinet meeting. It should be noted that the Prime Minister could leave certain decisions off the agenda if he wished, and Mr. Trudeau did so. At the outset of the Trudeau regime it was noted that the committee system tended to function much as it did in the Pearson days. The various committees met weekly, and a large number of committee decisions were questioned by ministers in meetings of the full cabinet, even by ministers who had participated in the original decision. Consequently the system appeared to be breaking down. Ministers apparently were going to cabinet committee meetings unprepared to discuss matters on the agenda and then waiting to raise objections at full meetings. It was then decided that weekly committee meetings did not give ministers sufficient time to prepare; consequently most committees met every two weeks, ministers appeared to be better prepared, and fewer decisions were reviewed by the full cabinet. A former minister said, "If thirty decisions are taken by Cabinet committees, twenty-two to twenty-five are not questioned in the Cabinet."[23]

In the beginning of the Trudeau regime eight cabinet committees were set up, four of which were designated as co-ordinating committees and four as subject committees. The four co-ordinating committees were Priorities and Planning, Treasury Board, Legislation and Government Procedures (now the Committee on Legislation and House Planning), and Federal-Provincial Relations. The four subject committees were the Committee on External Policy and Defence, the Committee on Economic Planning (later Economic Policy), the Committee on Communications and Urban Affairs (later Science, Culture and Information), and the Committee on Social Policy, which included matters having to do with the Departments of Labour and Manpower. It was found that the responsibilities of the Committee on Economic Planning were excessive, and so an additional subject committee, the Committee on Government Operations, was formed.

A number of *ad hoc* committees were also established, one to look into tax reform, and Prime Minister Trudeau has hinted that other committees deal with such problems as student unrest, but has refused to provide details, stating, "The arrangements made by the Cabinet for the discharge of the business for which it is collectively responsible are matters for the Cabinet itself and are not customarily disclosed."[24] As a result, one could not find out the exact membership of any committee, probably because if membership was known certain areas and groups would complain of being deprived of representation on key committees. It is known, however, that the Prime Minister has acted as chairman of the Committee on Priorities and Planning and of the Committee on Federal-Provincial Relations. The President of the Privy Council acted as chairman of the Committee on Legislation and House Planning, and the President of Treasury Board, of course, acted as chairman of that committee. If procedure was similar to that in the Pearson cabinet, membership in the subject committees was determined mostly by the relationship between the subject and the particular responsibility of each minister.

The most important of the Trudeau cabinet committees was the Committee on Priorities and Planning, composed of the senior members of the cabinet, concerned mainly with the development of broad policy objectives for the government and the assignment of priority ranking to these objectives. "The priorities are set in broad terms: objectives to be achieved, the amount of effort and resources to be directed toward each, the increase or decrease in the emphasis to be accorded to general areas of government action."[25] Of course, a very close relationship existed between the Committee on Priorities and Planning and the other cabinet committees. This was a two-way relationship; that is, the decisions of the Committee on Priorities and Planning affected the deliberations of the other committees but according to the then Secretary of the Treasury Board: ". . . the programs and 'internal priorities' developed by the functional committees in turn become elements or considerations in the work of the Priorities and Planning Committee."[26]

One of the results of the committee system was that the cabinet met less frequently than it did under previous Prime Ministers. In the period July 1, 1970, to June 30, 1971, the cabinet met 75 times, whereas in the period July 1, 1966, to June 30, 1967 (under Mr. Pearson) it had met 139 times. At the same time in 1970-1971 there were 311 cabinet committee meetings compared with 120 under Mr. Pearson. The first Trudeau cabinet then was obviously functioning far less frequently as a collegial body and thus its role as a mechanism of accommodation was altered.

Earlier procedure, then, involved proposed legislation being fully discussed by the entire cabinet. Under the system introduced by the Trudeau government, only legislative proposals upon which a cabinet committee could not agree were normally discussed by the full cabinet, with all concerned ministers kept informed of policy proposals and committee decisions. The exception to both the earlier and the present method of operation seems to be legislation relating to the budget.

Some confusion exists as to whether or not the cabinet discusses the budget. In 1944 the budget was considered and discussed at a cabinet meeting.[27] This seems to be an unusual case, more frequently very few people are aware of budget proposals. Speaking of budget preparation during the Diefenbaker administration one writer noted, "No one knows what is in it except the Minister of Finance, his deputy and a small core of senior departmental officials who help to prepare it. Even the Prime Minister and the rest of the Cabinet are not made aware of the contents until a day or two before. . . ."[28] Miss LaMarsh writes, ". . . the Cabinet did not know of the Budget's contents until the day of the Budget itself and that was in accord with usual practice."[29] After the first budget of the Pearson government, the cabinet was briefed on the budget's contents a few days in advance, and under the Trudeau government the same procedure seems to be followed. It was reported on October 27, 1968, that "Mr. Benson briefed the Cabinet on his financial proposals Monday",[30] which was several days prior to the budget speech in the House of Commons. One former minister in the Trudeau cabinet said, "The contents of the budget in 1970 were revealed on the day the Minister of Finance made his budget speech in the House of Commons."[31] In 1971 Mr. Trudeau told the House of Commons that ". . . the considerations in preparation for the budget are discussed in a Cabinet committee, and I am a member of that committee."[32] This was an unusual situation due to the fact that large-scale changes in tax policy were anticipated with the budget, but normal practice is for the Minister of Finance and the officials in the Department of Finance to originate budget provisions. It appears that normally under the Trudeau administration the Prime Minister discusses the budget with the Minister of Finance about two weeks prior to its presentation to the House of Commons, and other members of the cabinet are briefed a few days before the budget speech.

The reason for the secrecy and caution surrounding the budget is to prevent a minister from inadvertently revealing budget secrets, thus causing reaction in the stock market, etc. The practice is similar to the one followed in Great Britain, where the contents of the budget are revealed to the cabinet a few days before the budget is brought down in the House of Commons. This procedure is unfortunate, in that it prevents the experience of the cabinet from being utilized in the preparation of the budget and makes a mockery of the idea of cabinet responsibility, since ministers must assume responsibility for something they have had little or no voice in preparing. It also illustrates the great influence of the civil servants who advise the Minister of Finance on this matter, and it would appear that the budget is one very significant governmental proposal over which the civil service still retains paramount influence.

The Cabinet Secretariat

In addition to revamping the cabinet committee system, the cabinet secretariat was also substantially upgraded during the first Trudeau administration.

For many years the cabinet functioned without a secretariat. There were a few employees in the Privy Council Office who looked after routine matters, such as filing minutes, drafting Orders-in-Council, etc. These operations were under the direction of the Clerk of the Privy Council, who was regarded as the senior Canadian civil servant. The staff was very small; in 1918, for example, there were only four employees in the Privy Council Office. The only records kept of cabinet meetings consisted of Orders-in-Council and minutes that required government action. In 1919 a Senate Committee on the Machinery of Government recommended the establishment of a secretariat, but nothing was done until 1939, except that for a period after World War I a secretary was appointed for the Cabinet Committee on Reconstruction and Development. No actual minutes were kept of this committee's meetings, however. As a consequence of the lack of a secretariat, "the decisions of the Ministry in the exercise of the formal executive authority of the Governor-in-Council were recorded in the most precise form. Their conclusions on matters of policy, however, remained unrecorded unless of such a nature as to require formal action subsequently on the part of Council."[33]

In 1940 Mr. Arnold Heeney was appointed Clerk of the Privy Council and also began to act as secretary to the cabinet. (It was not until 1975, however, that the title of Secretary to the Cabinet was formally established by law, although all incumbents of the position of Clerk of the Privy Council have acted as secretary to the cabinet since 1940.) In the beginning, most of Mr. Heeney's time was spent on secretarial duties with the War Committee of the Cabinet, drawing up the agenda and preparing and circulating documents to committee members. "Minutes of the meetings of the War Committee are kept by the Secretary and the decisions made are not only recorded but sent to the Minister concerned. The Secretary acts as a liaison officer. . . . "[34] The cabinet secretariat also followed up decisions taken by the War Committee. As time went on, the cabinet secretariat became more closely involved with the cabinet proper, preparing the cabinet agenda under the direction of the Prime Minister, circulating relevant documents, and following up cabinet decisons. Mr. Heeney attended cabinet meetings, and recorded any conclusions reached, and prepared a minute on the important aspects of each matter raised in cabinet. Ministers were also provided with a written note of decisions, and these were followed up by the cabinet secretariat, functioning as the Privy Council Office. At the time there was a Government Business Committee to consider routine Orders-in-Council, and the cabinet secretary decided which items would go to this committee. As the volume of work grew, so did the size of the Privy Council Office to meet the demands of the cabinet and its committees. Secretarial duties for committees were usually carried out by members of the staff of the Privy Council Office, or occasionally by civil servants assigned for the purpose from other departments of government. For a time there would be some meetings of the cabinet when no official was present; usually one cabinet meeting a week was held to discuss political matters when the secretary was absent and no minutes were kept.

In contrast to the United Kingdom, the Privy Council Office and cabinet secretariat are not distinct from each other. As Mr. King explained, "There is no formal or official body known as the Cabinet Secretariat. Employees of the Privy Council perform duties of a secretarial character in connection with committees of the Cabinet and committees of officials established by the Cabinet."[35] The records kept during the King-St. Laurent period were quite informal. Mr. St. Laurent described the procedure as follows: "Summary minutes are kept but these are not authenticated. They are simply memoranda of the discussion and deliberations. . . . The only documents that do have an official character are the recommendations to His Excellency, the Governor General."[36] Later in his remarks Mr. St. Laurent provided an illustration of the informality that sometimes attends important government business when he said that when the cabinet passed Orders-in-Council that had to be tabled in the House of Commons at once " . . . they are communicated to His Excellency by telephone and his assent is obtained while the messenger is on the way to Government House to get them signed."[37]

After 1945 the size of the staff of the Privy Council Office was increased, and it began to provide advice to the Prime Minister and the cabinet on policy, but the advisory role remained secondary to the secretarial role. It was alleged that under Mr. St. Laurent, the then Clerk of the Privy Council, Mr. J.W. Pickersgill, was consulted by the Prime Minister quite frequently on policy matters. This was denied, however, by Mr. St. Laurent.[38]

When Mr. Diefenbaker became Prime Minister there were three assistant secretaries of the cabinet, each of whom was responsible for keeping specific departments informed on cabinet matters. One former assistant secretary of the cabinet stated in a confidential interview that there were times during the Diefenbaker regime when it was difficult for officials to determine exactly what the cabinet had decided. The officials frequently had to have a quick *post mortem* after some cabinet meetings to decide what the consensus actually had been. Moreover, cabinet minutes were sent out to ministers three or four weeks late, so they were of dubious value.[39]

The cabinet secretariat cannot be said to have become permanently established until 1957, when Mr. Diefenbaker and Mr. St. Laurent, during the transfer of the administration, agreed that the secretary of the cabinet in future would be the custodian of cabinet papers, and it would be his responsibility to determine which of these would be made available to succeeding governments. Prior to Mr. St. Laurent's assuming office " . . . there were no files in the Prime Minister's office except personal files. . . . Up to that time every Prime Minister from Confederation on took everything away. Nothing was left but the filing cabinets."[40]

Under the Pearson administration there were four assistant secretaries of the cabinet to deal with specific areas of responsibility corresponding to the responsibilities of the various committees, but their functions were mainly clerical and they had little influence on the determination of policy.

Since Mr. Trudeau became Prime Minister the Privy Council Office has become responsible for more than secretarial duties. The change in its position is probably best illustrated by the growth in the number of its personnel. Under Mr. Pearson the Privy Council staff had numbered 142.[41] At the end of 1971 it numbered 239[42] and by March 1975 the staff had increased to 352.[43] The Privy Council Office was divided into three divisions: Plans, Operations, and Federal-Provincial Relations, each under a deputy secretary of the cabinet. An assistant secretary of the cabinet and a secretariat was appointed for each cabinet committee; that is, each committee had a permanent staff that prepared committee agendas, followed up committee decisions, and did research into matters of interest to the committee, thus providing on occasion some policy input of its own.

The Plans Division of the Privy Council Office was closely linked with the four co-ordinating committees of the cabinet, and each assistant secretary of the cabinet for these committees reported to the deputy secretary (Planning). The deputy secretary was not involved in secretarial duties and thus was free to develop policy proposals independently — that is, proposals for government policy could be developed in the Privy Council Office itself, as well as in government departments. The Plans Division was also given responsibility for legal policy and advice and for the organization of procedure within the Privy Council Office.

A Machinery of Government Secretariat was also established within the Plans Division to advise the Prime Minister on how governmental responsibilities ought to be allocated among various departments and agencies. The secretariat also provides advice on personnel selection and on ways to improve communications between the Privy Council Office and other government departments and agencies. The secretariat also plays a role, along with other sections of the Plans Division, in drafting major policy statements about the future direction of government policy.

When a department wishes to submit a policy proposal, it is forwarded to the Privy Council Office in the form of a memorandum, signed by the responsible minister. The proposal is then examined by the Planning Division of the Privy Council Office in the light of government objectives. Sometimes policy panels are set up to review these proposals. Membership on such panels is varied, consisting of officials of the Privy Council Office, members of the staff of the Prime Minister's Office, academics, businessmen, labour leaders, and others. The proposal is then referred to the appropriate cabinet committees for consideration or returned to the department. The Planning Division also has the responsibility of deciding which committee is to examine a particular proposal, but is not a particularly significant responsibility, since according to one official 95 per cent of the proposals clearly come under the terms of reference of a particular committee. Usually then the assignment is made automatically by an official in the Privy Council Office, the Registrar of Cabinet Documents.

The Operations Division is responsible for providing administrative and clerical assistance for the cabinet subject committees. There is an assistant secretary to the cabinet and a secretariat for each committee, and they are responsible for managing the flow of proposals in and out of the committees and to and from the cabinet itself.

Prior to a policy proposal being discussed at a cabinet committee meeting, the secretariat gathers together all the information pertinent to the proposal, summarizes it, and circulates it to all cabinet members (not simply members of the committee). It also circulates the agenda and all supporting memoranda to *all* ministers prior to both cabinet meetings and cabinet committee meetings. The secretariat also informs all departments concerned if a proposal for cabinet or cabinet committee discussion will be affecting them. The secretariat records all decisions taken at cabinet committee meetings and at meetings of the full cabinet, advises all departments of decisions that will affect them, and follows up decisions to ensure that they are implemented. It also provides a liaison service among government departments by ensuring co-ordination among their planning units.

The Privy Council Office must also brief the Prime Minister on policy matters and on matters leading up to policy decisions. Thus he knows everything that goes on in cabinet committee meetings — who is in favour of proposals, who is opposed and their reasons, which enables him to anticipate responses to policy suggestions in the cabinet or House of Commons.

A recent development (1975) has been the establishment of the office of Secretary to the Cabinet for Federal-Provincial Relations and a Federal-Provincial Office distinct from the Privy Council Office. In effect, a new department of government has been set up, with the Prime Minister serving as minister of that department, indicating the increasing importance of inter-relationships between the two levels of government and the pre-eminent role of the Prime Minister in dealing with these relationships.

These changes represent an attempt to rationalize policy making but it should be noted that the process has added immensely to the influence of the Prime Minister, to whom the Privy Council Office is directly responsible. By providing a source of policy input independent of the government departments, the role of departmental civil servants has been greatly reduced, a situation that will be discussed later.

The Prime Minister's Office

A third innovation of the Trudeau government was the establishment of a major policy and executive centre in the Prime Minister's Office, distinct from the Privy Council Office.

There is evidence to suggest that the members of the Prime Minister's personal staff exercise considerable influence on government policy, influence of a type formerly restricted to civil servants. It is alleged, for example, that the decisions to reduce Canada's commitment to NATO and to phase out the Department of Indian Affairs[44] were taken contrary to the recommendations of the departments most closely involved but on the advice of the Prime Minister's personal staff. One outstanding example of a shift in influence was the decision to send one of Mr. Trudeau's personal assistants, Professor Ivan Head, to Biafra, rather than an official of the Department of External Affairs, to negotiate with the Nigerian government regarding relief flights into Biafra,[45] as well as on other missions. When the location of the new Quebec airport had been decided Mr. Trudeau " . . . fired off his regional advisor, Pierre Levasseur, to Quebec to break the news. . . . "[46] According to one senior civil servant the Prime Minister's principal secretary from 1968-72, Marc Lalonde, was ". . . really an Assistant Prime Minister. He is in charge of the whole flow of advice going to the Prime Minister and no policy will be accepted unless he likes it."[47]

The Prime Minister's Office has always had two functions, that of providing service (handling correspondence, etc.) and providing political advice. It is in this second capacity that the Prime Minister's Office acquired new importance under Mr. Trudeau. In a press release dated July 31, 1968, the Prime Minister described the functions of the office:

> The basic concept of the organization (P.M.O.) is that in addition to the usual personal assistance necessary to the discharge of his daily routine the Prime Minister's Office should include units responsible for policy advice, for maintaining close contacts with individuals and groups in all areas of the country, for initiation of policy proposals and for information.

As in the case of the Privy Council Office, change in the size of the staff indicates a change in the role of the office. For many years the Prime Minister's staff consisted of a few clerical employees. Thus, under Prime Minister Bennett: "The standard office equipment for Prime Ministers was two or more private secretaries — one bilingual — and a small staff of Civil Service stenographers capable of handling routine correspondence without direction."[48] Mr. King augmented the staff somewhat, and it continued to grow, so that by the time Mr. Pearson left office his staff amounted to forty people. According to a return tabled in the House of Commons there were 98 people in the Prime Minister's Office on March 3, 1975, of which only 23 had been appointed by the Public Service Commission, and one had been seconded from the Department of External Affairs.[49]

A large part of this expansion consisted of personnel necessary to deal with clerical duties " . . . half of the staff of the Prime Minister's Office today works in the correspondence section",[50] but there was also a substantial increase in advisory staff. The leading figure in the Prime Minister's Office is the Principal Secretary who, in his own words:

> . . . is the Prime Minister's chief of staff and main personal advisor. He attends most meetings between the Prime Minister and P.M.O./P.C.O. staff; with the approval of the Prime Minister, he may attend any Cabinet committee meeting; he attends or is represented at the weekly staff meetings of the P.C.O. for the purpose of liaison and co-operation between that office and the P.M.O. . . . he provides the Prime Minister with advice on a variety of policy matters and fulfills any assignment that the Prime Minister decides to give him.[51]

In addition to advice from his Principal Secretary, the Prime Minister also receives information and advice from four desk officers, each one responsible for a particular area of the country — Maritimes, Quebec, Ontario and the West. The duties of the desk officers were described as:

> . . . to improve the liaison between the Prime Minister and those voluntary organizations which concern themselves with issues and problems common to many Canadians; to act as an additional source of information and advice to the Prime Minister on matters upon which he has

requested such information and advice; to be of assistance to Members of Parliament in their dealings with the Prime Minister and his office. . . . Problems of citizens which come to the attention of the regional desks will be referred to the Prime Minister, a Member of Parliament for that area, a Governmental Department or other appropriate agency. . . .[52]

In fact the regional desks did not serve any purpose whatsoever insofar as opposition Members of Parliament were concerned, and few were even aware of the name of the desk man for their area. What the regional desks did was provide the Prime Minister with information and advice on political matters in their specific regions, supplementing and in some cases replacing the information provided by cabinet members and individual Members of Parliament.

The desk men, however, were not seasoned politicians and tended at times to be abrasive and tactless in dealing with politicians and senior civil servants. This attracted a great deal of attention and criticism, and as a result the Prime Minister's Office maintained a very high profile from 1968 to 1972. The results of the 1972 election, however, seemed to reflect adversely on the quality of the advice supplied by the staff of the Prime Minister's Office. "Some critics of the office felt that an unbalanced reliance upon technology rather than common-sense politics had scuttled the campaign. . . ."[53] Thus during the period of minority government the office maintained a very low profile, a practice which has continued since the election of 1974. It should be noted that since 1972 greater stress has been placed on political experience in recruiting staff for the Prime Minister's Office.

Other members of the Prime Minister's staff are charged " . . . with ensuring that the government and party have and maintain a comprehensive and coherent program."[54] Thus the staff of the Prime Minister's Office provides him with an in-depth political analysis of proposed policies and programs, something he cannot normally expect from the Privy Council Office. The Prime Minister's Office is kept aware at all times of developments in the Privy Council Office, since all policy documents are forwarded from the P.C.O. to the P.M.O. Members of Mr. Trudeau's staff attend committee meetings in the Privy Council Office, form part of policy panels, and help decide cabinet committee agendas. Even when a policy decision has been taken in a cabinet committee, the Prime Minister's Office can advise the Privy Council Office to leave the decision off the cabinet agenda or insist that the decision be referred back to the committee, so that the decision might be temporarily set aside. Ministers who have announced disagreements with a committee decision might on occasion be contacted by a member of the Prime Minister's Office and urged to withdraw their opposition. Decision making then is influenced by the personal staff of the Prime Minister as well as by the staff of the Privy Council Office. The technical administrative procedures followed by the Trudeau government thus also serve to concentrate even more power in the hands of the Prime Minister.

Efficiency and Rationality in the Canadian Cabinet

The changes in the decision-making process instituted by the Trudeau government were made with a view to making the process more efficient and rational. Efficiency and rationality, however, may be counter-productive in a consociational democracy. The consociational model is more likely to stress incremental decision making; i.e. the process of muddling through, emphasizing always the maintenance of the system rather than a grand design. One writer who served as an executive assistant for several years has said that a basic fact of Canadian government is that "efforts at social change through government policy must take second place to the requisites of keeping the federal system together."[55] It may be that the Canadian model has built in features that limit rational decision making. "Rational decision making is thought of as the gathering of all pertinent facts, canvassing the alternatives for action and selecting the one which will produce maximum results through a thought process . . . excluding the emotions and the subconscious."[56] Under a rational decision-making process, decision making tends to become depoliticized, which in effect may be dysfunctional to the existing political system because rationality may exclude sensitivity to particular groups or regions, which in turn stimulates a lack of confidence among such groups in the system. It would seem that decisions in the first Trudeau administration were being taken to a very large extent in cabinet committees that did not contain representatives from all groups, and while such committees may very well be highly sensitive to all groups and regions in Canada, they may not appear to be so — that is, the decision-making process instituted under Mr. Trudeau does not exactly fit the consociational model.

At any rate, a cabinet that reflects social and other divisions to the extent that the Canadian cabinet does is not likely to be efficient in making decisions. The skills and attributes required for this kind of decision making are not necessarily automatically possessed by cabinet ministers, who are usually appointed more with their representative role in mind than their ability to provide policy leadership or to manage a government department. Consequently it should not be surprising that the initiative for policy leadership has tended to pass into the hands of the civil service and to the Prime Minister himself.

NOTES

[1]A.D.P. Heeney, "Cabinet Government in Canada", p. 283.

[2]*Ibid.*, p. 285.

[3]Canada, House of Commons, *Debates.* (August 7, 1956), p. 7126.

[4]Robert Fortier, Clerk of the Senate, letter to author, September 23, 1971.

[5]W.L. Morton, "The Formation of the First Federal Cabinet". *Canadian Historical Review*, Vol. XXXVI, No. 2 (June, 1955), p. 123.

[6]Canada, House of Commons, *Debates.* (February 23, 1953), p. 2319.

[7]J.W. Pickersgill and D.F. Forster, *The Mackenzie King Record*, Vol. II, p. 15.

[8]*Ibid.*, p. 28.

[9]*Ibid.*, p. 135.

[10]Peter Aucoin, "Theory and Research in the Study of Policy Making in Canada", in G. Bruce Doern and Peter Aucoin eds., *The Structure of Policy Making in Canada*, p. 15.

[11]Donald Creighton, *Dominion of the North*, second ed. (Toronto; Macmillan, 1957), p. 432.

[12]H. Blair Neatby, "William Lyon Mackenzie King", in R.L. McDougall ed., *Canada's Past and Present: A Dialogue, Our Living Tradition*, fifth series. (Toronto; University of Toronto Press, 1965), p. 5.

[13]J.W. Pickersgill and D.F. Forster, *The Mackenzie King Record*, Vol. 4. (Toronto; University of Toronto Press, 1970), p. 35.

[14]Richard Simeon, *Federal Provincial Diplomacy.* (Toronto; University of Toronto Press, 1972), p. 293.

[15]Roger Graham, *Arthur Meighen*, Volume 1, p. 196.

[16]Gordon Robertson, The Changing Role of the Privy Council Office". *Canadian Public Administration*, Volume 14, No. 4 (Winter, 1971), p. 489.

[17]James Eayrs, *The Art of the Possible*, p. 13.

[18]A.D.P. Heeney, "Cabinet Government in Canada", p. 289.

[19]Hon. W.E. Harris, "A More Business Like Parliament". *Queen's Quarterly*, Volume LXIII, No. 4 (Winter, 1956), p. 545.

[20]Peter Newman, *Renegade in Power*, p. 343.

[21]Gordon Robertson, "The Changing Role of the Privy Council Office", p. 490-491.

[22]Canada, House of Commons, *Debates.* (February 27, 1969), p. 6014.

[23]*Interview.* (October 7, 1971).

[24]Canada, House of Commons, *Debates.* (June 18, 1969), p. 10, 302.

[25]Gordon Robertson, "The Changing Role of the Privy Council Office", p. 495.

[26]A.W. Johnson, "The Treasury Board of Canada and the Machinery of Government of the 1970's", p. 352.

[27]J.W. Pickersgill and D.F. Forster, *The Mackenzie King Record*, Vol. II, p. 30.

[28]Peter Dempson, *Assignment Ottawa*, p. 254.

[29]Judy LaMarsh, *Memoirs of a Bird in a Gilded Cage*, p. 64.

[30]*Ottawa Citizen.* (Tuesday, October 22, 1968), p. 1.

[31]*Interview.* (October 7, 1971).

[32]Canada, House of Commons, *Debates.* (June 2, 1971), p. 6291.

[33]A.D.P. Heeney, "Cabinet Government in Canada", p. 285.

[34]R. McG. Dawson, "The Impact of War on Canadian Political Institutions". *Canadian Journal of Economics and Political Science*, Vol. VII, No. 2. (May, 1941), p. 187.

[35]Canada, House of Commons, *Debates*. (February 10, 1947), p. 246.

[36]*Ibid*. (April 27, 1953), p. 4438.

[37]*Ibid*.

[38]*Ibid*., p. 4434.

[39]*Interview*. (August 5, 1969).

[40]Canada, House of Commons, *Debates*. (August 28, 1958), p. 4266.

[41]*Ibid*. (March 25, 1970), p. 5457. (starred question # 326).

[42]*Ibid*. (December 20, 1971), p. 10, 610. (starred question # 1893).

[43]*Ibid*. (March 3, 1975), p. 3705 (starred question # 1522).

[44]Anthony Westell, *Paradox: Trudeau as Prime Minister*, p. 202.

[45]*Ibid*., p. 179.

[46]Walter Stewart, *Shrug: Trudeau in Power*, p. 178.

[47]*Interview*. (January 7, 1972).

[48]Ernest Watkins, *R.B. Bennett*. (Toronto; Kingswood House, 1963), p. 169.

[49]Canada, House of Commons, *Debates*. (March 3, 1975), p. 3705. (starred question # 1522).

[50]*Ibid*. (December 9, 1974), p. 2073.

[51]Marc Lalonde, "The Changing Role of the Prime Minister's Office". *Canadian Public Administration*, Vol. 14, No. 4 (Winter, 1971), p. 522.

[52]Canada, House of Commons, *Debates*. (March 12, 1969), p. 6508.

[53]Thomas d'Acquino, "The Prime Minister's Office: Catalyst or Cabal?" *Canadian Public Administration*, Vol. 17, No. 1 (Spring, 1974), p. 63.

[54]Marc Lalonde, "The Changing Role of the Prime Minister's Office", p. 523.

[55]Lloyd Axworthy, "The Housing Task Force: A Case Study", in Bruce Doern and Peter Aucoin, eds., *The Structures of Policy Making in Canada*, p. 135.

[56]John M. Pfiffner, "Administrative Rationality". *Public Administration Review*, Vol. XX, No. 3 (Summer, 1960), p. 126.

Chapter V

The Cabinet in Profile

This chapter will provide a statistical analysis of the 379 individuals who have served as cabinet ministers from July 1, 1967, to October 30, 1974. The analysis is divided into four periods. The first, from 1867 to 1896 (29 years), corresponds to the period of Conservative domination of the federal cabinet from the time of Macdonald to the time of Laurier. The second, from 1896 to 1921 (25 years), covers the interim between the advent of the Laurier cabinet and that of Mackenzie King. The third period, 1921 to 1948 (27 years), covers the "King era", and the final period 1948-1974 (26 years) brings the period under analysis to 1974.

Table 5-1 provides a geographical analysis of cabinet membership during the four periods by province.

TABLE 5-I

**Membership of the Canadian Cabinet 1867-1974
by Province of Residence**

	1867-1896	1896-1921	1921-1948	1948-1974	Total	%
Quebec	32	24	29	41	126	33.2
Ontario	23	25	31	36	115	30.3
N.S.	14	6	8	3	31	8.2
N.B.	9	7	10	5	31	8.2
Man.	2	6	5	6	19	5.0
P.E.I.	2	1	3	3	9	2.4
B.C.	3	3	5	11	22	5.8
Alta.		4	2	6	12	3.2
Sask.		2	4	3	9	2.4
Nfld.				5	5	1.3
Total	85	78	97	119	379	100.0

Age of Cabinet Ministers

The average age at which ministers enter the cabinet has shown remarkably little variation over the years. Members of Macdonald's first cabinet became ministers at an average age of 50.2 years. The average age of entry to the cabinet for the period 1867-1896 was 49.4 years, and for the first 107 years the average age of members entering the cabinet was 50.1 years, slightly more than the average age of Members of Parliament for the same period, which has consistently remained at 49.5 years. (Unpublished figures prepared by Dr. Roman March and made available to the author). In recent years, however, there has been some indication that the average age is decreasing; ministers appointed during Mr. Pearson's tenure had an average age of 47.9 years, and those who have entered Mr. Trudeau's cabinet have averaged 44.5 years of age. The very moderate overall change in average age, however, indicates that the process of selection is relatively impervious to demographic changes in the overall population. As will be pointed out later, a very large proportion of cabinet ministers are businesspeople, lawyers, and other professionals who usually spend only a relatively brief period of time in the cabinet. It may be necessary then for potential ministers to establish themselves well in their professions or businesses before entering politics and becoming cabinet ministers as a full-time career, and this accounts in part for the relatively late age at which individuals enter the cabinet. Prof. Ward's study of the House of Commons, in which he pointed out that it has become increasingly difficult for younger people to enter the House of Commons because of limited financial resources, tends to verify this explanation. This was not likely the case, however, in the early years when

> . . . Parliaments contained large numbers of "gentlemen" who could possibly afford to enter politics at a younger age than their successors. They held commissions in the local militia, and were probably either closely related to active politicians or were their junior law partners; in any case the path into federal politics was made smooth for them in ways which do not seem to operate now.[1]

It is true, however, that for members of the legal profession, membership in the House of Commons may prove helpful to a professional career, so that the explanation offered above is only partially correct. The recent trend towards entry into the cabinet at an earlier age seems partially to reflect that, after a period of aging, the Canadian population appears to be becoming more youthful. It is clear, however, that in terms of age cabinet members do not reflect the age composition of the adult population of Canada, the younger groups being considerably under-represented. (The terms "under-represented" and "over-represented" are applied in a statistical sense and simply mean a greater or less proportion of cabinet ministers who possess a given attribute than the whole Canadian population).

There is considerable variation among the provinces as to the ages at which individuals enter the cabinet, as illustrated in Table 5-II. It should be pointed out that there seems to be a tendency for ministers from the western provinces to enter the cabinet at a later age than those from other provinces. This may be partially accounted for by Ward's argument cited above, in that in the early days there was no established society in western Canada and consequently fewer "gentlemen" than in the older, more established provinces.

TABLE 5-II

Average Age at Time of Appointment of Cabinet Ministers by Province

	1867-1896	1896-1921	1921-1948	1948-1974	1867-1974
National Average	49.4	51.4	51.8	48.2	50.1
Quebec	49.4	51.4	51.9	44.8	48.8
Ontario	49.9	51.9	50.4	48.7	50.1
Nova Scotia	49.8	52.7	53.7	46.3	51.1
New Brunswick	48.5	52.0	55.6	54.2	52.4
Manitoba	43.0	44.3	56.6	53.7	50.4
Prince Edward Is.	47.0	51.0	47.3	47.0	47.5
British Columbia	52.3	54.3	46.6	54.1	52.2
Alberta		54.7	55.5	47.3	51.2
Saskatchewan		52.0	50.7	47.3	49.9
Newfoundland				54.0	54.0

Sources: *Canadian Parliamentary Guide*
Guide to Canadian Ministries Since Confederation
Who's Who in Canada

The age of entry to the cabinet for ministers from Quebec is quite different from that of other provinces. Table 5-III illustrates that the age of French-Canadian ministers entering the cabinet is somewhat lower than the average from the rest of Canada and considerably lower than the average age of English-Canadian cabinet ministers from Quebec.

Ward has already noted that "Quebec returns an unusually large number of young members and fewer elderly ones. . . . ",[2] and this is presumably reflected in elevation to the cabinet at an earlier age. The reason for this may be that there is less competition for membership in this particular elite among French Canadians, in that the elite may find other avenues of self-expression. The fact that politics in Quebec tends to be more familial may make it easier for younger people to enter Parliament and the cabinet at an earlier age than is the case with members from other provinces. Moreover, as indicated by Table 5-XVI, French-Canadian ministers have historically been more secure in their

TABLE 5-III

Average Age at Time of Appointment of Cabinet Ministers
from Quebec by Party and by Ethnic Origin

	1867-1896	1896-1921	1921-1948	1948-1974	1867-1974
Fr. Cdn. Conservatives	45.9	49.7	51.7	46.2	48.0
Non-Fr. Cdn. Conservatives	55.0	53.7	69.0+	38.0+	54.5
Total Conservatives	49.9	50.9	53.7	45.5	49.8
Fr. Cdn. Liberals	48.4	51.7	51.3	44.0	47.6
Non-Fr. Cdn. Liberals	47.0+	51.3	50.5	46.7	49.0
Total Liberals	48.2	51.6	51.0	44.5	47.9
All Fr. Cdns.	46.9	50.9	51.4	44.7	47.8
All Non-Fr.	54.3	52.7	53.1	45.4	51.8
Total For Province	49.4	51.4	51.9	44.8	48.8

Sources: *Canadian Parliamentary Guide*
  Guide to Canadian Ministries Since Confederation
  Who's Who in Canada
+ one individual

positions as ministers, and more likely to receive patronage positions than English-Canadian ministers as a reward, and this may encourage entry into the cabinet at an earlier age.

Table 5-IV indicates the age of entry of ministers in the major (i.e., long-lasting) ministries in Canada, by party. The table shows that in general Liberals tend to become ministers at an earlier age than Conservatives, especially in the latter periods under study. This is probably because Conservative Prime Ministers, when coming to power after a long period of opposition, have felt obliged to appoint a large number of "old guard" supporters as a reward for past loyalty. There will probably be a large number of veteran Members of Parliament who will feel that they are entitled to cabinet positions. A Liberal Prime Minister, however, after the party has been in power a long time, will possibly be interested in appointing younger people to rejuvenate and renew the cabinet and forestall charges that the cabinet is elderly and too long in power. Mr. King's appointment to the cabinet of Abbott, Chevrier, and Martin in April 1945 may be an example here. The Prime Minister is also able to move older ministers into other positions, such as the Senate, thus making room for new blood, and is less indebted to an "old guard".

TABLE 5-IV

**Average Age of Entry of Cabinet Ministers by
Ministry and Party**

Ministry	Conservative	Liberal
Macdonald (1)	50.2	
Mackenzie		48.1
Macdonald (2)	51.9	
Laurier		50.5
Borden	52.4	
King		51.7
Bennett	52.8	
King		52.1
St. Laurent		46.8
Diefenbaker	52.0	
Pearson		47.9
Trudeau		44.5

Sources: *Canadian Parliamentary Guide*
Guide to Canadian Ministries Since Confederation
Who's Who in Canada

Religion of Cabinet Ministers

Table 5-V provides an analysis of the religion of members of the Canadian cabinet and illustrates the close attention paid by Prime Ministers to the problem of getting as balanced a representation of the major religious denominations as possible. For many years, however, the proportion of Roman Catholics in the cabinet was considerably less than their share of the Canadian population, but this has been increasing over time, partly because more emphasis has been placed on having French Canadians, who are Catholic as well, in the cabinet. In addition the overall increase in the size of the Roman Catholic population has made this group more significant politically and thus made it necessary to provide them with more recognition.

The Anglican denomination does not claim as many adherents in the cabinet now as was the case early in Canada's history. There is now a close correlation between cabinet membership and the size of the Anglican population in general, as is true of the Roman Catholic representation. It is interesting to note, however, that the Anglican influence among English Canadians in Quebec appears to have been unusually strong (Table 5-VI). Fifteen of the 26 non-French-Canadian members of the cabinet from Quebec have been Anglican and the sole non-Roman Catholic French Canadian was also an Anglican.

TABLE 5-V

**Religious Affiliation of Cabinet Ministers
and Religious Affiliation of the Population of Canada by Percentage**

Denomination	Affiliation of Cabinet Members 1867-1896	Affiliation of Popul'n 1871 Census	Affiliation of Cabinet Members 1896-1921	Affiliation of Popul'n 1901	Affiliation of Cabinet Members 1921-1948	Affiliation of Popul'n 1931	Affiliation of Cabinet Members 1948-1974	Affiliation of Popul'n 1971	Affiliation of Cabinet Members 1867-1974
Roman Catholic	31.7	42.9	29.5	41.6	32.0	39.6	47.8	46.2	36.4
Anglican	24.7	14.8	23.0	12.9	19.6	15.8	13.4	11.7	19.5
Pres.-Meth.-Cong. United	12.9	33.0	37.3	33.6	39.2	29.2	28.6	21.5	29.6
Baptists	2.4	6.8	3.7	5.9	7.2	4.2	1.7	3.1	3.7
Other Protestant	23.5	2.5	5.2	5.9	1.0	6.6	5.1	10.3	8.2
Other	4.8		1.3	.1	1.0	4.6	3.4	7.2	2.6
Total	100.0	100.0	100.0	100.0	100.0	100.0	100.0	100.0	100.0

Sources: *Canadian Parliamentary Guide*
Canada Year Book
Guide to Canadian Ministries Since Confederation
The Canadian Directory of Parliament
Who's Who in Canada

TABLE 5-VI

Religious Affiliation of Cabinet Members from Quebec by Party 1867-1974

Party	1867-1896					1896-1921					1921-1948					1948-1974					1867-1974				
	R.C.	An	Un*	Pr†	O	R.C.	An	Un*	Pr†	O	R.C.	An	Un*	Pr†	O	R.C.	An	Un*	Pr†	O	R.C.	An	Un*	Pr†	O
Fr. Cons.	13					10					8					11					42				
Eng. Cons.		3	1	5	1	2	1	1					1				1				2	5	3	5	1
Total Cons.	13	3	1	5	1	12	1	1			8		1			11	1				44	5	3	5	1
Fr. Lib.	8					6	1				14					23					51	1			
Eng. Lib.		1				1	2				1	4	1			4	2				6	9	1		
Total Lib.	8	1				7	3				15	4	1			27	2				57	10	1		
Fr. Cons. & Lib.	21					16	1				22					34					93	1			
Eng. Cons. & Lib.		4	1	5	1	3	3	1			1	4	2			4	3				8	14	4	5	1
Total	21	4	1	5	1	19	4	1			23	4	2			38	3				101	15	4	5	1

*Includes Methodists, Congregationalists prior to 1926 when the United Church of Canada was formed.

†Presbyterians

Sources: *Canadian Parliamentary Guide*
   Canada Year Book
   Guide to Canadian Ministries Since Confederation
   The Canadian Directory of Parliament
   Who's Who in Canada

In the first period under study (1867-1896) a large number of cabinet ministers are described as "Protestant" in the various sources consulted. It is likely that most of these were members of those churches which later formed the United Church or the continuing Presbyterian Church and, if this was the case, then it is clear that members of this group have been consistently over-represented in the cabinet, and that this situation persists. The oft-heard description of the cabinet as being representative of the WASP establishment, while not completely accurate in view of the strong Roman Catholic representation, is to some extent justified by the very large number of members of the Anglican and Methodist-Presbyterian-United tradition who have achieved cabinet rank. It should also be pointed out that this latter tradition seems to account for most cabinet ministers in the western provinces, which is to some extent explained by the lack of an "establishment", which is usually Anglican, present in other parts of Canada.

It is obvious that the smaller denominations are considerably under-represented in the Canadian cabinet and consequently the cabinet is not representative of the Canadian population in general. Again, socio-economic reasons may help to explain the situation and, since the "others" column represents over thirty denominations, it is unlikely that any cabinet could be representative of all religions, even if this was desirable. It should be pointed out that cabinet ministers and parliamentarians in general appear to be very anxious to be identified with some religion; no cabinet minister has indicated that he was or is a non-believer.

Ethnic Background of Cabinet Ministers

Closely related to the matter of religion is the ethnic background of cabinet ministers. Table 5-VII provides an analysis of their ethnic backgrounds, and it is clear that the non-French, non-English segment of the Canadian population is substantially under-represented. The "other" segment of the Canadian population, while increasing rapidly in terms of the total Canadian population, has not yet been able to penetrate the elite comprising the cabinet, as reflected not only in terms of ethnic background but also with reference to religion, as illustrated above.

Educational Background

The educational background of cabinet ministers is also considerably different from that of the general population. Tables 5-VIII and 5-IX provide an analysis of this aspect, and it is clear that a university education is almost a necessity for entry into the cabinet. Table 5-VIII indicates that 249 or 65.7 per cent of all cabinet ministers have attended university, and the proportion of ministers who have university backgrounds

TABLE 5-VII

Ethnic Background of Cabinet Ministers 1867-1974

	1867-1896			1896-1921			1921-1948			1948-1974			Total Cabinet Ministers 1867-1974	
	No. of Cabinet Mins.	% of Cabinet Mins.	% of Pop. Census 1871	No. of Cabinet Mins.	% of Cabinet Mins.	% of Pop. Census 1901	No. of Cabinet Mins.	% of Cabinet Mins.	% of Pop. Census 1931	No. of Cabinet Mins.	% of Cabinet Mins.	% of Pop. Census 1971	#	
British	64	75.0	60.7	60	77.0	56.7	69	71.3	51.8	73	61.3	44.4	266	70.2
French Cdn.	21	25.0	30.9	18	23.0	30.9	25	25.7	28.2	40	33.6	28.7	104	27.4
Icelandic							1			1	.8		2	.5
German			8.4			12.4	2	2.0	10.0	1	.8	26.9	3	.8
Ukrainian										1	.8		1	.3
Other										3	2.7		3	.8
Total	85	100.0	100.0	78	100.0	100.0	97	100.0	100.0	119	100.0	100.0	379	100.0

Sources: *Canadian Parliamentary Guide*
Canada Year Book
Guide to Canadian Ministries Since Confederation
The Canadian Directory of Parliament
Who's Who In Canada

TABLE 5-VIII

Educational Background of Cabinet Ministers by Province 1867-1974
(Absolute Figures)

	1867-1896			1896-1921			1921-1948			1948-1974				Total Univ.	Non U
	Class. Coll.	Univ.	Non U	Class. Coll.	Univ.	Non U	Class. Coll.	Univ.	Non U	Class. Coll.	Univ.	Non U	Non Class. Coll.		
National	13	31	41	3	49	26	1	70	26	0	99	20	17	249	113
Quebec	13	12	7	3	19	2	1	26	2		37	4	17	94	15
Ontario		9	14		15	10		22	9		30	6		76	39
N.S.		5	9		2	4		5	3		3	0		15	16
N.B.		3	6		4	3		6	4		4	1		17	14
Man.		1	1		4	2		3	2		5	1		13	6
P.E.I.		0	2		1	0		1	2		2	1		4	5
B.C.		1	2		1	2		4	1		9	2		15	7
Alta.					2	2		0	2		3	3		5	7
Sask.					1	1		3	1		3	0		7	2
Nfld.								3	1		3	2		3	2

Sources: *Canadian Parliamentary Guide*
Canada Year Book
Guide to Canadian Ministries Since Confederation
The Canadian Directory of Parliament
Who's Who In Canada

TABLE 5-IX

**Educational Background of Cabinet Ministers
by Ministry**

Ministry	University	Non University
Macdonald (1)		
(1867-1873)	11	14
Mackenzie	10	13
Macdonald (2)		
(1878-1891)	15	15
Laurier	24	9
Borden	23	13
King (1)		
(1921-1930)	26	17
Bennett	29	6
King (2)		
(1935-1948)	35	9
St. Laurent	29	5
Diefenbaker	32	6
Pearson	35	6
Trudeau	38	7

has steadily increased, so that in the Trudeau ministry only seven ministers (15.6 per cent) had not attended university. Table 5-IX, showing the educational background of ministers serving in the ministries, illustrates the growth in the importance of a university background. The percentage of the members of the first Trudeau cabinet having a university background corresponds almost exactly with Porter's figures for the Canadian political elite (84.5 per cent versus 86 per cent).[3] This situation, indicating that the level of education achieved by members of the Canadian cabinet is considerably above that of the general population, appears to be similar to that in the United States, where it has been claimed that political figures must " . . . display a considerable amount of personal achievement before their political chances are very good".[4] Personal achievement refers to other factors as well as education, but a university education may be one indicator of achievement.

Occupational Background of Cabinet Ministers

It will come as no surprise that cabinet ministers are " . . . usually lawyers, businessmen or other persons high on the socio-economic scale and frequently occupy other positions of community leadership".[5] Table 5-X provides an analysis of occupational background by period. Table 5-XI provides a similar analysis by province.

TABLE 5-X

Occupations of Cabinet Ministers 1867-1972

Period	Lawyer		Business person		Journalist		Doctor		Farmer		Educator		Public Servant		Engineer		Others		Total
	#	%	#	%	#	%	#	%	#	%	#	%	#	%	#	%	#	%	#
1867-1896	48	56.5	22	25.9	4	4.7	4	4.7	2	2.3	1	1.1	2	2.3	1	1.2	1	1.2	85
1896-1921	44	56.4	15	19.1	6	7.6	7	9.0	2	2.6			2	2.6			2	2.6	78
1921-1948	52	53.6	20	20.6	1	1.0	6	6.2	4	4.2	4	4.2	5	5.1	3	3.1	2	2.0	97
1948-1972	57	47.9	35	29.4	4	3.4			5	4.2	10	8.4	2	1.7	1	.8	5	4.2	119
Total	201	53.6	92	24.3	15	4.0	17	4.5	13	3.4	15	4.0	11	2.9	5	1.2	10	2.6	379

Sources: *Canadian Parliamentary Guide*
Canada Year Book
Guide to Canadian Ministries Since Confederation
The Canadian Directory of Parliament
Who's Who In Canada

TABLE 5-XI

Occupation of Cabinet Ministers by Province of Residence 1867-1974

Prov.	Lawyer	Business person	Journalist	Doctor	Farmer	Educator	Public Servant	Engineer	Others	Total
Quebec	90	16	5	5	2	3	2		3	126
Ontario	50	38	3	7	2	3	4	2	6	115
N.S.	15	8	2	2		1	2	1		31
N.B.	17	9	1	1		2	1			31
Man.	10	6		1	1	1				19
P.E.I.	2	3	1		2	1				9
B.C.	9	5	2	1	1		1	2	1	22
Alta.	4	3	1		3	1				12
Sask.	2	2			2	3				9
Nfld.	2	2					1			5
Total	201	92	15	17	13	15	11	5	10	379

Sources: *Canadian Parliamentary Guide*
Canada Year Book
Guide to Canadian Ministries Since Confederation
The Canadian Directory of Parliament
Who's Who In Canada

It will be noticed from Table 5-X that lawyers have made up the majority of the cabinet during the entire history of Canada, although their relative importance appears to be declining slightly. The vocations of farming, journalism, and medicine are less relevant as far as the cabinet is concerned, while business and education appear to have become more important. Farming and medicine have both become so complicated that it is no longer possible for people in these fields to easily interrupt their careers for careers in politics. Doctors were quite prominent in earlier years, and the situation in Canada may have been similar to that in the United States, where it was found that doctors were more prominent in political life because ". . . the subject matter of medicine was much less technical, the achievement and rewards of practice were much lower, the work was less demanding, doctors were not trained to such specialized skills or to strong commitment to their careers, and the profession was much less solidary."[6] The journalists who entered politics in the early years were often self-employed journalists *cum* businessmen, who owned their own papers and thus were better able to devote time to politics, while employing others to look after their business interests. Few journlaists today are in such a position. Most important of all possible explanations is that the Canadian elite has changed due to changes in the structure of Canadian society and the Canadian economy.

The fact that in Canada " . . . lawyers constitute the high priesthood of the political system"[7] is not a startling discovery. This is similar to the situation in the United States, and Porter gives several possible explanations as to why this is so. One of his arguments is that lawyers " . . . are about the only persons for whom sustained political activity is not incompatible with the career system."[8] In addition, the training and skills of a lawyer " . . . tend to give him an advantage in the race for office if not actual training for filling the office once it is achieved."[9] These skills include mediation, compromise, verbal manipulation, etc. The absence in Canada of a substantial, independently wealthy aristocracy has also encouraged lawyers to enter politics, for as both Matthews and Porter observe, a society without an aristocracy devoted to political matters usually turns to lawyers for this purpose. As noted earlier, a period in politics may be helpful to a lawyer in building up his practice.

The importance of businesspeople and educators may be partially explained by the fact that they, too, are better able to leave their usual occupations for a career in politics than are people in most other professions. The growth of large corporations has made it easier for businesspeople to transfer in and out of business careers more easily than when most businesspeople were individual entrepreneurs rather than members of corporate bureaucracies. The growth in the demand for educators has provided a market for individuals trained in this field who have not been successful politically. It is still true, however, that in a highly competitive society, where occupational success is the most highly valued goal, it is lawyers who can best take the risks of a hazardous political career.

However, it is important to note that of 29 individuals recruited into the cabinet by Mr. Trudeau, ten have been businesspeople, twelve have been lawyers, three farmers, three journalists, and one a teacher. Thus in the Trudeau cabinet at the end of 1974 the legal profession was less prominent than in any other cabinet. The increasing number of businesspeople entering the cabinet over the years tends to confirm the thesis that the higher the degree of industrialization, the larger the proportion of businessmen participating in politics.[10]

The Tenure and Exit of Cabinet Ministers

Table 5-XII demonstrates that the average tenure of cabinet ministers has been 5.2 years. While it is difficult to compare the tenure of ministers from various provinces, since some provinces have had very few ministers, it may be interesting to compare the terms of office of ministers from Quebec (Table 5-XIII) with those of ministers from outside Quebec. French-Canadian ministers from Quebec appear to have served for briefer periods in the cabinet than their non-French colleagues, regardless of party. This may be related to the difficulty of the Conservatives to

TABLE 5-XII

Average Service of Cabinet Ministers by Years

	1867-1896	1896-1921	1921-1948	1948-1974*	Average
Canada-Wide	5.4	5.5	5.7	4.1	5.2
Province					
Quebec	4.3	4.2	6.1	3.3	4.5
Ontario	7.4	6.1	5.7	4.0	5.7
N.S.	4.3	6.5	5.4	9.0	5.3
N.B.	7.4	3.3	3.6	3.7	4.7
Man.	2.0	8.2	2.8	4.4	4.9
P.E.I.	2.5	5.0	3.3	4.0	3.5
B.C.	3.0	6.7	6.0	5.4	5.4
Alta.		7.3	10.0	3.3	5.8
Sask.		2.0	11.0	6.0	7.5
Nfld.				4.5	4.5

*As of Oct. 30, 1974

TABLE 5-XIII

Average Service for Cabinet Ministers from Quebec by Party in Years*

	1867-1896	1896-1921	1921-1948	1948-1974	Average
Fr. Cons.	5.6	1.9	2.1	2.4	3.2
Eng. Cons.	3.6	6.7	5.0	6.0	4.6
Total Cons.	4.7	3.3	2.4	2.7	3.6
Fr. Lib.	3.2	5.0	8.3	3.9	5.3
Eng. Lib.	4.0	7.0	6.5	2.5	5.7
Total Lib.	3.3	5.6	7.8	3.7	5.4
French	4.7	3.2	6.1	3.3	4.3
English	3.6	6.8	6.3	3.7	5.1
Provincial Average	4.3	4.2	6.1	3.3	4.5

Sources: *Canadian Parliamentary Guide*
Canada Year Book
Guide to Canadian Ministries Since Confederation
The Canadian Directory of Parliament
Who's Who In Canada

*As of October 30, 1974

find suitable ministers from Quebec. A second reason may be that in the past French-Canadian ministers (and their families) have not felt at home in Ottawa and have returned to their native province for that reason. Some support for this argument is found in a survey conducted for the Royal Commission on Bilingualism and Biculturalism[11], which revealed that 50 per cent of French-Canadian Members of the House of Commons in the 26th Parliament (1963-1965) did not feel at home in Ottawa. Some Quebec ministers may have used their Ottawa position as a stepping stone to a position in Quebec politics, as in the case of Mr. Lesage. In addition, the greater likelihood of French-Canadian ministers receiving a patronage appointment (as indicated by Table 5-XVI) would be reflected by a briefer tenure in the cabinet.

Directly related to the term of office of ministers is the mode of exit from the cabinet, as illustrated in Table 5-XIV. Over the 107-year period 33.5 per cent of all members of the cabinet left as the result of the defeat of the government or as the result of a personal defeat (4.2 per cent). Another 22.2 per cent resigned for personal reasons, 6.3 per cent died in office, 7.7 per cent were still in office, and the balance, 26.1 per cent, were moved into more secure positions in the Senate, on the bench, or in the public service. In one sense, then, elevation to the cabinet can be a

TABLE 5-XIV

Exits of Cabinet Ministers 1867-1974
(as percentage of total)

Reason	1867-1896	1896-1921	1921-1948	1948-1974	1867-1974
Resigned	22.4	28.0	22.7	17.6	22.2
Govt. defeated	37.8	32.1	41.2	25.2	33.5
Lost seat	1.0		1.0	9.2	3.4
Not renominated			1.0	1.7	.8
Died in office	7.1	10.3	7.3	2.5	6.3
Received govt. appointments	31.7	29.6	26.8	19.3	26.1
Senate	(3.5)	10.3)	(8.2)	(10.9)	(8.4)
Judiciary	(10.5)	(9.0)	(12.4)	(2.5)	(8.2)
Lt. Gov.	(17.7)	(2.6)	(1.0)	(2.5)	(5.5)
Other		(7.7)	(5.2)	(3.4)	(4.0)
Still in office				25.5	7.7
Total	100.0	100.0	100.0	100.0	100.0

promising move, in that the chances are slightly better than one in four that the minister will find himself appointed to a more secure patronage position. On the other hand, the chances are better than one in three that he will lose his position abruptly at the hands of the electorate.

Over time there has been a considerable shift in the type of position filled by a minister after he leaves the cabinet (Table 5-XV). In the period 1867-1896, the position of Lieutenant Governor appears to be the most attractive, but since 1896 only six cabinet ministers have gone directly from that position to that of Lieutenant Governor, compared with fourteen in the first period. Again, this fact helps to confirm Ward's suggestion that in the early days there were many more well-to-do "gentlemen" in Canadian politics who might be interested in the social prestige this position would bring. It should also be remembered that in the early years after Confederation the position of Lieutenant Governor did involve considerable authority and power as well as political activity, making it far more than the social or honorific position it is today, which would make it more attractive. At the same time, the social burdens of the position, and hence the expenses, were quite high; this may have restricted it to "gentlemen" and making it less attractive to cabinet ministers today.

Under Mr. King, as shown by Table 5-XV, the Senate and judiciary became especially important as repositories for former cabinet ministers, but both seem to have declined in importance in recent years. The

TABLE 5-XV

Exits of Cabinet Ministers by Ministries

	Resigned	Govt. Defeated	Lost Seat	Not Renominated	Died	Senate	Appointed to Judiciary	Lt. Gov.	Other Govt. Pos'ns.	Still in Office
Macdonald (1)	7	4	1		4		3	6		
Mackenzie	5	10				1	3	4		
Macdonald (2)	7	6			1	2	2	4	2	
Laurier	6	8			4	3	4	2	2	
Borden	15	5			3	5	3		4	
King (1)	15	10			5	5	2			
Bennett	1	18				1	1	1		
King (2)	7	5	1		3	2	9		6	
St. Laurent	2	10			1	1	1		1	
Diefenbaker	8	21	2		1	4	2	2		
Pearson	7		4	2	1	8	1	1	2	7
Trudeau	3		4				1			22

Sources: *Canadian Parliamentary Guide*
Canada Year Book
Guide to Canadian Ministries Since Confederation
The Canadian Directory of Parliament
Who's Who In Canada

TABLE 5-XVI

Exists of Cabinet Ministers, Nationally and
for Provinces of Quebec and Ontario (Percentages) 1867-1974

	Resigned	Govt. Defeated	Lost Seat	Not Renom- inated	Died	Senate	Appointed to Judiciary	Lt. Gov.	Other† Govt. Pos'ns.	Still in Office
National	22.2	33.5	3.4	.8	6.3	8.4	8.2	5.5	4.0	7.7
Fr. Cdn. Quebec	16.8	27.4	3.1	1.1	8.4	9.5	14.7	5.3	5.3	8.4
Eng. Cdn. Quebec	34.4	31.3			12.5		9.3			12.5
Prov. of Quebec	21.2	28.3	2.4	.8	9.4	7.1	13.4	4.0	4.0	9.4
Ontario	30.4	31.3	1.0	1.0	6.0	8.7	5.2	6.0	2.6	7.8

Sources: *Canadian Parliamentary Guide*
    Canada Year Book
    Guide to Canadian Ministries Since Confederation
    The Canadian Directory of Parliament
    Who's Who in Canada

†Includes Appointments to — Government Boards and Commissions
                            — Diplomatic Positions
                            — Speakership of Senate and House of Commons
                            — Parliamentary Library
                            — Collector of Customs

judiciary is likely to become even less significant, due to the recent changes in the procedure for appointing the judges instituted under Mr. Pearson and continuing under Mr. Trudeau.[12] This procedure involves consultation with a committee of the Canadian Bar Association on judicial appointments, although final responsibility remains with the cabinet.

The exits of ministers from Quebec shows a pattern somewhat different from that of the rest of Canada (Table 5-XVI). French-Canadian ministers are less likely to leave the cabinet because of defeats, either governmental or personal, or for personal reasons and are more likely to enjoy a patronage reward on leaving the cabinet than most members of the cabinet. It would also appear that non-French-speaking ministers are less secure in their cabinet positions than French colleagues, both nationally and from the province of Quebec. A comparison of the exits of cabinet ministers from Quebec and Ontario indicates that patronage appointments to the bench are relatively more common in Quebec than in Ontario. On a Canada-wide basis, 26.1 per cent of all cabinet ministers received patronage appointments, but 34.8 per cent of French Canadians have received such appointments. This may help account for the briefer tenure in office of French-Canadian ministers noted in Tables 5-XII and 5-XIII.

POST-CABINET CAREERS

An analysis was made of the subsequent careers of those ministers who were members of the House of Commons who resigned from the cabinet for personal reasons or left the cabinet because of a government defeat. Table 5-XVII indicates that rewards are not confined to those who are promoted while still cabinet members. Of those who resigned from the cabinet for the reasons cited above, 44.3 per cent returned to private life, 25.7 per cent remained active as Members of the House of Commons for some time after leaving the cabinet, 4.3 per cent entered municipal or provincial politics (and in one case, British politics) and the remaining 25.7 per cent eventually received some form of government appointment. Thus, combining the data on Table 5-XIV and 5-XV, one may conclude that over one-third of all individuals entering the cabinet are appointed eventually to some form of non-elective office. In addition many former cabinet ministers became prominent members of the business community after their terms in the cabinet, which is itself a form of reward.

A comparison of the figures for Quebec and all of Canada in Table 5-XVIII shows that a much lower proportion of French-Canadian ministers remain in Parliament after they have left the cabinet, and a higher proportion receive subsequent appointments. These figures are partially accounted for by the Liberal victories of 1896 and 1963, which resulted in

TABLE 5-XVII

**Post-Cabinet Careers of Ministers Holding Seats in the House of Commons
Who Left Cabinet for Personal Reasons or
because of Defeat of Government 1867-1974 (as percentage)**

	1867-1896	1896-1921	1921-1948	1948-1972	1867-1974
Returned to Private Life	35.1	53.3	45.2	42.4	44.3
Remained in House of Commons	27.1	17.8	24.2	31.8	25.7
Appointed Lt. Gov.	5.4	4.4	6.5	1.5	4.3
Appointed to Senate	10.8	6.7	14.5	4.6	9.0
Appointed to Judiciary	8.1	8.9		3.0	4.3
Appointed to Patronage Position	8.1	6.7	4.8	12.1	8.1
Entered Politics at Provincial or Municipal Level	5.4	2.2	4.8	4.6	4.3
Total	100.0	100.0	100.0	100.0	100.0

Sources: *Canadian Parliamentary Guide*
Canada Year Book
Guide to Canadian Ministries Since Confederation
The Canadian Directory of Parliament
Who's Who In Canada

many Quebec ministers being unseated and by the explanations offered with regard to tenure of office discussed on page 116. It should be noted, however, that English-Canadian ministers from Quebec also receive a higher number of appointments than the national figure. The small number of ministers involved, however, does not make comparisons with the rest of Canada especially useful.

Business Connections of Members of the Cabinet

There has always been a close connection between members of the cabinet and the Canadian business community. This was true at Confederation and has continued to the present time.

The deep involvement of the Canadian government in economic activities (particularly with railways) and the wide-spread patronage practices at the time of Confederation and since are not without their disturbing aspects. The interest of members of the cabinet in expanding the economy and frontiers of Canada was only partly inspired by a sense of patriotism. "That the government had become so deeply involved in

TABLE 5-XVIII

Comparison of Post Cabinet Careers of Ministers from Quebec and All of Canada Holding Seats in the House of Commons Who Left Cabinet for Personal Reasons or Because of the Defeat of Government 1867-1974

	Quebec French	English	Total Quebec	All Canada
Returned to Private Life	45.5	50.0	46.8	44.3
Remained in House of Commons	15.9	16.7	16.1	25.7
Appointed Lt. Gov.	9.1		6.5	4.3
Appointed to Senate	13.6	11.1	12.9	9.0
Appointed to Judiciary	4.5		3.2	4.3
Appointed to Patronage Position	9.1	16.7	11.3	8.1
Entered Politics at Provincial or Municipal Level	2.3	5.5	3.2	4.3
Total	100.0	100.0	100.0	100.0

Sources: *Canadian Parliamentary Guide*
Canada Year Book
Guide to Canadian Ministries Since Confederation
The Canadian Directory of Parliament

railway financing must also be attributed to politicians who did not hesitate to mix business with politics. No less than six of the original directors of the Grand Trunk were members of the Canadian Cabinet."[13] This connection between business and members of the cabinet has continued to be a source of controversy up to the present. A close connection between business and government did not seem to be as inconsistent with prevailing opinion in the early years of Confederation as it did later. Thus it was that Sir Charles Tupper, who served simultaneously as High Commissioner to Great Britain and as a member of Macdonald's cabinet, had no compunction in accepting from the Canadian Pacific Railway Company in 1885 " . . . $100,000 of its common stock then selling at $45.00. . . ."[14] in appreciation for his services as High Commissioner for Canada in selling their bonds. Even prior to becoming High Commissioner, Tupper had had close links with business. When he became Secretary of State in 1876 he was a director of several important companies including the Bank of British Columbia, the General Mining Associates London, and he was chairman of the

South Africa Cable Company, all of which involved renumeration for him.

The practice of ministers continuing their outside business associations persisted for a good many years, although the number of ministers thus involved decreased in number. One of the staunchest opponents of this questionable practice was Sir Robert Borden. When Laurier appointed Aylesworth as Minister of Justice in 1906, Borden argued that Aylesworth should not serve as Minister of Justice while still engaged in private legal practice. Laurier himself could hardly be expected to sympathize with Borden since he was at that time a director of the Mutual Life of Canada and had been since 1890.[15] When Borden himself became Prime Minister, he insisted that his ministers divorce themselves from their outside business connections. The practice of permitting outside affiliations was resumed under King and was bitterly criticized. "The Minister of Justice (Gouin) is a director of the Bank of Montreal . . . also a director of the Cockshutt Plough Company . . . a director of the Montreal City and District Savings Bank, of the Royal Trust Company, of the Mount Royal Assurance Company, of the Mutual Life Assurance Company. . . ."[16] A motion was presented in 1922 that would have had the effect of preventing members of the cabinet from holding outside directorates. Mr. King was opposed to the idea. "In the long run we will gain more in virility in our public life by leaving some matters to conscience and honour rather than by seeking to enforce prohibitions that may be too severe and too drastic. . . ."[17]

The close relationship between business and the cabinet has continued over the years, although the relationship is not as direct as it once was. One of the leading members of Bennett's cabinet was the Hon. C.H. Cahan, who had been a leading Montreal businessman prior to his entry into the cabinet, and Bennett himself, in addition to being a highly successful corporation lawyer, was even more successful in various business enterprises. C.D. Howe, who joined Mr. King's cabinet in 1935, had been a highly successful construction engineer who, on becoming a cabinet minister, sold out his interest in the C.D. Howe Company. The company, however, continued to receive government work under its new ownership, and among the company's employees at this time were Mr. Howe's son and son-in-law.

One of the more interesting features of the relationship between business and the cabinet has been the ease with which individuals have been able to cross over from one area to another. Hon. C.A. Dunning, who served as Minister of Finance from 1935 to 1939, became chairman of the board of Ogilvie Flour Mills and of the Sun Life Assurance Company shortly after leaving the cabinet. Another minister who entered the cabinet under Mr. King, Brooke Claxton, resigned his position in 1954 to become Canadian vice-president of the Metropolitan Life Insurance Co.

Hon. Walter Harris, Minister of Finance, under Mr. St. Laurent, became president of the Victoria and Gray Trust Co. after his personal defeat and the defeat of the St. Laurent government in 1957.

Under Mr. St. Laurent there arose two cases that created a considerable amount of controversy. It was discovered that the Hon. George Prudham, Minister of Mines and Technical Surveys, had not divested himself of his private business interests on entering the cabinet. The opposition was very critical of this, but was even more critical of the fact that Hon. J.J. McCann, Minister of National Revenue, remained a director of the Guaranty Trust Company, although his department was frequently engaged in negotiations with that company. Dr. McCann refused to resign this position, even though it was surely an embarrassment to the Prime Minister and his colleagues in the cabinet.

Mention has already been made of the entry of Senator Wallace McCutcheon into the Diefenbaker cabinet. Senator McCutcheon " . . . had resigned twenty-seven major corporate directorships to enter politics."[18] Hon. Donald Flemming and Hon. William Hamilton, who served in Mr. Diefenbaker's cabinet, became senior business executives after leaving the cabinet.

Mr. Pearson's cabinet included five prominent members of the Canadian business community: Hon. Walter Gordon, Hon. J.R. Nicholson, Hon. Robert Winters, Hon. C.M. Drury, and Hon. Mitchell Sharp. The latter two had been deputy ministers in federal government departments and had then entered business before entering active politics. Mr. Gordon and Mr. Winters both returned to careers in business on leaving the cabinet, and another of Mr. Pearson's ministers, Hon. Maurice Sauvé, became Vice-President, Administration, Consolidated-Bathurst Company Limited after leaving the cabinet. Mr. Pearson himself became a director of several companies after his retirement from politics.

Similar problems have arisen over the years in Great Britain, and legislation has been passed to safeguard against conflicts of interest. In the United Kingdom, ministers must now resign all directorships, public or private, paid or unpaid, except directorships or offices held in connection with philanthropic institutions, and even these must be resigned if there is any possibility of a conflict of interest. Ministers must divest themselves of controlling interests in any companies, and of any shares, whether controlling or not, in concerns closely associated with a minister's own department. They are also required to avoid speculative investments in securities on which they have or may be thought to have early or confidential information.

In Canada the practice developed over the years of requiring cabinet ministers in the federal government, as in the case of Mr. Winters and Mr. Kierans, to resign all directorships before taking office. In many cases the management of their private affairs was turned over to a trustee, such as a trust company, which then managed the assets of the minister without reference to him. There was, however, no firm regulation to that effect, and the possibility of a conflict of interest still existed, especially in those cases where cabinet members had interests in private or family companies.

Under Mr. Trudeau more specific guidelines have been set down with reference to conflict of interest. Ministers are now required to resign any directorships they may hold in profit-making corporations and must sever all active business, commercial, or professional associations while they are members of the cabinet. Four options are available with respect to investments:

1 total divestment of assets;
2 the establishment of a blind trust, where the trustee can make investment decisions without reference to the owner and the only information provided the owner is the actual value of the assets;
3 the establishment of a frozen trust, where the minister's holdings are maintained as they are at the time of the formation of the trust;
4 registration of a declaration of property holdings with a registrar, with the declaration available for public inspection. The registrar advises ministers on matters covered by the government's policy on conflict of interest and all transactions are a matter of public knowledge.

These guidelines, while more formal and stringent than earlier practices, have been criticized because they do not cover the assets of spouses or minor children and thus do not absolutely preclude the possibility of a conflict of interest.

The description of the Canadian cabinet, then, is in fact a description of an elite, in that the cabinet is patterned to a very large extent on the Canadian socio-economic elite, with French Canadians being better represented in the cabinet than in other major elite groups. The analysis points up the fact that a cabinet career is relatively brief, that it does hold promise of some more permanent rewards but at some risk. Porter has remarked that "where the political career is unstable and taken up for an interstitial period only, during a career devoted to something else, the political system will probably be strong in administration and weak in creativity."[19] This leads to the cautious and prudent style of leadership noted earlier as being characteristic of a consociational democracy.

NOTES

[1]Norman Ward, *The Canadian House of Commons, Representation*, 2nd. ed. (Toronto; University of Toronto Press, 1963), p. 120.

[2]*Ibid.*

[3]John Porter, *The Vertical Mosaic*, p. 388.

[4]Donald Matthews, *The Social Background of Political Decision Makers*. (New York; Random House, 1954), p. 28.

[5]Howard A. Scarrow, "Three Dimensions of a Local Political Party", in John Meisel, ed., *Papers on the 1962 Election*. (Toronto; University of Toronto Press, 1962), p. 56.

[6]William A. Glaser, "Doctors and Politics". *American Journal of Sociology*, Vol. LXVI (November, 1960), p. 234.

[7]John Porter, *The Vertical Mosaic*, p. 392.

[8]*Ibid.*, p. 393.

[9]Donald R. Matthews, *U.S. Senators and Their World*. (New York; Random House, 1960), p. 33.

[10]Rosalio Wences, "Electoral Participation and the Occupational Composition of Cabinets and Parliaments". *American Journal of Sociology*, Vol. 75, No. 2 (1969-70), pp. 181-190.

[11]David Hoffman and Norman Ward, *Bilingualism and Biculturalism in the Canadian House of Commons*, p. 190.

[12]Canada, House of Commons, *Debates*. (November 30, 1967), p. 4896.

[13]Sister Teresa Burke, *Canadian Cabinets in the Making*, p. 10.

[14]Saunders, *Life and Letters of Sir Charles Tupper*, Vol. II, pp. 60-61.

[15]L.M. Sprung, Vice-President of the Mutual Life Assurance Company of Canada, Letter to author. (March 16, 1970).

[16]Canada, House of Commons, *Debates*. (March 20, 1922), p. 242-3.

[17]*Ibid.* (March 24, 1922), p. 1099.

[18]Peter Newman, *The Distemper of Our Times*, p. 158.

[19]John Porter, *The Vertical Mosaic*, p. 406.

Chapter VI

The Cabinet and the Prime Minister
Macdonald to King

It has been alleged that there has recently developed " . . . a new pattern in Canadian politics, the emergence of the Prime Minister, who has always been a powerful figure as the single dominant force in government. . . . "[1] This is in fact not a new development, for the Prime Minister has normally been the dominant figure; those prime ministers who failed to be dominant have not been kindly judged by the electorate or by history. What is true is that the present Prime Minister appears to have more control over the policy-making apparatus than his predecessors, but it would also appear true that the powers of the Prime Minister have been greatly exaggerated.

Various factors contribute to the power of the Prime Minister. Reference has already been made to the emphasis given to his position as a result of the representation principle, but there are other important factors as well. The Prime Minister's role as party leader and master of his cabinet, his influence over policy making, his special relationship with the Crown, and the Prime Minister's own style and personality are all important in this regard.

The Prime Minister as Party Leader

Normally the Prime Minister is master of his party. He has been elected party leader via a national party convention, and as long as he can keep members of the party convinced that he will retain office and win elections, his power is overwhelming. If a prime minister is in a strong position insofar as the electorate is concerned, it is unlikely that the party will be anxious to replace him. Moreover, as party leader (see Chapter X), the Prime Minister has control over the party organization. In the past he has appointed the leading party officials, including organizers, and thus controls, or is in a position to control, party strategy. He is like a general in command of an army; his authority is almost absolute within the party. He alone authoritatively expresses the views of the party, and every plank in its platform requires his approval. The Prime Minister can threaten to resign, leaving the party and the cabinet with the problem of finding an immediate successor. Threats of resignation must not be made too frequently, but it should be noted that this was a tactic not infrequently adopted by Mr. King. During 1944, for example, Mr. King told members of the cabinet at least twice that he would resign as party leader if they did not support him. Like most prime ministers, however, Mr. King was at pains to see to it that there was no potential successor in sight, and thus was usually able to win his point.

As party leader, the Prime Minister can claim that he owes his position to the grass roots of the party, not to the parliamentary caucus or to the cabinet, because he has been elected via a party convention. He can claim also that he, and he alone, has received a mandate from the party, a claim that is especially useful in times of conflict with caucus or cabinet, for no one else can make that claim. He can argue that the members of caucus and the cabinet owe their positions to him; they will be aware of this debt and hence reluctant to oppose him. Mr. King " . . . more than once silenced the parliamentary wolves by emphasizing that he was the representative and leader of the party as a whole, not merely of the parliamentary group".[2] It was said of Mr. Diefenbaker that, "He had led the party for victory through the use of his political sense, and everyone was expected to trust this sense between elections."[3] Since the numerous cleavages in Canadian society prevent the polarization of political parties around issues, the political struggle tends to revolve around the personalities of the party leaders rather than around questions of alternative choices of action. Thus elections have more and more become personality contests, enabling a Prime Minister to claim that his support *qua* Prime Minister comes from the public who voted for him rather than for any particular policy or program. It can even be argued that under the present system the only mandate a Member of Parliament has is to follow his leader, since the party's policy is the policy of the leader. There is no question but that usually a Prime Minister, as a result of his control over the party, can be sure that his party's backbenchers will support him and the cabinet in the House, and in public, however they may oppose him in caucus.

It should be remembered, however, that there are realistic limits to the power of the Prime Minister with regard to the party. The need to conciliate group and regional interests will prevent a prime minister from favouring one section of the party over another for fear of alienating party supporters. Thus it is unlikely that he will ever advocate extreme policies in an ideological sense, and his leadership will have more of a conciliatory character than a bold or dynamic one.

The Prime Minister as Master of His Cabinet

The Prime Minister derives great power from his mastery over the cabinet. "He has in his gift the highest executive offices in the state, and although he is limited, by custom and convention in his distribution of them, his problem is not usually one of persuading men to accept Cabinet appointments but of choosing among the aspirants."[4] His power to appoint and dismiss cabinet members and to allocate portfolios gives him a very decisive influence over the political futures of his colleagues, since he is able to encourage the careers of some and to impede the careers of others. This ability is illustrated by an event that took place when Mr. Bennett was forming his cabinet. C.H. Cahan, a prominent Conservative, told the Prime Minister that he would enter the cabinet only if he were appointed Minister of Justice. Mr. Bennett in turn presented Mr. Cahan with an ultimatum himself: Either agree to serve in the far less glamorous position of Secretary of State or remain on the back benches. Cahan became Secretary of State. Even the fact that at times the Prime Minister must take into his cabinet those who in the past have been his enemies can have the beneficial result for him of silencing them; that is, the doctrine of cabinet responsibility will force them, at least in public, to support him. Thus Mr. Diefenbaker took Mr. Balcer into his cabinet, even though the latter was politically antagonistic to the Prime Minister. This antagonism was publicly muted while Mr. Balcer served as minister.

It has been noted in Chapter II that the Prime Minister does not have absolute freedom in appointing ministers. He is also limited in his ability to dismiss ministers, although constitutionally his right cannot be disputed. Although Prime Minister King was strongly opposed by Power, the Minister of National Defence for Air, during the Conscription Crisis of 1944, he made no move to dismiss him because of Power's standing in the Liberal Party and his influence in Quebec. Similarly, in 1962 Diefenbaker did not attempt to fire Hees, the Minister of Trade and Commerce, or Sévigny, the Associate Minister of National Defence, even though they had opposed him in cabinet and were trying to have him replaced. There have been very few firings from the cabinet in Canadian history, the most noteworthy being the cases of Tarte, Ralston, and Dupuis, but these were unusual cases. Tarte, Laurier's Minister of Public Works, had spoken out in 1902 in favour of higher tariffs, which was contrary to cabinet policy. Ralston advocated conscription in 1944, an issue that King feared would offend Quebec and endanger Canadian unity as well as losing support for him in Quebec. Dupuis became involved in an unsavoury scandal in 1965. The more normal course of events is for cabinet ministers to resign when they cannot get their own way on policy, rather than for the Prime Minister to dismiss a minister in order to get *his* way. Neither Mr. Hellyer nor Mr. Kierans were asked to resign by Mr. Trudeau; they took the initiative themselves because they could not reconcile their ideas on policy with those of the Prime Minister and their cabinet colleagues. The possible political consequences make it a very unwise procedure to dismiss a cabinet minister who has high standing in the party or who represents an important segment of Canadian society. It can be argued, then, that the Prime Minister's ability to appoint and to dismiss ministers can be exaggerated; political reality limits him severely.

It should be noted, however, that after the 1974 federal election, Mr. Trudeau asked three of his ministers to resign, apparently because their performance had not lived up to his expectations. One of these was the minister from New Brunswick and another was the sole Jewish member of the cabinet. They were both immediately replaced by another member from New Brunswick and a second Jewish member so that the representation principle was not impaired. The fact that there was no great public outcry over these resignations may be a manifestation of the deference of the groups represented by these particular ministers. Nevertheless, calling for resignations on the basis of dissatisfaction with performance is a rare thing in cabinet government in Canada.

The Prime Minister does have a free hand in managing the operations of the cabinet. He controls the agenda through the Privy Council Office and thus can decide what is to be discussed — and possibly more important, he can decide what will not be discussed. During cabinet meetings he acts as chairman and is thus in a position to guide the discussion along the lines he wishes. He can also terminate discussions and assess the feelings of the cabinet. The last word is always his. Mr. Diefenbaker remarked, "The Prime Minister must always have the last and decisive word."[5] A minister who disagrees with a prime minister then is in a very difficult position. His choice is a very simple one: He can resign or he can accept the Prime Minister's view. The fact that there have been very few resignations from the Canadian cabinet over matters of policy indicates quite clearly the decision most ministers have taken. The consequences of a minister's resigning are extremely serious in terms of his political career. If he resigns, he risks losing the favour of the party and will probably have difficulty in securing the party's nomination at the next election, although it is quite possible that a minister who has forfeited his chance for advancement by resigning from the cabinet would not be interested in attempting to be re-elected, as in the case of Mr. Kierans. When a minister resigns from the cabinet over policy he is likely to be written off politically by the party and he can look forward to a bleak political career. The cases of Hon. H.H. Stevens and Hon. J.L. Ralston come to mind in this connection. Stevens resigned from Bennett's cabinet after he was criticized by the Prime Minister for his public attacks on big business. He then established the Reconstruction Party, devoted to the reform of capitalism. The party elected only one member in the election of 1935, Stevens himself, who remained in Parliament until 1940. Ralston retired from political life in 1945, a year after his resignation. The doctrine of cabinet solidarity has the effect of muzzling the Prime Minister's opponents and thus his position is greatly enhanced.

It should be remembered, however, that again there are realistic limitations to the power of the Prime Minister. In many instances cabinet ministers are powerful in their own right either because of their personal ability, as in the case of Edward Blake in the Mackenzie cabinet, or C.D. Howe under King and St. Laurent; because of the interests they represent, as in the case of Cartier in Macdonald's first cabinet or Lapointe under King from 1921 to 1941; because of their role in the party, as in the case of Flemming in Diefenbaker's cabinet, or for a combination of these factors, as with Gardiner, Minister of Agriculture in King's cabinet after 1935. To antagonize such men could have serious repercussions and thus again emphasis must be placed on the process of conciliation rather than on arbitrary action. A prime minister who persistently imposes his will on the cabinet ,runs the risk of polarizing opinion in his cabinet as well as alienating certain groups or interests that ministers represent. At the time of the Cuban crisis in 1962, a majority in Mr. Diefenbaker's cabinet[6] favoured placing the Canadian armed forces on the alert. "Nevertheless the Prime Minister overruled the majority choice and ordered that Canada's defence squadrons should not be alerted."[7] It was shortly after this and several similar incidents that Mr. Diefenbaker began to lose control of his cabinet.

It should be noted that a prime minister cannot indefinitely prevent the cabinet from discussing matters uncongenial to him. Matters under public discussion cannot be left for long undiscussed by the cabinet, and other important matters, which may be unknown to the public, cannot be ignored indefinitely. Parliament, pressure groups (including the civil service), or the press will eventually bring pressure to bear to have these matters considered by the cabinet. In 1964 the Pearson cabinet had not discussed the attempted bribery of an executive assistant to the Minister of Citizenship and Immigration on behalf of narcotics smuggler Lucien Rivard, and when the matter was raised in the House of Commons by an opposition member,[8] Eric Nielsen, the cabinet was unprepared and without a strategy for dealing with Mr. Nielsen's allegations. Again, in 1970 it was only after massive public pressure that the government began to contribute to Biafran relief. To indefinitely postpone discussion of an issue and to allow problems to pile up would probably lead to instability in the political system.

It is not likely in a prime minister's interest to keep matters that a minister wishes to discuss off the cabinet agenda. Under Mr. Trudeau, a minister who opposes a cabinet committee decision has the right to discuss it further in a meeting of the full cabinet. He may be urged not to disagree by the Prime Minister or members of the Prime Minister's staff, but several people interviewed indicated that ministers are not inhibited under Mr. Trudeau in this regard.

There is no doubt however that the Prime Minister as chairman of the cabinet and as chairman of the chief co-ordinating committee has a great advantage over the other ministers. He is better informed on a wide range of issues than his ministers and this in itself is sufficient to make him the most powerful minister in the cabinet.

When a prime minister loses control of his cabinet, as in the case of Mackenzie and Diefenbaker he is likely to lose his power entirely. The cabinet is normally made up of the leading men of the party so that loss of control over the cabinet can lead to the loss of control over the party. By keeping a check on the cabinet the Prime Minister is in effect retaining his mastery over the party. Mackenzie, Bowell and Diefenbaker all had great difficulty in controlling their cabinets and eventually lost control of the party. It should be noted that one of the reasons Bowell succeeded Thompson as Prime Minister was because the cabinet was afraid his rival, Tupper, would ". . . be their master. . . ."[9] Bowell, as it turned out, was not master of his cabinet and it soon disintegrated. Laurier, by contrast, was in a far different position. Thus it was said of him: ". . . from first to last the Prime Minister was first in fact as in form — to the end he remained the one indispensable man in government."[10]

The Prime Minister and Policy Formation

As noted earlier, the power of the Prime Minister over policy formation has been substantially increased under Mr. Trudeau as the result of the changes in the Privy Council Office, in the Prime Minister's Office, and in the cabinet committee system. The centralization and co-ordination taking place in the Privy Council Office enables the Prime Minister to have access to information that is not easily available to his colleagues. Because extensive use is now made of cabinet committees, because it is the Prime Minister who appoints the members of the committees, because he may decide, through the Privy Council Office, what items of business go to a particular committee, and because, through the Privy Council Office and the Prime Minister's Office, he is fully informed on developments taking place within cabinet committees, he is certainly the best-informed person in the cabinet. It can be argued that since membership on cabinet committees is closely related to the functional nature of a minister's department, the Prime Minister's ability even to select cabinet committee members is restricted. The Ministers of External Affairs and National Defence can hardly be left off the cabinet committee on External Affairs and Defence, the Minister of Finance could not be left off the cabinet committee of Priorities and Planning, and the Minister of National Health and Welfare could not be easily left off the Committee on Social Policy. The Prime Minister, however, still decides which portfolio will be assigned to a minister, and possibly he derives more power from this fact than from his ability to appoint and dismiss ministers, since it appears that there are fewer constraints on the Prime Minister's power to appoint to a *particular portfolio* than to appoint or to dismiss. Thus Mr. Diefenbaker may not have had much choice in appointing Mr. Balcer or in keeping him in office, but he could make him Solicitor-General, a relatively minor cabinet position. The Prime Minister can affect policy priorities for a government department by appointing as minister an individual who shares his ideas on what policy is desirable in that department, and he can transfer ministers whose policies he dislikes.

It might be argued that the civil service, being a permanent and professional body, can counterbalance the influence of the Prime Minister over policy. It should be pointed out, however, that the Prime Minister has practically unlimited power to make appointments to his office, uninhibited by the usual restraints of the Public Service Commission or Treasury Board, and such appointees, because of their proximity to the Prime Minister, can frustrate the civil service's policy influence. Moreover, while senior civil servants may appear before parliamentary committees, Mr. Trudeau has not permitted the Clerk of the Privy Council to appear before such committees and answer questions regarding policy. Such immunity from parliamentary scrutiny surely enhances the Prime Minister's influence over policy making.

Again it is important to note that the Prime Minister's influence over policy can be exaggerated. The scope of governmental activity is so diverse and involves so many complex and technical details that it is impossible for one man to master them all. The point is that the position provides great potential for influence and pressure, and one would normally expect a prime minister to make extensive use of this potential.

It should be noted that the Prime Minister has a special role in the co-ordination of policy. He is the ultimate co-ordinator in the cabinet and must decide disputes that cannot be resolved elsewhere. This requires him to maintain a delicate balancing act. He must exercise general control but avoid undue interference; he must keep informed and avoid being accused of meddling with his ministers' activities. One of the attributes of a successful prime minister is the ability to maintain this balance.

The Prime Minister and the Crown

The Prime Minister also draws strength in the cabinet from his special relationship with the Crown, since he is the only person who can advise the Governor General to dissolve Parliament and call an election. It is unlikely that this is a very effective weapon when there is a quarrel in the cabinet, because using it implies a divided party and under such circumstances an election is not beneficial to the Prime Minister or to the party. The power to dissolve is not a power over the cabinet, and its importance in contemporary times has been exaggerated. Only in very exceptional circumstances would it be sensible for a prime minister to recommend or threaten to recommend a dissolution during a cabinet crisis. The power to advise a dissolution can, however, be a power over the opposition, especially for a minority government. When the Liberal government lost a parliamentary vote in 1968 on a budget resolution, Mr. Pearson presented a bill to Parliament that in effect stated that the lost vote did not involve a vote of non-confidence in the government. The Créditiste party agreed to support this bill, since its members did not want an election at that time. The power of dissolution is especially useful to the Prime Minister in that it enables him to choose an election date that will be advantageous to his party.

The Prime Minister then is the leading figure in the cabinet; the nature of the office provides him with so much power that he is, of necessity, dominant but by no means all-powerful. The extent to which he dominates his cabinet, however, depends on how he chooses to use the potentialities of his office, on his own personality and temperament, on the political situation in which he finds himself, and on the relationship he is able to establish with his cabinet colleagues. Thus the success of a prime minister in asserting his claim to leadership depends on his personal qualities and on his administrative and political skill.

If the Prime Minister then occupies so pre-eminent a role in the governing of Canada, it is important to examine the behaviour of the occupants of the office to see if any distinctive style of conduct can be noted, and if any relevant generalizations can be made regarding the way in which prime ministers have conducted themselves in office.

It was Macdonald who set the pattern for all subsequent prime ministers. The ways in which he and his successors have carried out their responsibilities have been affected by their individual temperament and style, but there are at the same time certain important factors and techniques that every prime minister must take into account in carrying out his duties.

Macdonald as Prime Minister

Macdonald possessed many talents useful to him as Prime Minister. One of the most important of these was his keen sense of the political. He was always aware that his position as Prime Minister depended on his position as party leader, and he never neglected his responsibility as a politician.

> . . . Sir John paid little enough attention to the proper work of the
> several departments over which he at various times presided. . . . But
> he never neglected his work as leader and he took most excellent care to
> keep on the best of terms with his supporters. . . . Politically speaking
> Sir John attended to the one thing needful and let the rest take care of
> itself.[11]

As party leader Macdonald considered himself supreme, and as one of
his colleagues remarked:

> . . . His manner was in fact imperious. He had been chosen to lead his
> party, and he considered it was his duty to lead it in the fullest sense of
> the term. . . . He therefore tolerated little or no interference by his
> lieutenants in matters of party strategy — always save and except when
> Sir George [sic] Cartier occasionally put his foot down. . . .[12]

This exception was important, for it illustrates that Macdonald understood that Cartier had to have special influence as the leader of one of
the most important groups in his cabinet. In fact there was little need for
interference, for Macdonald had a genius for strategy. He was often
referred to as "Old Tomorrow" because of his habit of delaying matters
until a more propitious time. He recognized that it was not necessarily
sufficient to receive a thin majority of approval, that it was politically
more advantages to delay passage until more enthusiastic support could
be mobilized, usually through the use of his powers of persuasion.

Macdonald also managed to remain in control of his cabinet. "He
was fond of power and he never made any secret out of it,"[13] Laurier
remarked at the time of his death. His colleagues were always well
aware of this, yet he did not exclude them from decision making and
rarely acted autocratically in cabinet. He relied on persuasion rather
than exerting his authority, although it would appear that he usually
took the initiative on policy matters. He selected men for his cabinet
who were not overly ambitious ". . . but men who could be relied upon
to support and maintain the policy and measures which, as the chosen
Conservative leader — he carefully planned and mapped out. . . ."[14] It
would appear that he usually received the acquiescence of his cabinet,
but it is also worth noting that he was able to delegate responsibility to
his ministers and leave them free to run their own departments.

In a consociational democracy one of the most important attributes
of a leader is the ability to act as a conciliator. Macdonald's ability here
was demonstrated as he went about forming his first cabinet. His ability
to bring into his cabinet men of opposing cultural, regional, religious,
and ethnic interests and to be able to have them work together with a
fair amount of harmony showed him to be a conciliator *par excellence*.
Goldwin Smith was moved to write of him, "The task of his political life
has been to hold together a set of elements, national, religious, sectional
and personal, as motley as the component parts of any crazy quilt,

activated [sic]'each of them by paramount regard for its own interest."[15]

Macdonald's talent as a conciliator required great flexibility, and this flexibility manifested itself in other ways as well. He was, for example, prepared to accept ideas from any source provided these ideas were useful to him. "He originated no great principle. He appropriated, however, freely from others when an opportunity offered or when he thought another's ideas would lead him to or keep him in office."[16] He was not a contemplative man; the supreme test of any policy was in its results. He was flexible and possessed an abundance of common sense.

Another important feature of Macdonald's style was his use of caution.

> [He] seldom studied out or submitted legislation in advance of public opinion. . . . When the efforts of his opponents or friends however had crystallized public opinion in favour of any particular measures and the people generally began to demand them, he was quite ready to give way and equally efficient in framing and passing legislation to carry out the popular will.[17]

Conciliation, flexibility, and caution can be expected in a consociational democracy, but Macdonald's leadership did not produce a dull and unexciting style of politics. At times he could be daring and a visionary; the National Policy is a monument to this, but he acted this way only when the political climate was favourable. Unlike some of his successors, Macdonald did not attempt to point the way to the public, but rather he waited until public opinion had indicated which direction it wanted to go and then he assumed leadership, a tactic emulated by his most successful successor, Mr. King.

Thus in Macdonald one found a Prime Minister who remained master of his party. He was able to control his cabinet without unduly dominating it. He placed great stress on conciliation and persuasion and consequently was both cautious and flexible. Yet his personality was such that in difficult times he could impose his will on his colleagues while still retaining their support. In obtaining such support he was able to make the members of his cabinet feel they were not only serving him, but their party and their country as well. Thus he kept them committed to the Canadian system. That he was able to find men who would behave in this fashion is illustrative of his ability to judge and select men and is also evidence of the loyalty that his personality could inspire.

Alexander Mackenzie

Alexander Mackenzie, who succeeded Macdonald as Prime Minister in 1873, was a far different man, who went about his duties as Prime Minister in a completely different way and had a very different style. Some of these differences in style were due to the political situation as it then existed; others were due to the personality of the man himself.

Mackenzie's strength within the Liberal Party was never as strong as that of Macdonald in the Conservative Party, and he did nothing to enhance his position as party leader. Thus his weakness as a party leader made it difficult for him to exert his authority, especially over Edward Blake. He appeared at times to have lost control of his cabinet to Blake and sometimes to Cartwright, mostly because of his lack of status in the party. The evidence that he no longer controlled the cabinet weakened his position no only with the party, but with the electorate as well.

The intermittent presence of Edward Blake in the cabinet was the cause of some of Mackenzie's difficulties. Blake's participation in the Mackenzie government is one of the few instances in Canadian government where the Prime Minister has had to contend with a potential rival in his cabinet. Other prime ministers have seen to it that their position was not threatened, but Blake was so influential and so capable that it was essential for Mackenzie to have him in the cabinet. To entice him in, Mackenzie was forced to make concessions to Blake that were to cause him problems later on. These concessions, which had to do with modifying the government's policy with respect to railway construction in British Columbia, led to great controversy later. Mackenzie was also unable to retain control over his cabinet. He involved himself in so many interests that he had little time to think through his problems. To a considerable extent this was not his fault. His cabinet was plagued with a lack of ability and much of the burden of the administration fell on Mackenzie personally. Mackenzie attempted to combine the office of Prime Minister with that of the position of Minister of Public Works. The administration of this department, which was one of the most important in the government at that time, took an inordinate amount of time, and in taking on such heavy responsibilities, Mackenzie committed a serious error. As a cabinet colleague noted: "Had he devoted one-tenth part of the time and energy to the task of organizing and keeping his party together which he bestowed on the work of his Department, the result would have been very different."[18] Because Mackenzie neglected his duties as leader of the party, he was unable to make a claim on the loyalty of his supporters. Since he refused to engage in many of the patronage practices of his day, as a matter of principle, many supporters of Macdonald remained in government service. As a result, his political opponents were quickly informed of the government's plans.

The presence of so many political enemies in high places in the civil service made it impossible for Mackenzie to delegate authority to civil servants as Macdonald could do. At any rate it is unlikely that Mackenzie's temperament would have made it possible for him to delegate responsibility. "He had felt it his duty, however, not only to know the details of his own department, but also the cause of proceedings in some of the other departments, and the explanations which devolved upon the Minister in charge were often undertaken by the Prime Minister."[19] As a result, Parliament and the country lost confidence in the government because it was obviously depending excessively on the talents of one man. Mackenzie tried from time to time to shuffle his cabinet so that he could share responsibility more, but he was usually not successful.

Mackenzie was a man of stern, upright, and inflexible convictions, and it is possible to argue that such a man will experience great difficulty if he becomes Prime Minister of Canada. Conciliation and pragmatism are difficult for those of unbending principle, which makes the task of managing a cabinet extraordinarily difficult. Mackenzie found it difficult to compromise even in trifling matters. Inability to compromise or conciliate makes it difficult for the individual to tolerate differences of opinion within the cabinet, a characteristic which, in a country as diverse as Canada, can be fatal. A man who attempts to be dictatorial in cabinet but who does not have an attractive and inspiring personality is not likely to be an effective Prime Minister. Mackenzie continually ". . . offended by his inflexibility, his lack of tact and his air of rectitude."[20]

It should be noted that never at any time was Mackenzie's character or integrity questioned, but these qualities were not sufficient to make him great. He was unable to combine his basic honesty with an attractive temperament that would inspire loyalty. Thus while he was prone to interfere with details of administration, he was unable to do so without antagonizing his subordinates, unlike other prime ministers who could interfere at times without stirring up a great deal of resentment. His personality, combined with the political circumstances under which he laboured, made his task extremely difficult and his term of office was not a success, in spite of all his hard work and personal integrity.

It was Mackenzie's misfortune to be Prime Minister at an especially awkward and difficult time in Canadian history. Had he possessed some of the attributes of Macdonald he might have been able to compensate for his lack of luck, but since this was not so he cannot be judged as a successful prime minister.

Sir Wilfrid Laurier

Laurier's model as Prime Minister was Macdonald. His remark (noted earlier) that Macdonald was fond of power and made no secret of it could be applied equally well to Laurier himself. Like Macdonald, Laurier was a genius at conciliation and compromise who nevertheless was able at all times to remain undisputed master of his cabinet and party. Laurier's personality was of great help to him in this regard.

"Perhaps the most salient feature was his personal charm which evoked among his colleagues a loyalty and affection unusual among politicians."[21]

Laurier possessed one important advantage over his Liberal predecessor, Mackenzie: he was the undisputed master of the Liberal Party and he always paid close attention to his position as party leader. To some observers, Laurier's control over his party was the key to his success as a statesman. "It has not always been realized that Laurier's opportunities for statesmanship were made possible by his capacity as a politician."[22] He controlled his party to a large extent through skilled use of the tool most readily available to him at that time, patronage, and he made sure that all the important appointments remained within his power. This was consistent with the very practical and realistic view he took of politics. "Reforms are for oppositions. . . . It is the business of Governments to stay in office."[23] It was his control over the party that enabled him to present his colleagues with a *fait accompli*; their only alternative to submitting to his policy was to unseat him, a most difficult task in the light of his strength within the party.

Laurier was careful to avoid becoming so involved with the business of government that he would be forced to neglect his duties as party leader. Unlike Macdonald and Mackenzie, he did not take on any departmental responsibilities and took little interest in the details of government. This attitude possibly enabled him to remain cool in times of stress, to approach problems in a somewhat detached frame of mind. He once said in a speech, "For my part, so long as I have the honour to occupy my present post you shall never see me carried away by passion or prejudice or even enthusiasm. I have to think and consider."[24] Such a view assured an analytic approach to the problem confronting the cabinet. It is true that this analytic approach might revolve around the question of what was politically feasible, but it prevented a highly emotional approach to problems that later marred the record of other prime ministers who were so very much in control of their parties.

One important point about Laurier ought to be noted, and that is that he did not tolerate rivals in the cabinet. It is true that he made commitments to Sifton before the latter entered the cabinet, but he never permitted Sifton to threaten his position. Sifton resigned once from the cabinet and when Laurier invited him to return, Sifton laid down terms which, if accepted, would have given him great influence over policy and the succession. Laurier would have none of it, and Sifton remained outside the cabinet.

Laurier was fortunate in securing as cabinet colleagues men who were not only competent but who were also valued political allies as well. He was determined to get the men he wanted, men who would not only serve as capable cabinet colleagues, but who, because of their political position, would provide him with the support he needed to maintain the Liberal Party in power. Once he had convinced them to enter the cabinet, he was able to keep them loyal to himself and thus to maintain his own position as Prime Minister and as leader of the party. The key then to Laurier's success was an astute political mind combined with a strength of character that enabled him to inspire the confidence and devotion of those around him.

Laurier's ability in this connection became apparent as soon as he took office. He was able to persuade four provincial politicians — Blair of New Brunswick, Fielding of Nova Scotia, Mowat of Ontario, and Sifton of Manitoba — to leave their comfortable positions and enter his cabinet, and at the same time maintain peace among his backbenchers. Having brought together a powerful team (probably as close to a cabinet of all the talents as Canada has ever had), he was able to remain its master. It was difficult and tiring work for him, but he was successful in maintaining harmony, and he did so partly through the somewhat contradictory practice of seeing that each minister had a great deal of independence while assuming a highly autocratic stance as master of the whole cabinet. He believed in giving each minister as much latitude and responsibility as possible. He permitted ministers to speak their minds, and one of Mr. King's biographers makes the comment that, while in Laurier's cabinet, King, although very much a junior member" . . . expressed himself freely and firmly when he felt strongly on subjects under discussion."[25] At times, however, when Laurier made up his mind on an issue there was no question but that he would have his way. One of his favourite tactics for accomplishing his own ends was to present the cabinet with a *fait accompli*. He would come to a decision and put it into effect, depending on the affection and respect in which his colleagues held him as well as on his tremendous ability to smooth over ruffled feathers to prevent trouble. This was the great advantage Laurier had over Mackenzie, a fund of personal charm that enabled him to impose his will on his colleagues without encountering a great deal of resistance. When ministers were difficult, however, Laurier could be decisive and ruthless. When he lost confidence in a minister's ability to deal with a problem, he intervened directly, as with Mackenzie and Mann in 1903. When Tarte caused difficulties he was dismissed, and when Mulock made an embarrassing error he was overruled ". . . with a dispatch that left Mulock breathless."[26]

As a leader of the Canadian people, Laurier imitated Macdonald and was in turn imitated by King. He was no moulder of public opinion; he was cautious, flexible and prudent. He recognized the virtues of inaction and was well aware that too often to act was more harmful politically than to do nothing. He was inclined to play it safe and thus was able to say to a friend, "Men who have the responsibility of practical politics will always find it safer to let things as they are, though they may be theoretically insufficient, if satisfactory to the people."[27] This requires restraint and the avoidance of any kind of messianism and in the past has seemed to be a guarantee of success. In Laurier's terms success was measured by one's ability to stay in office, and by this standard Laurier had reason to be satisfied with his achievement.

Sir Robert Borden

Laurier's successor, Sir Robert Borden, has a far better reputation as a statesman than as a politician. Someone once described a statesman as one who thinks of the next generation while a politician is one who thinks of the next election. With Laurier the emphasis was on elections; this was not true of Borden.

In spite of an abundance of common sense, Borden was not as successful a party leader as Laurier. He was ". . . more interested in national problems than party problems, he was an imperious man who was impatient with the little details and the niceties of party management. . . ."[28] He did not accept the notion of Macdonald and Laurier that it was unwise for Canadian political leaders to attempt to lead public opinion. A statesman intent on leading public opinion in Canada must be in a position where he influences the opinion of the various segments of society that go to make up the Canadian public. Borden was unable to do this, for he never understood Quebec. The problems of preserving and protecting the French-Canadian culture and identity were of much less interest to him than pan-Canadian problems, and thus he tended to ignore French-Canadian sensitivities. An inability to appreciate the special needs and problems of French Canada has been responsible for many of the difficulties in which Canadian prime ministers have found themselves; Borden, Meighen, and Diefenbaker all were troubled by this lack of sensitivity. It was soon clear to residents of Quebec than in Borden's cabinet none of the French Canadians were among the more influential members. He paid dearly for this, and many of his party's problems in Quebec originated with Borden himself.

Borden's lack of interest in political matters made him impatient of political niceties and sometimes led him to act in an authoritarian manner. Mr. Meighen noted this in his introduction to Borden's memoirs when he wrote, "Waste of time in Parliament or in Council was a burden for him to endure. When he came to a conclusion as to what was in the public interest he wanted that thing done and was impatient of restraints imposed by the clamourings of what the Press calls 'Public Opinion'."[29] This attitude was reflected in one of his own comments in his diary in 1917 regarding a discussion in council on the possibility of a coalition government: "The discussion was lengthy and eventually became so wearisome that I interposed, informing my colleagues that they had made me sufficiently acquainted with their views, that the duty of decision rested with me and that I would subsequently make them acquainted with my conclusions."[30] In order to avoid such wearisome discussions, Borden and the ministers directly concerned would not infrequently settle the matter among themselves, a tactic later employed by Mr. St. Laurent, who also disliked "wasting time" on discussions. Borden once had a discussion with Sir Thomas White respecting estimates and tariffs and he told Sir Thomas ". . . he and I would settle tariff matters and thus avoid protracted discussion in Council."[31]

The problem with this approach was that Borden did not have the ability to communicate the wisdom of his decisions. As illustrated by his difficulties with Monk (see page 35), the division of opinion within the caucus and cabinet over the question of financial aid to railways and on the question of French language rights in Ontario, Borden frequently had difficulty in persuading party supporters to follow the course of action that he preferred and had settled on. He was at times inclined to ignore the caucus, and often the support he received for his ideas was not nearly so enthusiastic as it might have been had he been more aggressive as a party leader and less so as Prime Minister. Consultation with his colleagues was not unknown, but if consultation took place too frequently Borden became irritated, and there are many references in his diary to colleagues "pestering" him for advice.

In spite of his lack of the "common touch", Borden at times showed a very deft hand in dealing with his more troublesome colleagues. Instead of firing the bombastic Sir Sam Hughes, for example, and thus provoking a great public row, Borden merely detached from Sir Sam the responsibility for all the important branches of the military administration and assigned them to others. Hughes remained a minister for quite some time with a portfolio so reduced in significance that it was difficult for him to greatly harm or embarrass the government. Borden wrote, ". . . while I felt that his continued presence in the government was a handicap rather than a support, I determined to let him continue until I was perfectly sure that his dismissal would not entail any serious danger to my administration, "[32] reminiscent of the tactics of "Old Tomorrow."

Borden was well aware of his limitations as a politician, and to some extent he compensated for this by bringing seasoned politicians into his cabinet and relying on them for political advice. He appointed Rogers as Minister of Public Works, and Rogers subsequently became known to the Liberals as the Minister of Elections. Later Borden relied on men like Sifton and Rowell for political advice.

Borden came to office with many fixed ideas, and as a result he could not compromise to the extent that Laurier could. He was nevertheless inclined to be pragmatic — not so much because he recognized the political desirability of such an approach to politics, but rather because he was a practical man who never seemed to need a theoretical base of any kind to justify his actions. Lloyd George said that Sir Robert Borden ". . . was always the quintessence of common sense, always calm, well-balanced, a man of co-operating temperament, invariably subordinating self to the common causes."[33]

The longer Borden remained in office, the more effective he became as Prime Minister. Paradoxically, some of this success was due to his lack of ability as a politician. Prior to 1917, Borden had great problems with his own party, but after the formation of the Union government on a two-party basis he had fewer political problems. He delegated more and more power (indeed he was abroad much of the time from 1917-1920) and seemed to inspire those around him more. Professor Dawson remarked that it was only in 1917 that Borden ". . . seemed to acquire a breadth of view which had hitherto been noticeably absent. He became in a real sense the master of his Cabinet and the leader of his Parliament and of his people."[34]

Borden's deficiencies as Prime Minister may be traced back to two problems, his inability to perceive his role as a party leader and his inability to understand Quebec. They were offset to some extent by his steadiness and his pragmatic outlook, but they also led to a rift in the Canadian body politic that is yet to be healed. As a consociational engineer Borden was a failure.

Arthur Meighen

Arthur Meighen, Borden's successor as Prime Minister, possessed some of the defects that had caused Borden problems. Like Borden, Meighen never seemed to understand French Canada and in turn, French Canadians disliked him intensely. Bourassa, writing in *Le Devoir*, said of him: "Mr. Meighen represents in person and temperament, in his attitudes and in his past declarations the utmost that Anglo-Saxon jingoism has to offer in the way of brutality, all that is most exclusive, most anti-Canadian."[35] Thus it should not be surprising that during the 1925 federal election the Conservatives' strategy ". . . was to persuade the voters to forget all about Meighen; he could hardly intrude where obviously he was not wanted."[36]

Meighen not only misunderstood French Canada, he misunderstood his own role as party leader. He was inclined to be dogmatic and very self-confident, which led to arrogance and an unwillingness to trust the judgment or to accept the advice of colleagues. As a result, both the party and the cabinet became almost a one-man show, with unfortunate consequences. He tended to rely on his own judgment rather than that of more experienced and politically sensitive colleagues and at times severely limited discussion on policy in cabinet meetings.

Meighen's dogmatism and temperament resulted in a very weak cabinet. "Painfully inept in his understanding of both politics and men, Meighen surrounded himself with associates who lacked experience and whose knowledge of Canada was confined chiefly to Toronto and its environs."[37] Such weakness is to be expected if the cabinet is to be led by a man such as Meighen. Strife will be avoided by selecting as ministers men who will defer to their leader and who are personally congenial to one another, and a common regional background is useful here. Under such circumstances the cabinet acts neither as a federal nor consociational body.

There was another important characteristic that caused Meighen difficulty. He was temperamentally incapable of being cautious. No one could ever refer to him as "Old Tomorrow", and he never appreciated the political advantages of inaction. His notion of leadership was somewhat unrealistic. He expected the cabinet to proclaim the policy, usually his own policy, and the party to accept it and carry it out without question. As a result, under Meighen the Conservative Party became very much a one-man affair. Other prime ministers have also seen to it that the party and cabinet accept their ideas on policy; the difference lies in the method of convincing them to do so. The fact that a policy proposal has been enunciated by a leader may be sufficient reason in itself for the proposal to be accepted by the cabinet and party, if the leader has a very strong hold over the public, but under other circumstances more devious techniques of persuasion will have to be used, involving conciliation and compromise. His most sympathetic biographer has noted, "He made little effort to ingratiate himself, to cultivate that being of friendliness which enabled some men of opposing views to enjoy cordial relations outside the chamber. . . ."[38]

Meighen believed that it was his duty and responsibility to specify a position on public issues.

> . . . if the whole political process was not to be carried on in an atmosphere of mass confusion, parties and their leaders had to adopt clearly defined positions on the questions of the day and hold to them consistently. These positions, based on a conception of the public interest, ought to be adhered to even if in so doing one went against the grain of public opinion courting defeat.[39]

Under such conditions the accommodation and compromise essential in a consociational state were not possible, and Meighen was too impatient a man to take the time to permit a consensus to be reached. "He though hard debate followed by decision was better than a consensus arrived at in confusion."[40]

Meighen cannot be judged a success as Prime Minister. Some of the qualities he admired least in men appear to be those most desirable in a prime minister. It is obvious that a successful consociational engineer must be prepared to compromise and to conciliate, to act at times as a skilled politician carefully appeasing various sectors of his party, sometimes being content with much less than his original objective. This was a role for which Meighen was peculiarly ill-fitted.

R.B. Bennett

R.B. Bennett, like Arthur Meighen, ran the Conservative Party as a one-man show, with disastrous results. He was able to retain his hold over the party not because of any deep affection for him or confidence in him, but because he was the source of most of its funds. This made the party extremely dependent on him at a time when under other circumstances steps might have been taken to replace him, and he was able to treat party officials the same way as he treated cabinet ministers — as subordinates. Thus, while Bennett remained master of the party, it was mostly because of his financial support rather than because he was able to inspire his supporters with confidence or because of his organizational skill. Sir Robert Borden wrote of him that ". . . his neglect to direct or to authorize effective or indeed any organization is guiding the party to ultimate overwhelming defeat."[41]

Bennett was also very much the master of his cabinet, but again his style led to great difficulties. He had come to the position of Prime Minister after a highly successful career in law and in business. Much of his success was achieved by following a very distinctive style; in business Bennett tended to operate exclusively on his own. This habit was bound to cause problems when Bennett came to be Prime Minister, for Bennett lacked two important qualities essential to a prime minister — the ability to readily delegate responsibility and the ability to say no when demands are being placed on his time.

The result was that Bennett was easily the most overworked Prime Minister in Canada's history. He took on too much responsibility to himself by insisting on holding several positions in the government simultaneously and acquired too much responsibility by refusing to give his cabinet colleagues a free hand. The errors of his ways were pointed out to him by King shortly after Bennett became Prime Minister, during the debate on the Speech from the Throne.

> My honourable friend holds at the present time the positions of Prime Minister, President of the Council, Secretary of State for External Affairs and Minister of Finance. He is leader of the House of Commons and as leader of the government he has as well other duties to perform . . . it is neither good for his own health nor for the health of the people he represents . . . the business of Cabinet government was devised as a means of giving to the country the benefit of many minds, of freeing it from the tyranny of a single mind . . . it was intended that safety was to be found only in a multitude of councillors.[42]

One of Bennett's biographers notes, "If the Chief thought he should be consulted on the whole field of activity most [Cabinet members] acquiesced; it was easier and less dangerous. In that way Bennett brought back on himself a volume of work that ought to have been disposed of by others."[43]

Bennett often did not even go through the motions of consulting with his cabinet colleagues. Other prime ministers have behaved thus, but not to the extent Bennett did. Thus when he announced his New Deal program in a speech on July 2, 1935, none of his colleagues knew beforehand details of the program. But Bennett's proclivity for taking all responsibility to himself had unfortunate consequences. Introduction of much of his New Deal legislation was delayed and critical time lost simply because Bennett fell ill and there was no one else sufficiently well informed to replace him as sponsor of the legislation. He centralized administration so much in his own person that other ministers had little or no input into the policy-making process.

There is one aspect of Bennett's tenure that should be carefully noted. Even though he treated his cabinet colleagues like schoolboys and insisted on supervising almost all departments himself, there was only one resignation from the cabinet over a matter of principle, that of the Hon. H.H. Stevens. It would seem that his ministers were not prepared to accept the political consequences of disagreement with their chief, for in spite of his lack of popularity within the country and the party, his power was so great as to deter his colleagues from disagreeing with him or from leaving the cabinet. When election time came, however, his ministers deserted him, and in 1935 eight of the original members of his cabinet refused to stand for re-election. The financial control Bennett exercised over the party was not enough to encourage many of its strong men to support him, and so they left.

Bennett also failed as a consociational engineer. He failed to understand Quebec and insisted on treating it as a province like the others and often relied on theNova Scotia born St. James Street lawyer, C.H. Cahan, as his lieutenant in that province. He did not learn from his English-speaking predecessors that a prime minister ought to have a senior French-Canadian minister to keep the lines of communication open to the province of Quebec. He antagonized Quebec at a time when there was great dissatisfaction in that province with the Liberal Party, and thus missed a very important political opportunity.

Bennett was, like Alexander Mackenzie, a man of deep religious convictions and, as in the case of Mackenzie, these convictions had political repercussions. He tended to be inflexible and unable to compromise and, equally important, he tended to be insensitive to those around him. Thus he failed to inspire either confidence or loyalty, and this complicated a situation already perilous because of his wish to do everything himself. Ministers seemed to be prepared to allow him to do so in order to avoid working with him, and because of this and possibly because the party relied on him so much for funds, no challenger arose, as in the case of Mr. Diefenbaker years later.

NOTES

[1]Walter Stewart, "Pierre Elliott Trudeau Is the President of Canada". *Maclean's*, Vol. 83, No. 6 (June, 1970), p. 36.

[2]D.V. Smiley, "The National Party Leadership in Canada: A Preliminary Analysis". *Canadian Journal of Political Science*, Vol. I. No. 4 (December 1968), p. 382.

[3]*Interview*. (February 6, 1970).

[4]F.W. Gibson, ed., *Cabinet Formation and Bicultural Relations*, p. 174.

[5]*Interview*. (May 25, 1970).

[6]P.V. Lyon, *Canada in World Affairs*, Vol. XII. (Toronto; Oxford University Press, 1968), p. 37.

[7]Patrick Nicholson, *Vision and Indecision*, p. 160.

[8]Canada, House of Commons, *Debates*. (November 23, 1964), p. 10379ff.

[9]Cartwright, *Reminiscences*, p. 343.

[10]O.D. Skelton, *The Life and Letters of Sir Wilfrid Laurier*, Vol. II, p. 162.

[11]Richard Cartwright, *Reminiscences*, p. 125.

[12]James Young, *Public Men and Public Life*, Vol. II. (Toronto; Wm. Briggs, 1902), p. 77.

[13]Quoted in J.W. Willison, *Sir Wilfrid Laurier and the Liberal Party*, Vol. II. (Toronto; C.M. Morag Co., 1903), p. 28.

[14]Young, *Public Men and Public Life*, p. 324.

[15]Goldwin Smith, in *This Week*, February 28, 1884; quoted in Burke, *Canadian Cabinets in the Making*, p. 171.

[16]J.S. Willison, *Reminiscences, Political and Personal*. (Toronto; McClelland & Stewart, 1919), p. 188.

[17]Young, *Public Men and Public Life*, p. 412.

[18]Cartwright, *Reminiscences*, p. 124.

[19]W. Buckingham and C.W. Ross, *Alexander Mackenzie, His Life and Times*. (Toronto; Rose, 1892), p. 441-442.

[20]Margaret Ormsby, "Prime Minister Mackenzie, the Liberal Party and the Bargain with British Columbia". *Canadian Historical Review*, Vol. 21, No. 2 (June, 1945) p. 173.

[21]Paul Stevens, "Wilfrid Laurier, Politician" in M. Hamelin ed., *The Political Ideas of the Prime Ministers of Canada*. (Ottawa; University of Ottawa Press, 1969), p. 71.

[22]*Ibid.*, p. 69.

[23]Quoted in *Ibid.*, p. 74.

[24]Quoted in Mason Wade, *The French Canadians*, Vol. I. (Toronto, Macmillan, 1968), p. 480.

[25]Fred McGregor, *The Fall and Rise of Mackenzie King*, 1911-1919. (Toronto; Macmillan, 1962), p. 41.

[26]Joseph Schull, *Laurier*. (Toronto; Macmillan, 1966), p. 374.

[27]Public Archives of Canada, *Wilfrid Laurier Papers*, Laurier to A.O. Jeffry, 21 January 1904.

[28]R.C. Brown, "The Political Ideas of Robert Borden", in M. Hamelin ed., *The Political Ideas of the Prime Ministers of Canada*, p. 105.

[29]Arthur Meighen, *Introduction to Robert Laird Borden, His Memoirs*, Vol. I, p. viii.

[30]Henry Borden, ed., *Robert Laird Borden, His Memoirs*, Vol. II, p. 720.

[31]*Ibid.*, Vol. I, p. 392.

[32]*Ibid*, p. 571.

[33]Lloyd George, *War Memoirs*, Vol. IV. (Ivor Nicholson and Watson, 1932), p. 1743.

[34]R. MacG. Dawson, in a review of Henry Borden, ed., "Robert Laird Borden — His Memoirs". *Canadian Journal of Economics and Political Science*, Vol. 5, No. 1 (February, 1939), p. 95.

[35]Quoted in Mason Wade, *The French Canadians*, Vol. 2., p. 783.

[36]Roger Graham, *Arthur Meighen*, Vol. II. (Toronto: Clarke Irwin, 1963), p. 325.

[37]John R. Williams, *The Conservative Party in Canada*. (Durham; Duke University Press, 1956), p. 49.

[38]Roger Graham, "Meighen in Debate". *Queen's Quarterly*, Vol. LXII, No. 1 (Spring, 1955), p. 30.

[39]Roger Graham, "Some Political Ideas of Arthur Meighen", in M. Hamelin, ed., *The Political Ideas of the Prime Ministers of Canada*, p. 112.

[40]*Ibid.*, p. 108.

[41]Henry Borden, ed., *Letters to Limbo*. (Toronto; University of Toronto Press, 1971), p. 147.

[42]Canada, House of Commons, *Debates*. (September 9, 1930), p. 17.

[43]Watkins, *R.B. Bennett*, p. 170.

Chapter VII

The Cabinet and Mackenzie King

The significance of Mackenzie King's impact on Canada is still hotly debated. It is curious that there should be such a debate, in that King managed to remain Prime Minister for a longer period of time than anyone else, and presumably he was able to do so because of some qualities that caused the electorate to favour him over his rivals. Yet to a very large extent King has become a symbol of what many observers believe to be the national failings of Canada. He is accused of being responsible for mediocre politics, for having no purpose but to remain in office, of unparalleled timidity, of having institutionalized dullness and equivocation in Canadian politics, of being bland and uninspiring. All this criticism is made even though while King was Prime Minister Canada made tremendous strides as an autonomous nation, participated successfully in World War II, laid the foundation of the welfare state, and assumed an international identity, and when Mackenzie King ceased to be leader of the Liberal Party it was far stronger and more popular than it was when he became its leader in 1919.

It is the contention of this study that King was the Prime Minister *par excellence* of Canada. That his personality, methods, and style might not be considered suitable for the position today does not alter the fact that he, above all others, suited the times and the office. It is his ability and style in filling the office of the Prime Minister that are of interest in this study.

For several years after his election as leader of the Liberal Party King's position was insecure, but ". . . by a combination of good fortune, personal loyalties and skill [he] established his supremacy within seven years."[1] King's electoral successes were unquestionably the major factor contributing to his longevity as party leader, but these electoral successes were in turn due to his understanding of his role as a political leader, for he thought that ". . . the real secret of political leadership was more in what was prevented than in what was accomplished."[2]

The most obvious aspect of King's personality as a leader was his political sensitivity. He was always sensitive to the political implications of the alternatives confronting him and his cabinet colleagues. Because of this sensitivity and because he was prepared to delegate a great deal of authority to ministers (and at times to party officials), King was able to build up a sense of confidence and loyalty within the cabinet and within the party. Lacking the personal attributes that drew men to Macdonald and Laurier, King substituted for them confidence in himself as a sensitive political leader.

Although King professed to be a strict Presbyterian with the usual Presbyterian reservations about dancing, the consumption of alcohol, and other frivolities, his religious principles were sufficiently flexible to permit him to indulge in spiritualism. Similarly in political matters, his convictions allowed him a great deal of flexibility. Dogma and definitions were dangerous. "Definitions always seemed to him to be dangerously inflexible; they also seemed unnecessary because King was pragmatic."[3] He once said, "Politics is not a matter of the ideal thing but of doing what is best to meet circumstances and difficulties that present themselves from day to day."[4] Thus leadership to him consisted not of asserting one's power, but rather in getting a consensus acceptable to all. Thus King could by no means be described as a political philosopher or a man of ideas. "He was necessarily concerned with immediate problems and choices of action. To govern is to choose — to decide what is necessary, what is desirable, what is possible."[5]

Mackenzie King did have one very firm conviction which had great effect on his political conduct. One of his secretaries remarked, "Among his robust convictions I recall his belief that the really important people in the world were the *conciliators*."[6] A conciliator is of necessity flexible in mind and purpose, traits that served King well as Prime Minister but traits which to some observers appeared rather as indecisiveness and weakness. Often decisions seemed to be taken more with the needs of the moment in mind than some great vision of the future. In the context of 1972, when "visionary" politics were the fashion, King seemed to have been uninspiring, cautious and parochial, but given the context of his own times, King's style was eminently satisfactory. He never tried to achieve anything that he did not feel he had a good chance of obtaining and thus he avoided two serious political pitfalls; he did not build up high expectations among his supporters and then disappoint them, and he did not often have to apologize for failing to achieve a previously determined objective. King realized that in order to stay in office, he had to be flexible so as to conciliate. It is not surprising that he wanted to stay in office when he had such great confidence in himself as being the right man for the position. Extreme men and extreme policies were dangerous in Canadian politics. He once wrote to a friend: "The extreme man is always more or less dangerous but nowhere more so than in politics. In a country like ours it is particularly true that the art of government is largely one of seeking to reconcile rather than to exaggerate differences — to come as near as may be possible to the happy mean."[7]

One clear indication of King's political sagacity was his manner of dealing with the province of Quebec. He made sure that he had a trusted and competent lieutenant who would faithfully look after political matters in Quebec without endangering his own position as party leader or Prime Minister. He understood what Quebec, in his day, required of Ottawa such things as autonomy in political appointments, patronage, etc. It should be noted, of course, that the problem of satisfying Quebec in those days was less difficult than today, for the demands made by Quebec on Ottawa emphasized cultural autonomy; economic policy and cultural survival were not closely linked. Frequently Quebec's demands meant doing little or nothing; there was no danger to the federal system by satisfying them.

King was singularly fortunate in his choice of Quebec's lieutenants. In Lapointe and St. Laurent, King found men who were able to retain the confidence of Quebec and the respect of English Canada while at the same time remaining loyal to their leader. King usually managed in his cabinet selections to surround himself with capable men who could be counted on not to threaten his role as leader. His judgment of men was usually sound, both in terms of selecting men who could competently serve as ministers and in anticipating what his enemies might do. During the conscription crisis for example he was able to accurately foresee Ralston's reactions; he saw that Ralston was not personally ambitious and thus was able to deal with him accordingly. He had the ability to persuade men to take on difficult assignments and make them believe that what they were undertaking was of tremendous importance. He was a master at both conciliation and persuasion.

King was able to maintain mastery over his cabinet for nearly all of his term in office, while at the same time being able to give each member a great deal of freedom in his own department. Only on one occasion did he lose control, and that was in 1947, a year before his retirement and when he was in poor health. This was over the issue of whether to withdraw from the U.N. temporary commission for Korea, on which membership for Canada had been accepted without his knowledge and consent. King gave in on this issue, and it is significant that from that time on his influence waned considerably and he ceased to be the dominant figure in the cabinet. But the freedom King granted to his ministers was by no means absolute. "King deliberately gave his colleagues wide authority within their own departments. They were expected to inform Cabinet of their decisions, but the decisions were questioned only if King sensed that there were political implications which could not be ignored."[8]

There was only one area in government where King refused to

share power, and that was in foreign relations. Until 1946, it was the custom for the responsibility for foreign affairs to be assumed by the Prime Minister, so that in conducting Canada's foreign policy on his own it might be argued that King was merely doing what he encouraged his own ministers to do — that is, run their own departments independently. Foreign policy, however, is a matter that affects many areas of government, and in insisting on a free hand Mr. King was doing something more than exercising one of the traditional prerogatives of the Prime Minister; he was enhancing his own power and emphasizing that he was far more than *primus inter pares* in the cabinet. As Canada became increasingly involved in foreign affairs and as the Department of External Affairs grew in size and prestige, it was natural that the political head of the department would become more significant. The fact that this office was attached to the office of the Prime Minister substantially increased the power and prestige of the Prime Minister within the cabinet, a fact King understood quite clearly.

When he first took office, King was very careful to consult the cabinet on matters pertaining to External Affairs. At the time of the Chanak crisis in 1922, he refused to make any comment until the cabinet had met. As he became more confident and as External Affairs began to impinge more directly on Canada, he relied less on the cabinet. When he went to meet Hitler in 1937, he did not take any of his colleagues with him, and during the Munich crisis he would not even allow his colleagues to read the ". . . coded cables from London . . . such was King's control of government and nation . . . that he could take foreign policy into his own hands and direct it as he pleased."[9] At times his colleagues could be influential. Lapointe played a major role in convincing King that Canada should repudiate the stand of the Canadian delegate at the League of Nations who had supported sanctions against Mussolini as a result of his invasion of Ethiopia. Most of the time he would at least go through the motions of cabinet consultation and, being the best informed person in the cabinet on the subject, he would get his own way, but he was careful to preserve the veneer of consultation. Thus when proposals regarding an Imperial Joint Board for Defence were advanced while he was in London in 1944, he said that he ". . . could not begin to speak without approval of the Government and I certainly would not bind my colleagues to anything that would involve commitments. I said that such success as I had had with government and with my Parliament, was the result of allowing all my colleagues their fair share of responsibility of consideration of policy. . . ."[10] King, then, never employed the tactic so useful to Laurier, that of presenting his colleagues with a *fait accompli*. He did not have the personality that would enable him to accomplish this, and he probably knew it. But he did possess great powers of persuasion, so that it could be said:

The Cabinet seldom, if ever, reached a conclusion of which he really disapproved, but he often postponed or even abandoned courses he would have liked to take because of the opposition of his colleagues, and only rarely did he insist on getting his own way when a clear majority of his colleagues dissented. . . .[11]

But King managed to develop tactics that enabled him to get his own way quite frequently. He was fond of Macdonald's method of delaying matters when there were strong differences of opinion. Sometimes he would not bring up contentious matters until the end of a cabinet meeting. Starved and tired ministers would then give way, and King would win his point. He also learned the virtue of patience. A former American Ambassador to Canada, J.P. Moffatt noted that ". . . if he saw that opinion was running against him, he would as presiding officer postpone bringing a problem to the point of decision time after time until ultimately some change of circumstances would shift the balance of opinion to his side. . . ."[12]

King was, of course, an extremely pragmatic man who had a very strong belief in the idea that a consensus could always be obtained. It was his prerogative as Prime Minister to decide when a consensus had been reached, and his decision was rarely questioned. On one occasion there was a brief discussion on a matter, then Mr. King stated his understanding of the consensus of cabinet. Mr. Howe, then a junior minister, questioned Mr. King's understanding and was coldly ignored and never again questioned Mr. King's conclusion that there was a consensus.

King also carefully guarded his prerogatives as Prime Minister. He rarely consulted others on appointments to the cabinet and often ignored advice from important political figures. The premier of Ontario, Mr. Hepburn, was under the impression that he had helped bring about the election of the Liberal government in 1935 and thus ought to be consulted about the composition of Mackenzie King's cabinet. He proceeded to provide unsolicited advice, which was ignored. King appointed St. Laurent to his cabinet on his own initiative after secret negotiations and without consulting other ministers. His acting in this way strengthened the idea that Mr. King was at all times in charge and increased his authority within the cabinet. He also reserved the right to intervene directly in department affairs when he deemed it necessary. When, after the end of World War II, he learned that the ocean liner *Queen Mary*, which had been chartered by the Department of National Defence to bring back Canadian troops from Europe, was to dock at New York rather than Halifax, he immediately called in the responsible official, dressed him down, and told him that in future the *Queen Mary* would have to dock in Halifax. When the official protested that part of the agreement with the ship's owners stated that the ship would dock in New York because the captain disliked bringing his ship into Halifax harbour and ". . . one does not tell the Captain of the *Queen Mary* where to dock his ship," King replied, "I am the captain of this ship and the *Queen Mary* will dock in Halifax." He then picked up the phone, contacted Sir Winston Churchill, and asked him to speak to the Cunard officials. On her next voyage the *Queen Mary* docked at Halifax.[13]

King could also be ruthless, although his reputation in this respect has been exaggerated. He disposed of difficult ministers without regret, as in the case of Ralston, and brought about the political destruction of many of his enemies, as with the Progressives. His task of disposing of ministers and political associates as in the case of Gen. Lafleche, an ineffective wartime minister, and Ralston, was made easier by his practice of not becoming personally friendly with his associates. He was careful, however, not to let the public see too much of this side of his personality. His diary reveals that King was in fact a vain and arrogant man, but he never appeared so in public. He said of George Drew, "He has an arrogant manner worse than either Meighen or Bennett and has a more bitter tongue than Meighen. This helped to destroy these men and the party. Having that type of man as an opponent has been the best asset I have had."[14] King knew the type of man the public was averse to — that they would prefer a bland man to an arrogant man, and his public behaviour reflected this knowledge.

King always made sure that he had no rivals in the cabinet. He encouraged personal feuds among his ministers, as between Dunning and Gardiner, knowing that divisions within the cabinet prevented ministers from uniting against him. No national figure developed beside him, and when he was faced with a rebellious cabinet, he could count on putting the rebellion down by putting the question as to who was prepared to take over from him. He also made sure that too much power would not be concentrated in the hands of any one minister, unless he was sure, as in the case of C.D. Howe, that the individual was not personally ambitious. When he attended the inaugural meeting of the United Nations in 1945, for example, he divided up his responsibilities, having one minister serve as Acting Prime Minister, another as Acting Secretary of External Affairs, and still another as Acting President of the Privy Council.

By effectively controlling his cabinet, King controlled the party, since the members of the cabinet dominated the party. King was also successful in establishing a national office for the Liberal Party, and in Norman Lambert he found a capable organizer who was usually prepared to do his bidding. King was never satisfied with the organization of the party, another indication of the importance he attached to political matters. Control of the party always rested in his hands, however, and as long as the party won elections, members did not appear to be unduly dissatisfied with the state of affairs.

Under King, the Canadian bureaucracy expanded enormously, both in size and influence (see Chapter XI). During his long term of office King appointed numerous deputy ministers and other senior officials and had great confidence in their ability. Such men as Norman Robertson, Dana Wilgress, and Clifford Clark in External Affairs, Hector MacKinnon of the Wheat Board, O.D. Skelton and Robert Bryce in Finance all influenced King a great deal. A competent and experienced administrator himself, King relied to a great extent on the advice of civil servants, and this marked to some extent a shift in power away from the cabinet, partly due to King's ". . . philosophy of a paternalistic state run not by politicians but by brilliant administrators."[15] King was sympathetic to such men and allowed them considerable influence in formulating policy. The advent of the war also contributed to the growth of the influence of the civil service, since of necessity it had to be more independent because of the large number of decisions that had to be taken. Cabinet ministers could not possibly supervise everything, and thus much power was delegated to civil servants whom King trusted and who could work effectively and inconspicuously. But he gave close attention to senior appointments so that there would be no obstacle in the civil service to his objectives.

The advent of World War II also caused King to make several interesting innovations in the cabinet. During this period the position of secretary to the cabinet became more important, a cabinet committee system was developed with one committee (the War Committee) acting with the power of the full cabinet, and parliamentary secretaries were appointed. King was a reluctant innovator: "Instinctively, Mr. King recoiled from efforts to formalize an institution the genius of which, historically and in his own experience, had been its flexibility and informality."[16] He did make changes and, although they were often long overdue, when change was necessary it was made.

King's style changed as conditions changed, but in one thing he was always consistent: ". . . the keystone of his political reputation was the calculated identification of himself and his party with the cause of national unity."[17] As Prof. Underhill, one of his most severe critics, noted, King understood that ". . . the essential task of Canadian statesmanship is to discover the terms on which as many as possible of the significant interest groups of our country can be induced to work together in a common policy."[18] This is consistent with the role of a prime minister in a consociational democracy for "one of the conditions of prime ministerial success is an ability to maintain and operate successfully . . . a system of elite accommodation."[19]

It was in this manner that King directed the affairs of Canada for over twenty years. A delegator of authority who nevertheless managed to retain control, a conciliator who could impose his will at difficult times, a sensitive politician who was always attentive to the peculiar needs of Quebec, a man of action who nevertheless appeared to the world to be negative and passive, he presented to the world a bland and colourless image that masked a cunning, capable, and tough Prime Minister. This image was consistent throughout his career and probably contributed to the existence of stable government in Canada. To the public he was a simple man who inspired confidence, and to the cabinet he was the astute party leader and the indispensable man in the Canadian government.

NOTES

[1]Peter Regenstreif, *The Liberal Party of Canada: A Political Analysis*, Unpublished Ph.D. thesis. (Cornell University, 1963), p. 410.

[2]J.W. Pickersgill *The Mackenzie King Record*, Vol. 1., p. 10.

[3]H. Blair Neatby, "William Lyon Mackenzie King", p. 7.

[4]J.W. Pickersgill and D.F. Forster, *The Mackenzie King Record*, Vol. II, p. 319.

[5]H. Blair Neatby, "The Political Ideas of William Lyon Mackenzie", in M. Hamelin, ed., *The Political Ideas of the Prime Ministers of Canada*, p. 122.

[6]James Gibson, "Mackenzie King and Canadian Autonomy 1921-1946". *Canadian Historical Association Annual Report*, 1951, p. 20.

[7]W.L. Mackenzie King to A.E. Ames, January 29, 1937. Quoted in Blair Neatby, "The Political Ideas of William Lyon Mackenzie King", p. 129.

[8]H. Blair Neatby, "William Lyon Mackenzie King", p. 17.

[9]Bruce Hutchison, *The Incredible Canadian*. (Toronto; Longmans, Green & Co. 1953), p. 236-237.

[10]J.W. Pickersgill *The Mackenzie King Record*, Vol. I., p. 687.

[11]*Ibid.*, p. 7.

[12]Quoted in Nancy Hooker, ed., *The Moffatt Papers 1919-1943*. (Cambridge; Harvard University Press, 1956), p. 339.

[13]*Interview*. (July 5, 1969).

[14]J.W. Pickersgill and D.F. Forster, *The Mackenzie King Record*, Vol. IV, p. 348.

[15]John Porter, *Political Parties and the Political Career*, p. 54.

[16]A.D.P. Heeney, "Mackenzie King and the Cabinet Secretariat". *Canadian Public Administration*, Vol. 10, No. 3 (September, 1967), p. 371.

[17]Gerald C.V. Wright, "Mackenzie King: Power over the Political Executive", in T. Hocken ed., *Apex of Power*. (Scarborough; Prentice-Hall, 1971), p. 205.

[18]Frank Underhill, "The End of the King Era", in Frank Underhill, ed., *In Search of Canadian Liberalism*, p. 126.

[19]S.J.R. Noel, "The Prime Minister's Role in a Consociational Democracy", in Thomas Hockin, ed., *Apex of Power*, p. 106.

Chapter VIII

The Cabinet and the Prime Minister St. Laurent to Trudeau

Louis St. Laurent

King's successor as Prime Minister, Louis St. Laurent, was not a professional politician, and as a result his method of governing was quite different from that of his predecessor, Mr. King, first and foremost a politician, always ensured that the moves being taken by the government were appropriate to the political situation and that all possible political ramifications were canvassed before a decision was made. According to Mr. Pickersgill, who served as a civil servant under both Mr. King and Mr. St. Laurent and who also served as a minister in the St. Laurent cabinet, St. Laurent, on the other hand, ". . . with his sharp lawyer's mind made a decision by removing the human element from it and working it out like an algebraic equation. Then he tried to make it fit political reality."[1] The result was that policies and procedures were frequently adopted that were administratively sound and highly efficient but which failed to take account of possible political repercussions.

While King usually obtained a consensus by having all points of view thoroughly discussed, meeting argument with argument, and then proposing a line of action, in St. Laurent's time agreement as to what should be done was frequently reached *before* cabinet meetings. It was not unusual for ministers to submit to Mr. St. Laurent their proposals before cabinet meetings to ensure that he personally approved them. Since St. Laurent was reputed to be very capable at picking out flaws in an argument, ministers were careful to be very well briefed before going to him with policy proposals. Little time would be spent on them in cabinet. The result of this practical approach was that cabinet meetings were businesslike and to the point, with the Prime Minister playing the role of *primus inter pares*.

It was probably a mistake for Mr. St. Laurent to conduct himself as *primus inter pares*. There were several important side effects that eventually worked to the disadvantage of the parliamentary process, to Canadian federalism, and to the Liberal Party. Mr. St. Laurent delegated a great deal of authority without retaining the control Mr. King always had. The chief recipient of delegated power was the effective and capable C.D. Howe, who despite his ability had little political sense and was contemptuous of normal parliamentary procedure. Like Mr. St. Laurent, Mr. Howe stressed efficiency in government over political considerations. During this time administrative ability was stressed, and the running of the state to a large extent fell into the hands of senior civil servants. The Prime Minister began to lose control of his cabinet, and power drifted from his hands into those of his ministers and senior civil servants such as Bryce, Deputy Minister of Finance; Pickersgill, Clerk of the Privy Council; and Sharp, Deputy Minister of Trade and Commerce. Thus Mr. Drew, the leader of the opposition, was able to say quite accurately during the pipeline debate, "After all, while we know that the real and effective head of the government on this occasion is the Minister of Trade and Commerce [Howe], the Prime Minister is the nominal head."[2]

In fact Mr. St. Laurent ceased to be master of his cabinet, something that King had foreseen might happen early in St. Laurent's career as Prime Minister. In conversation with one journalist he ". . . suggested that the new Prime Minister ruled with too loose a rein in Cabinet. Soon St. Laurent would find that a Prime Minister cannot merely be first among equals. He must assert the authority residing in this office."[3]

St. Laurent then was far more lenient as Prime Minister than Mr. King and easier to work for. He trusted his ministers implicitly and tolerated situations that were politically unpalatable. The government emarked on various ventures that would never have received the approval of the cautious King, and St. Laurent even permitted some of his ministers to retain business connections that proved to be politically embarrassing, thus encouraging the idea that he was not really in control of his government. These circumstances did not even sit well with his ministers, although they were quick to take advantage of the situation. Howe remarked, "King was tough, you sort of wanted that at times from St. Laurent. He didn't wield a big stick like King did and make sure that no one stepped out of line."[4]

The result was a very congenial, easy-going cabinet. Mr. St. Laurent permitted his colleagues a relatively free hand in the administration of their departments. There were few cabinet disagreements and none so sharp as to split the cabinet, possibly because, with one or two exceptions, the members of the cabinet were very much alike in outlook and temperament. The cabinet consequently, in time, became insensitive to Parliament and to public opinion. Unanimity in the cabinet of a consociational democracy is probably in the long run a dangerous thing, in that the members cease to be truly representative of the groups and areas they represent. Having difficult colleagues in the cabinet may work against efficiency, but it does help ensure that various viewpoints are heard and taken into account. In St. Laurent's cabinet they appeared to be muted in favour of smoothness and efficiency, and the attitude seemed to develop that Ottawa knew best what was good for the rest of the country. Many important matters were settled by individual ministers and the Prime Minister or by the ministers and departmental officials. The decision-making process thus tended to lose its collegial nature, and the cabinet, when it did meet as a collegial body, acted more as a board of directors than as a political body, with Mr. St. Laurent acting as chairman.

Mr. St. Laurent also tended to delegate responsibility for party matters to others. Because of this extensive delegation, some ministers were able to control their areas like feudal lords. This would not have been so serious had the ministers been sensitive politicians, but many were not. Possibly because of St. Laurent's lack of experience in politics some of his appointments were not successful — "With only a restricted circle of close acquaintances and still distrustful of politicians he did not know well, he was inclined to choose those in whom he could place his trust because of their personal qualities."[5] Thus there were few real politicians in the cabinet. Mr. Gardiner remarked, "There weren't many in the St. Laurent Cabinet who were politicians . . . I don't think Mr. St. Laurent was a politician at all . . . he was a lawyer's lawyer . . . but that isn't politics."[6]

It can be argued that under Mr. St. Laurent Canada experienced efficient and sound government. However, during the period the Prime Minister ceased to be master of his cabinet and of the party. Consequently, the bureaucracy, which was relatively insensitive to the political aspects of decision making, became highly influential in this field, almost displacing cabinet ministers. For a time the country seemed to favour this emphasis on efficiency, as attested to by the Liberal election victories of 1949 and 1953, and it seemed that as long as the Liberal Party was successful at the polls, Mr. St. Laurent's position as party leader remained secure. But when an alternative appeared who was able to exploit the insensitivity of the government and who was thus politically appealing, the people voted the St. Laurent government out of office and the party was then quick to replace him as leader. It can be argued that Mr. Laurent himself decided to vacate the leadership in 1957, but it is likely that even if he had wanted to stay on as leader, there would have been great pressure within the party to replace him with a more aggressive person.

Mr. St. Laurent's errors were to excessively delegate responsibility to others, to overlook the political aspects of his position as Prime Minister, and to fail to learn from the examples of Macdonald, Laurier, and King. Consequently he was a failure as a consociational engineer, and under him the cabinet ceased to be a mechanism of accommodation but was not replaced by any other body that could perform this function.

John G. Diefenbaker

Mr. Diefenbaker, although an avowed admirer of Sir John A. Macdonald, tended more to imitate Mr. King as Prime Minister, with unfortunate results. Like Mr. King, Mr. Diefenbaker as Prime Minister was always acutely aware of the importance of political considerations, but unlike King he appeared to be lacking in administrative ability and experience, and the combination of a keen political consciousness and lack of appreciation for administration caused him great problems as Prime Minister.

In fairness, it must be remembered that prior to his becoming Prime Minister, Mr. Diefenbaker's administrative experience was limited to the problems associated with running a small-town lawyer's office and, briefly, the office of the Leader of the Opposition. To complicate his problems, on taking office in 1957 Mr. Diefenbaker had to construct a cabinet from among a contingent of Members of Parliament, only one of whom had ever had experience in a cabinet. This was the Hon. Earl Rowe, who had been a minister in Mr. Bennett's cabinet for three months (and who was not appointed to the cabinet by Mr. Diefenbaker). Thus, unlike Mr. King, Mr. Diefenbaker not only lacked experience in government himself, he also lacked colleagues who had had such experience. As a result his appointees were an unknown quantity to him in an administrative sense, and one would expect under these circumstances a considerable amount of supervision would have to be exercised by the Prime Minister, at least at the beginning of the administration. In addition, the Prime Minister was very suspicious of some of the senior men in the civil service, feeling that they were too favourably disposed towards their former masters in the Liberal Party. This suspicion was to some extent warranted, as shown by the fact that several senior civil servants later became ministers in the government of Mr. Pearson. As a result of all this, the efficient managerial group of the St. Laurent era was replaced by a more politically minded, less organized, but ambitious group under Mr. Diefenbaker. This new situation was reflected in the number of cabinet meetings. "In 1954, the Liberal Cabinet held 79 meetings, in 1955, 71 meetings — in 1956, 89 meetings and in 1957 up to June 13, 33 meetings. In the balance of 1957 the Conservative Cabinet held 78 meetings, and in the next four years it held respectively 134, 166, 157 and 144 meetings."[7]

During his term of office Mr. Diefenbaker tended to completely dominate the cabinet and the government. He tended to dominate not only the decision-making process within the cabinet, but he also tried at times to dominate the administration of the departments. One of his critics has said, "He ignored the normal delegation of authority and attempted to operate the federal administration through personal prerogative."[8] Other writers have accused him of the opposite — of over-delegating authority. "He was accused of being a one-man government; his fault was not that he governed too much, but that on occasion he governed too little. He appointed ministers and often allowed them to carry on as they would, even when they were wrong."[9]

Discussions with former cabinet ministers and others closely associated with Mr. Diefenbaker indicate that both criticisms were valid. He did tend to interfere, but if a strong-minded minister resisted this interference, then it would stop. Weak ministers who possibly did need supervision allowed him to constantly intervene in their activities. If Mr. Diefenbaker had himself been a good administrator, no serious harm might have been done. It would seem that this lack of ability soon became visible to his ministers, and they lost confidence in him. Thus Mr. Diefenbaker, unlike Mr. King, was unable to simultaneously delegate authority and to keep informed of developments within the departments. His methods tended to be clumsy and worked against the feelings of loyalty necessary for a prime minister to inspire in his cabinet colleagues. "His failure to delegate work and responsibility contained the seed of his own exhaustion. . . . His active supervision also betrayed a lack of confidence in his ministers or an ability to judge character, which undermined his ministers' respect for him and for themselves."[10] In one instance, a minister accepted an invitation to a dinner at the White House in Washington, shortly after the feud began between Mr. Diefenbaker and President Kennedy. The minister found, however, that he could not attend the dinner, as his department's estimates were suddenly called up in the House of Commons on the day of his scheduled departure, and several weeks before the date on which their presentation had been originally scheduled.[11] The minister suspects that this was arranged by Mr. Diefenbaker, who also liked to make important announcements himself, even though a minister had himself developed the policy to be announced on his own. Failure to give appropriate credit to ministers also increased discontent and stimulated the idea that the government was a one-man show.

Mr. Diefenbaker also imitated Mr. King in maintaining control over foreign policy. He asserted in the House of Commons that,

As Prime Minister I have always followed the course of not interfering with the ministers in the discharge of their responsibilities except that in regard to foreign policy I have followed the tradition of the United Kingdom, that the Prime Minister must take a particular interest in that field of national activity on which safety of the state so highly depends.[12]

Mr. Diefenbaker also attempted to emulate Mr. King's method of reaching a consensus in the cabinet. Where Mr. King would hear all sides of a question and then sum up the discussion and produce a decision based on what he believed to be a consensus (which might not be especially satisfactory to anyone but acceptable to all), Mr. Diefenbaker would insist on cabinet unanimity before a decision was taken on a particular matter. This meant that the decision-making process was slow and arduous, and as a result he and his cabinet frequently appeared indecisive. In cabinet at times it would seem that Mr. Diefenbaker did not assert himself sufficiently, and many important decisions were unduly delayed, causing the more competent ministers to become frustrated. On other occasions, however, Mr. Diefenbaker tended to force his own will against the majority of his colleagues. During the Cuban missile crisis of 1962, a majority of the cabinet favoured ordering Canadian forces to be alerted. The Prime Minister, after having stated earlier that such a move ought to have the approval of the cabinet before any action was taken, then opposed the idea in cabinet and prevented Canadian forces from being alerted. ". . . The Prime Minister's attitude was decisive. Had he favoured immediate action the Cabinet would certainly have gone along."[13] By forcing his will on the cabinet, Mr. Diefenbaker further frustrated his colleagues and undermined their confidence in him. King would probably have been more subtle and still produced a decision acceptable to him.

Mr. Diefenbaker was also unable to imitate Mr. King successfully because he seemed unable to choose competent men. King once remarked, "Sir Wilfred [Laurier] was right when he said that it does not do to cherish resentments in public life."[14] Mr. Diefenbaker cherished his resentments and tended to surround himself with people who had supported him through the years. It is true that circumstances required him to take into his cabinet many political enemies; indeed, during the period 1957-1962 he presided over a cabinet half of whose members had opposed his election as national leader in 1956, but he relied most closely on those who had constantly supported him. In doing so, he probably deprived himself not only of capable colleagues, but of much useful advice. One commentator suggested that both Mr. Diefenbaker and Mr. King had second-class brains; ". . . King was adroit in employing first-class people while Diefenbaker was too timid to tolerate better brains around him."[15] Another observer who was also very close to Mr. Diefenbaker has noted, "He often mistook mediocrity for loyalty and suffered fools where he would not have tolerated wise men."[16]

Even though he dominated the cabinet completely, Mr. Diefenbaker appeared to be so indecisive that he could not bring himself to dispose of cabinet ministers who had embarrassed him, as in the case of Mr. Sévigny, the Associate Minister of National Defence. In some instances, as in the Sévigny case, he guarded his prerogatives too closely and did not consult the cabinet at a time when advice from his colleagues would have been useful. The Royal Commission investigating the Munsinger scandal (Mr. Sévigny had had an affair with a prostitute, Gerda Munsinger, who was also a security risk) harshly criticized him for this. "Cabinet solidarity and joint responsibility are real factors. . . . Surely it would have been only fair and proper, and wise as well, to consult them as to whether . . . that Minister could continue in the Cabinet without risk to the national security."[17]

Possibly the greatest mistake Mr. Diefenbaker made was in his dealings with cabinet members from Quebec. His conduct here is reflected in the comment of one of his colleagues: "The prime requisite for influence with Mr. Diefenbaker was support for him over the years."[18] This support had not been forthcoming from the Quebec members and especially from the senior member, Mr. Balcer, who had opposed Mr. Diefenbaker's election as party leader. As noted earlier, Balcer was appointed to the relatively unimportant position of Solicitor-General and remained in that post through several cabinet shuffles, which antagonized French Canadians greatly. Mr. Diefenbaker did not select a trusted Quebec lieutenant as other Prime Ministers have done, nor did he have anyone in his office (which was woefully understaffed) to deal with specific problems in Quebec. As a result French Canadians felt ignored and poorly represented, and their resentment was clearly demonstrated in the elections of 1962 and 1963. In 1962 Progressive Conservative representation in the House of Commons was reduced from 59 members to fourteen and in 1963 it fell to eight members.

The St. Laurent cabinet and the Diefenbaker cabinet present a sharp contrast in decision making. Under St. Laurent, the process was decisive and efficient, with the bureaucracy being the major source of input. Under Diefenbaker, while there were few resignations from the bureaucracy (there were several notable resignations from the civil service at that time, notably Mitchell Sharp, then Deputy Minister of Trade and Commerce), it never worked as closely with the Progressive Conservatives as it did with the Liberals, and its input into the policy-making process was reduced. Because Mr. Diefenbaker insisted on cabinet unanimity and insisted that the political aspects of every problem be minutely considered, the efficiency of the policy-making process was sharply reduced; decisions were delayed and postponed, so that the cabinet reached almost a state of immobilism, and in time Mr. Diefenbaker lost control of his cabinet. Where Mr. St. Laurent's cabinet had been efficient but politically insensitive, Mr. Diefenbaker's was sensitive politically and highly inefficient. "At one point in 1959, forty-seven senior federal appointments — all of them the prerogative of the Prime Minister — were vacant at the same time."[19] Under such circumstances ministers became frustrated and either resigned from the cabinet or sought to replace Mr. Diefenbaker with someone else.

Mr. Diefenbaker was in firm control of the party, although the results of this control did not become evident until after his defeat as Prime Minister. He was very attentive to party matters and ". . . party officials always had priority over others when they wanted to see him."[20] He centralized a great deal of power over the party in his own office, which was greatly understaffed. His indecisiveness eventually led to his losing the support of many of the senior party officials as well as financial support, although he was relatively successful in retaining the support of the party faithful outside Quebec. The leaders of the various groups in the cabinet and party were muted, not in the name of efficiency as under Mr. St. Laurent, but as the result of the leader's insistence on depending on his own political instincts.

Mr. Diefenbaker's excessive reliance on his own political sagacity was the root cause of his failure. In attempting to imitate Mr. King, it would appear that Mr. Diefenbaker overlooked a basic difference between himself and his model. King was not a charismatic leader, and he did rely on others for advice and information. Mr. Diefenbaker also overlooked the fact that in a consociational democracy political sensitivity is not sufficient to enable a man to be a successful prime minister. Political sensitivity may make a man party leader, but once having attained office as Prime Minister he must develop other talents as well to retain his position as Prime Minister and as leader of his party. He must walk a narrow line between absolute control and excessive sharing of power in order to hold his cabinet together. Although Mr. Diefenbaker was able to bring together elites who were representative, his tragedy was that he could not hold them together, even though he had been immensely successful in arousing in the masses a sense of identity and pride in Canada that persists to this day.

L.B. Pearson

L.B. Pearson served as Prime Minister under conditions unique in Canadian history, in that during his entire term of office his party did not command a majority in the House of Commons. Other prime ministers have served under minority circumstances, but none for as long as Mr. Pearson, and his methods as Prime Minister must be analysed in the context of this situation. It should also be remembered that Mr. Pearson early in his career came into close contact with Mr. King who had a great deal of influence on him in the way in which he acted as Prime Minister.

One of the results of the minority situation was that Mr. Pearson was never in as strong a position as party leader as many of his predecessors. The constant threat of defeat in the House of Commons distracted attention away from him as leader, in spite of the fact that he led the Liberal Party back to power after a very severe electoral defeat.

Because of this situation, it can be argued that Mr. Pearson had even less freedom than most prime ministers in selecting members of his cabinet. He had to constantly avoid making appointments which would disturb party unity, and sometimes men were appointed to the cabinet whose main virtues were party loyalty and experience. Possible examples are Hon. Lionel Chevrier, who had represented an Ontario constituency after 1957, and Hon. George McIlraith, who had represented an Ottawa constituency since 1940. This produced a cabinet of varied reputation; it was later called everything from "the most impressive array of brains . . . and professional experts ever assembled in a Canadian Cabinet", by University of Toronto political scientist J.T. MacLeod,[21] to "a line up of drones, bores and inadequates", by newspaper columnist Douglas Fisher.[22] When in the course of Mr. Pearson's tenure various ministers embarrassed the government, it was not possible for him to be ruthless with them for fear of splitting the party in the House of Commons and bringing on an election. It would seem that when a government holds a minority of seats in the House of Commons, the Prime Minister's freedom of action within the cabinet and the caucus is very much restricted.

As in the case of Mr. Diefenbaker, Mr. Pearson has been accused both of interfering excessively with some of his ministers and of not consulting them sufficiently. Miss LaMarsh, Minister of National Health and Welfare, has stated that he prevented Mr. Hellyer, Minister of National Defence, from appointing a certain individual as his executive assistant, but this has been denied by Mr. Pearson. "I would consider an appointment of an Executive Assistant the special and personal prerogative of a Minister where he would not be required to consult the Prime Minister. . . . If he did not and a Prime Minister heard of a proposed appointment, knew the person in question better than the Minister, and that he would be most unsuitable then he could, and in some cases, should volunteer his opinion."[23] Peter Newman has also been critical, claiming that Mr. Pearson did not consult his cabinet sufficiently before becoming involved in major questions. Thus ". . . without consulting Cabinet, caucus or even his retinue of personal advisors . . . the Prime Minister decided to grab the initiative by introducing a new flag design."[24] Newman is incorrect. "Not only did I discuss the flag question in the Cabinet before a decision was made, it was also discussed in the caucus where the government was under strong pressure to proceed with a flag resolution without delay. Furthermore it had been a plank on our own election program in 1963."[25] Ministers interviewed who served under Mr. Pearson all felt that there had been no undue interference, although some ministers did note that, with the minority government situation, ministers had to be very careful not to embarrass the government, so that possibly the Prime Minister was more involved in decision making than he would have been in a majority government. Such a comment points up the unique problems encountered by a prime minister where even a minor miscalculation may have great political implications.

At times the Pearson cabinet appeared to be weak and indecisive. Referring to Newman again: "By not having any system of policy priorities, by succumbing to most of the pressures exerted on the administration they [the Cabinet] had lost command and had found themselves being controlled by events instead of controlling them."[26] In a minority government it is difficulty to see how events could be controlled as easily as with a majority, and it was very difficult to get cabinet members to concentrate on long-term priorities when they were not sure from one day to the next whether they would be in office or not. In fact an examination of the record of the Pearson government shows a considerable amount of legislation having been passed that would not have been introduced unless some set of priorities had been in existence.

Mr. Pearson did introduce some important innovations into the way in which the cabinet operated. He established a system of committees, and especially important was the establishment in 1968 of a cabinet committee on Priorities and Planning. The purpose of this committee was to provide a systematic assessment of overall priorities of expenditure to facilitate long-term planning. Under the circumstances, however, it was difficult to plan ahead in great detail. Unexpected developments forced the cabinet from time to time to shift course in order to avoid a defeat in the House of Commons, and sometimes this shift would make the cabinet appear disorganized and indecisive. The resultant publicity was unfavourable and resulted in a poor public image of the Pearson government. Mr. Pearson's procedure in arriving at a cabinet decision was quite similar to that of Mr. King. ". . . I always encouraged Cabinet Ministers to speak up, argue their case to their colleagues, who were also encouraged to speak. My philosophy was to let a Cabinet Minister, as far as possible, run his own show and that it was not my job to be interfering in details."[27] Frequently, however, discussion in cabinet was prolonged, and consequently many matters that should have been discussed by the cabinet were not mentioned because there was insufficient time. Moreover, because of the political situation considerable time was spent on trivial matters that had important political aspects and other matters were neglected. This was a source of great discontent to men such as the Hon. Robert Winters, who had been accustomed as a minister to the crisp efficiency of the St. Laurent regime and in business life to the smooth operations of the board of directors of a large company, and he found it difficult to function in this different environment. Allowance must be made, however, for the necessity for political considerations to have priority and it is difficult to see how the situation could have been avoided, although the Prime Minister could possibly have exhibited more firmness in meetings.

This is one area in which Mr. Pearson has been criticized severely. He was not a disciplinarian, as were most of his predecessors. "My style of conducting Cabinet meetings was relaxed, and informal . . . Mackenzie King never allowed anyone to smoke in Cabinet or have a coffee or any other kind of break. He was the headmaster! Mr. St. Laurent's Cabinet was more formal than were mine. . . ."[28] Possibly because of this informal atmosphere some of his ministers often revealed what was going on in cabinet in spite of admonitions from the Prime Minister. Divisions within the cabinet became public knowledge and caused dissatisfaction in the country. Cabinet disagreements are not uncommon in Canadian government, but usually the public is unaware of them until they become history. This was not the case, however, in the Pearson era and Mr. Pearson did not impose his will on his ministers in the way Mr. King or Mr. Diefenbaker could. An N.D.P. Member of Parliament, Colin Cameron remarked of Mr. Pearson, "A Prime Minister has to be capable on occasions of being a bastard. It is unfortunate that our Prime Minister is unable to be that sort of person. I might say in passing that the Right Honourable Leader of the Opposition [Mr. Diefenbaker] doesn't suffer from that disability."[29] There were possibly times when Mr. Pearson should have acted as a dictator rather than a mediator, although several of his ministers felt that had he done so the legislative output of his government would have been considerably reduced by this approach.

Mr. Pearson was Prime Minister at a time when relations with Quebec were at a very difficult stage. He was able to deal with the problem effectively. One of his methods in doing so was to try to secure as a Quebec lieutenant a minister who was trusted both within and without Quebec. Mr. Pearson's first choice as Quebec lieutenant was Hon. Lionel Chevrier who had been parachuted into the safe Montreal constituency of Laurier. Chevrier, however, was regarded as a "carpetbagger" by many French Canadians and thus was less effective in the role than had been anticipated. When Mr. Chevrier left the cabinet to become High Commissioner to the United Kingdom, he was succeeded as Quebec lieutenant by Hon. Guy Favreau. Mr. Favreau in turn was succeeded by Hon. Jean Marchand, who had complete authority over and responsibility for political activity there. Co-operative federalism as practised by Mr. Pearson seemed to be an acceptable concept in Quebec and illustrates quite clearly the flexibility of Mr. Pearson's methods. He did not repeat the mistake made by Mr. Diefenbaker; he was always conscious of Quebec's special needs and was most fortunate in having among his ministers from Quebec several men of outstanding ability.

Contrary to what many observers have said, Mr. Pearson appears to have been a highly astute politician. Certainly his cabinet colleagues regarded him as such; one veteran minister said, "He was a born politician, political to his finger tips."[30] He appeared to have an intuitive feeling for the public mood, very much like that of Mr. King. His political errors usually were more errors in timing than in tactics. The important point to note about Mr. Pearson is that, like all successful prime ministers, he managed to get his own way in most instances. Where he differed from other prime ministers was in his method of achieving the end. This method reflects his diplomatic background. Proposals would be made, resisted by members of the cabinet, withdrawn, and resubmitted with modifications satisfactory to all. Flexibility and pragmatism on the part of a prime minister with the cabinet probably reached a peak under Mr. Pearson, who understood, as an experienced diplomat, that a modified proposal does not necessarily bear with it the implication of defeat. Because of cabinet leaks, and because sometimes such tactics were used in Parliament, the impression created in the public mind was one of ineffectiveness and untidiness.

Mr. Pearson was also able to retain considerable control over his party during his term as Prime Minister. One of the ways in which he was able to accomplish this was by ensuring that his position as Prime Minister was not endangered excessively by the problems it encountered. Thus when the 1965 election failed to produce a Liberal majority, Mr. Gordon was allowed to take the blame for having advised the Prime Minister to call an election; this deflected criticism away from Mr. Pearson, who had made the actual decision. When Mr. Favreau and other ministers were severely criticized, Mr. Pearson's defence of them was restrained and as a result the government, rather than the Prime Minister, received most of the criticism. The government could survive this type of criticism; it is doubtful if it could have survived serious criticism of the Prime Minister. Through all of this, Mr. Pearson retained the loyalty of his ministers, who seemed to have genuine affection for him, unlike the situation with Mr. King, whose colleagues appeared to respect him but to have little affection for him. Possibly one reason for the continuing loyalty was the fact that he had virtually rebuilt the Liberal Party and guided it through some very difficult times and eventually to electoral victory. After such an achievement criticism was difficult.

Under Mr. Pearson's leadership several important innovations were made regarding party organization. He insisted, while still in opposition, that he be given an entire research staff, independent of the Liberal Party itself and for his personal use only, and when he became Prime Minister he continued to have his own research staff, thus preparing the way for the greatly enlarged staff in the Prime Minister's Office under Mr. Trudeau. He attempted, while still leader of the opposition, to make the party more democratic by organizing meetings such as the National Rally in 1961 and by restructuring the organization of the party to encourage more grass-roots participation. But whether in opposition or in government, the party remained under Mr. Pearson's control.

It should be obvious that the tactics followed by a prime minister in a minority government must differ substantially from those in a majority one. Caution is typical of Canadian governments, but becomes especially important when the government is in a minority, for then the cabinet must be prepared at all times to modify and alter its proposals and plans even when they have become public knowledge. The party must be kept united behind the leader, and this requires him to be more tolerant and less dictatorial than under other circumstances. In this situation the experience gained by Mr. Pearson in the diplomatic world was invaluable and was reflected by his willingness to make concessions, to be patient, and to be aware of the political implications of every move.

Pierre Elliott Trudeau

Mr. Trudeau is the first Prime Minister to have come to the office with an explicit philosophy of policy making. This philosophy can be discerned in the articles contained in *Federalism and the French Canadians*,[31] which has been referred to as Trudeau's political catechism. His main concern seems to be that reason and rationality be applied to all aspects of the policy-making process. He asserts that the modern state,

> . . . if it is not to be outdistanced by its rivals . . . will need political instruments which are sharper, tougher and more firmly controlled than anything based on mere emotionalism: such tools will be made up of advanced technology and scientific investigation as applied to the field of law, economics, social psychology, international affairs, and other areas of human relations; in short if not a pure product of reason, the political tools of the future will be designed and appraised by more rational standards than anything we are currently using in Canada today.[32]

The incrementalist approach to policy making then is no longer satisfactory, the rational approach is necessary. The rational approach, however, requires greater resources for the decision maker and greater control by him over the whole policy-making environment, in that he must be aware of all the alternatives and options available. This in turn requires structures to collect data as well as a strategy to determine priorities and to allocate resources. This in turn leads to a problem in a consociational and parliamentary democracy. How does one deal adequately with problems without giving serious offence to any one bloc and thus avoid disturbing the fragile equilibrium among the various Canadian interests while at the same time reconciling ". . . the mass, complexity and technical sophistication of the decisions required for government today with the continued handling of these decisions by the representatives of the people under a parliamentary system."[33]

The innovations introduced by Mr. Trudeau have been described elsewhere in detail. He has more clearly structured the policy-making system by enlarging and strengthening the Privy Council Office, the Prime Minister's Office, and the system of cabinet committees in order to rationalize the decision-making process and to provide him with more information and control over the policy-making process.

A second important aspect of Mr. Trudeau's philosophy is his stress on the importance of counterweights. In the introduction to *Federalism and the French Canadians* he says, "The theory of checks and balances . . . has always had my full support. It translates into practical terms the concept of equilibrium that is inseparable from freedom in the realm of ideas. It incorporates a corrective for abuses and excesses into the very functioning of political institutions. My political action, or my theory — in so much as I can be said to have one — can be expressed very simply: create counterweights."[34] Consequently the Privy Council Office, the Prime Minister's Office, and various commissions and boards have acted to counterbalance the influence of the departmental bureaucracy. Inputs into the policy-making process are to be derived from a large number of sources, each acting as a counterweight to the other. Rational decision making, however, seems to presuppose a set of values and priorities that are shared among the decision makers, yet there is no guarantee that the countervailing forces will have such values. They may simply react emotionally to a policy proposal or their reactions may be based on other values. Thus the final result may not actually arise out of purely rational calculation. There is also the possibility that decision makers faced with inputs from many sources may find themselves in a state of immobilism as a result of all the pressures on them. The establishment of a rational structure does not by itself guarantee the production of rational decisions and policies. Moreover, rationality may well have limited political value. In fact, the stress on rationality may well have contributed to the near-disastrous 1972 election results for the Liberals. The electorate cannot be counted upon to perceive issues in a rational way, and politicians must take this characteristic into account when communicating with the masses.

The Presidentializing of the Prime Ministership?

While all the innovations introduced by Mr. Trudeau were possible under the parliamentary system, it has been suggested by some critics that the effect of these innovations has been to fundamentally alter and transform the system and that ". . . Canada is moving towards a presidential system in everything but name."[35] Another critic has argued that

". . . the Canadian Prime Minister is inclined to think of himself as a crypto-president, responsible directly to the people. . . ."[36] An opposition member, however, has commented on the changes in the Privy Council Office and the Prime Minister's Office as follows: "In the main democrats should welcome these innovations . . . while it is undeniably true that the effectiveness of the Prime Minister has been increased by his staff, it is foolish to claim any change in principle in the constitutional position of Prime Minister [sic], which has always had primacy of power in our system of government."[37]

There can be no doubt that the various changes have enhanced the Prime Minister's power by increasing his control over the whole policy environment. Communications have been improved among the various components of the policy-making process, thus facilitating a more coordinated and rational method of policy development, with the Prime Minister as the central cog in the whole policy-making machinery, but it is doubtful if this means that Canada now has a presidential form of government as in the United States.

The first and obvious point to note on the question is that the presidential system in the United States involves a separation of powers among the executive, legislative, and judicial branches of government. No such clear-cut division of powers exists in Canada, and it can be argued that consequently the Prime Minister is in fact more powerful than the President. While the President does draw considerable strength from the fact that the constitution explicitly assigns executive power to him, legislative proposals made by him are frequently defeated or significantly altered in Congress; it is rare for such a fate to befall the proposals of a Canadian Prime Minister. In the matter of converting policy proposals into legislation, then, the Prime Minister has considerably more power than the President, in that he is not easily checked and his wishes, as reflected in proposed legislation, are usually translated into law.

There is one important check on the Prime Minister with which the President does not have to contend; that is, the Prime Minister must defend his policies in Parliament. He must explain himself to Parliament and thus to the country, for the press will report his remarks. This regular public conflict between the Prime Minister and the opposition is the essence of the parliamentary system and is not present at all in the presidential system. The President, if he wishes, need not defend himself or explain his policies; there is no compulsion for him to do so. The Prime Minister, on the other hand, has no alternative. He must face the opposition each day in the House of Commons. Thus it is unlikely that a Prime Minister could hold onto office as long as President Nixon did during the Watergate affair if he had had to face his opposition daily.

It has been argued that the new system of committees in the House of Commons has enhanced the ability of the House to check the Prime Minister. In fact, as shown in Chapter IX the committee system does not serve as an effective check because it operates within the context of strict party discipline, and it is difficult to see how such committees can check the Prime Minister and cabinet while the governing party has a majority on House committees. The typically American situation, where the chairmen of congressional committees become exceedingly powerful and are thus able to challenge the President, is not likely to arise in Canada, since according to a former Liberal whip, "The selection of chairmen [of House of Commons committees] is made in consultation with and following approval by the ministry."[38]

A check on the Prime Minister more effective than Parliament is the cabinet. While both the President and the Prime Minister can appoint and dismiss the members of their cabinets, it is necessary for the Canadian Prime Minister to carry his cabinet with him on policy matters, especially when many members of the cabinet have their own personal power bases. It is unlikely that a Prime Minister could triumph over a seriously divided cabinet for very long. In the American system, however, the cabinet does not make decisions; the President does. Presidents must conciliate and persuade as do Prime Ministers, but Prime Ministers persuade cabinet ministers within the accepted conventions of party discipline, cabinet solidarity, and cabinet responsbility. Presidents must persuade members of Congress without the advantage of such conventions, and without being able to dissolve the legislature. So the Prime Minister in balance probably has more power over the policy process than the President, although not simply because of changes instituted by Mr. Trudeau. The Prime Minister can force his will in difficult situations, but there are limits to his abilities to do so. That he is pre-eminent cannot be denied; that he is absolute is questionable.

It should also be noted that the President of the United States is limited to two terms of office, while there is no such limitation on the Prime Minister. Consequently, if a President wins a second term he becomes a "lame duck", less able to exert his will, while Canadian tradition imposes no such limitation. In fact, Canadian history seems to indicate that the longer a prime minister remains in office, the more powerful he becomes, so that again the Prime Minister appears to be more powerful. Historically it has been very difficult to remove a party leader without injuring the party, and it would be even more difficult to remove a party leader who was also Prime Minister.

It has been argued that the Canadian Prime Minister has less control over the civil service than the American President has over the American civil service and thus the Canadian civil service serves to check the Prime Minister. In the United States the senior policy advisors in the various departments are usually political appointees, not career civil servants, and thus a prime minister in order to turn the government into a presidential system ". . . would have to choose all the top policy advisors in the departments and make them responsible to him personally."[39] In fact there have been developments along these lines in Canada. The Prime Minister has tended to rotate deputy ministers far more frequently than was the case in the past, and there has been an explicit attempt to fill deputy ministerial and various quasi-independent agency and commission headships with appointees from outside the public service patterns. Some of these appointees have also been well-known Liberals, as in the case of Mr. Jean-Louis Gagnon, former head of Information Canada. The Prime Minister has also seen to it that civil servants in the Privy Council office are frequently rotated with the view of providing departments with a staff of senior men accustomed to an "overview" of government and who consequently have a point of view congenial to centralized planning. It is also argued that, in enlarging his own personal office and the Privy Council Office, the Prime Minister has in effect created a Presidential Office much like that of the President of the United States. Even these enlarged offices are miniscule in comparison with the ". . . twenty odd high powered personal assistants and a thousand civil servants in the executive office of the President."[40] The larger staff required by the President is the inevitable result of a basic difference between the two systems for, unlike the Canadian system, in the American one the President is the Executive and all policy is inevitably connected with the White House. One commentator has noted regarding Mr. Trudeau's innovations that he has ". . . altered the traditional lines between the senior officials, especially the deputy ministers and the Cabinet. Now they flow more directly through the Prime Minister's Office."[41] The net result has led to considerable control of the civil service by the Prime Minister, since power tends to be concentrated in the Privy Council Office and the Prime Minister's Office, and in that respect there is some basis for the argument that Canada has moved towards a presidential system. This development, however, may well be beneficial.

> Such assistance makes him [the Prime Minister] less dependent on the advice of bureaucrats in all departments who remain constant while governments come and go. A man who wishes to act in complicated situations can do so more intelligently by having a choice between advisers, testing the old against the new.[42]

The reduction of the influence of the civil service on policy making is not inconsistent with the traditions of the parliamentary system, but it is now true that the Prime Minister, like the President, does have access to more advice than that provided by the departmental civil service.

It has been argued also that one noticeable difference between the position of the Prime Minister and the President results from the fact that ". . . a key element of presidential control in the United States . . . is the Bureau of the Budget which interprets the President's overall priorities for the U.S. budget. The bureau is part of the presidential machinery."[43] In Canada such work is done by the Treasury Board and the Department of Finance, neither being located directly under the Prime Minister. But they are guided in their work by the priorities established by the Cabinet Committee on Priorities and Planning (of which the Prime Minister is chairman); furthermore, the membership of the Treasury Board is determined by the Prime Minister, who alone decides who is to be head of the Treasury Board. Thus while the Prime Minister's influence may not be as direct as that of the President, the difference in control is not great. This control is not new, however, and is consistent with parliamentary tradition in Canada. It should also be noted that the Prime Minister, like the President, at times is also directly involved in the preparation of the budget in Canada (see page 90).

On balance, the argument that the result of the changes brought about by Mr. Trudeau has led to a presidential form of government does not stand up. Great changes have been made, and in the process one of the effects has been to increase the Prime Minister's power and reduce that of the departmental bureaucracies. These changes are the result both of the enormous increase in the scope of government and a deliberate effort to ensure the primacy of responsible elected politicians over the bureaucracy rather than the result of an effort to alter the parliamentary system. It should be remembered that the Prime Minister of Canada normally has had great power and that an all-powerful bureaucracy is not compatible with a parliamentary system. The checks on the Prime Minister that have always existed are still present, and their effectiveness depends on how the Prime Minister wishes to use his power, on his ability to hold the cabinet together, and on his control over the party.

When Mr. Trudeau began enlarging his personal office staff and that of the Privy Council Office, there was some concern that political considerations would be neglected. Mr. Pearson commented:

> There is a danger that the operation will become excessively computerized and mechanical. A large number of capable young people have been brought in and given serious responsibilities, Harvard Business School types. What the office needs now is some seasoned political types who can realistically deal with the political problems which are always arising. It is futile to believe that either the P.M.'s office, the Cabinet or the government can be run as a business corporation. This was the problem Winters had. The people now in the new centre may tend to neglect the political aspects of government.[44]

The October 1972 election results seem to have confirmed Mr. Pearson's argument. Public reaction to the Trudeau cabinet's policies regarding unemployment, unemployment insurance, penal reform, and immigration has forced the Prime Minister to admit that

. . . some of the things we did went wrong. . . . We tried to find a solution. In some cases the solution didn't work as well as we liked so . . . the style will be to try and correct, certainly these sins of commission that we've made and to that extent we will change . . . I think that I would concede that we are more forced to listen [now] and I would also concede that probably as a result of that some of our legislation will be better.[45]

Pragmatism, however, seems to be almost as typical under Mr. Trudeau as under other prime ministers. In a speech at the Commonwealth Conference in 1969, he told the assembled prime ministers that ". . . they were not philosophers committed unswervingly to the ideal but politicians whose art was that of the possible."[46] Justification for arms sales to the United States, the establishment of diplomatic relations with China, and other policy decisions have been made on purely pragmatic grounds. Former ministers and others connected with the Trudeau cabinet remarked that discussions in the cabinet are as frequently concerned with the political significance of policy proposals as with their rationality and workability.

Mr. Trudeau has also made innovations with regard to the party (described in Chapter X), but these changes have not lessened his control. Some of the changes in the Prime Minister's Office may have enhanced his control; the regional desks, for example, can provide him with politically relevant knowledge about the country and also assist him in assessing the efficiency of Liberal backbenchers.

There was an expectation created among many people when Mr. Trudeau came to power and began to emphasize participatory democracy that this meant that the people would tell the cabinet what they wanted done and it would be done. The masters would speak and the servants obey. These expectations were unrealistic. Only in very rare situations is it possible for the people to express a reasonably clear opinion that can provide an unmistakable directive for Parliament and the cabinet. Normally public opinion is divided into so many segments that the cabinet cannot respond to popular direction; if it attempted to do so it would probably very quickly become immobilized. Prime Minister Trudeau noted before he entered politics that ". . . modern democracies hardly ever resort to the plebiscite — which requires each citizen to decide on what is often too technical a question. In contrast, the electoral system asks of the citizen only that he should decide on a set of ideas and tendencies, and on men who can hold them and give effect to them. These sets of ideas and men constitute political parties. . . ."[47] Mr. Trudeau's interpretation of participation means something quite different than what appears to be the popular understanding. He apparently means that a government should be so sensitive to the people (but without consulting them directly) that the people will obey because they want to obey, because they realize that their just demands are being met. "In this way democracy becomes a system in which all citizens *participate* in government: the laws in a sense, reflect the wishes of the citizens. . . ."[48] This places a heavy burden on the Prime Minister and cabinet and implies that a high degree of consensus exists among the Canadian people, something that up to the present seems to be lacking and which is not likely to be found in a consociational democracy. The October 1972 election results indicate clearly that there is no such consensus. The cabinet and Prime Minister failed to recognize the needs and problems of certain significant sections of Canada, such as the economic needs of western Canada and the expectations of urban Ontario, and in doing so they failed as consociational engineers.

Conclusion

The existence of numerous potentially conflicting groups make it impossible for the simple majoritarian form of democracy to work well in Canada.

> Consociational democracy violates the principle of majority rule. . . . In fragmented systems, many other decisions in addition to constitutional ones are perceived as involving high stakes and therefore require more than simple majority rule.[49]

The result of this situation is that the Prime Minister must spend much time and energy regulating conflicts that arise among the various groups, bringing about concessions and compromise, but without necessarily settling the conflicts or establishing large-scale consensus. Thus over the years certain conflict-regulating devices have developed; that is, procedures, arrangements, and rules that are potentially capable of making possible accommodations among antagonistic groups.

An examination of the careers of the Prime Ministers of Canada supports the assertion that, "In a fragmented society which contains numerous geographic, religious and racial conflicts the successful politician has been the man adept at negotiations and bargaining. . . . Success at this delicate business . . . depends on finding a formula for compromise."[50] This in turn demands certain personal qualities in Prime Ministers and has a definite effect on the style of politics practised at the federal level in Canada. The relative importance of these qualities will vary with the existent political situation, but the necessity for certain qualities remains constant.

The Prime Minister must in the first place be a skilled conciliator, which requires that he be prepared to regard political compromise as respectable and be willing to bargain with and accommodate his opponents. This in turn requires that the Prime Minister be cautious, flexible, pragmatic, and prudent.

The most successful prime ministers in terms of political longevity were Macdonald, Laurier, and King, and each exemplified the qualities noted above. All three during the course of their careers exhibited a practical, non-doctrinaire approach to the problems of the day, each was an opportunist, and each a master of the art of evolving policy gradually. Each was prudent and cautious and built support for various political compromises. None was a zealot or a reformer or a radical innovator. Each one was flexible, prepared to accept less than he originally asked for, and each felt free to borrow ideas from others. They were tolerant of others, including those who opposed them, and were patient in their political dealings.

Mackenzie, Meighen, and Bennett were all rigid men with fixed ideas and fixed principles, which made compromise difficult for them. They tended to be somewhat contemptuous of public opinion, being prepared to lead it rather than wait for it to develop. At times both Meighen and Bennett cast prudence aside and developed an aggressive, bombastic approach to problems, which did not seem to sit well with the electorate. It would seem that inflexible men and impatient men tend to be failures as prime ministers.

But other factors in addition to personal qualities are important if a prime minister is to be successful. It would seem that a prime minister must have control both of his cabinet and his party — that is, he must feel secure in his position. He can be effective only when he feels confident that what he does will not cause a split in his cabinet and party. The Prime Minister is expected to be both a conservator and an innovator. But he cannot innovate, he cannot risk change, if he is insecure, for then he may upset the delicate coalition that has brought him to office. Moreover, a prime minister who is insecure cannot function well because his authority will be in question; insecurity limits his ability to conserve as well as to innovate. Security can be achieved only if the Prime Minister engenders a sense of confidence in himself so that he is regarded as being indispensable by the other members of the political elite (his cabinet and the party elite).

Macdonald, Laurier, and King were all secure during most of their tenures in office — King despite the fact that many members of the political elite disliked him personally. His ability to sense the mood of the people and his ability to win elections made him appear indispensable, confirming Leon Dion's assertion that "if the political leader need not necessarily be loved, he must however be acclaimed."[51] Mackenzie and Diefenbaker serve as examples of Prime Ministers who at critical points in their careers did not have this security. Mackenzie was never master of his party and Diefenbaker lost mastery over his cabinet. It has been noted that as long as Borden and King were insecure they lacked authority over both cabinet and party.

In order to achieve security a prime minister has to employ several techniques. In the first place he must have a very keen sense of the political. A successful consociational engineer is highly sensitive to the political implications of all that he does. One important manifestation of this sensitivity results from his relations with Quebec. Mackenzie, Borden, Meighen, Bennett, and Diefenbaker all experienced great difficulties in their relationships with Quebec and thus never had the confidence of this important segment of Canadian society. They failed as consociational engineers because they were unable to win the support of one of the most important conflict groups.

The second requirement is that the Prime Minister retain mastery over his cabinet. This involves establishing a delicate balance between avoiding excessive interference with cabinet members while at the same time not delegating excessive authority, providing leadership without excessive control. One of the greatest tests of a prime minister's ability as a leader is to co-ordinate the work of the cabinet effectively. He must be able to procure through co-ordination the individual goals of his ministers and of the areas and groups they represent. He must be a good administrator himself or be sufficiently aware of the need for administration to surround himself with people who have this talent. Ministers must be left free to run their own departments while constantly being aware of the ultimate authority of the Prime Minister. It is clear that prime ministers who interfere excessively — as in the case of Mackenzie, Bennett, and Diefenbaker, will eventually lose the confidence of their ministers and their authority will be in question. A prime minister who delegates authority excessively, however, as in the case of St. Laurent, may bring about a situation where control over policy formation falls into the hands of a non-consociational body such as the civil service, with detrimental results to his own political career and to the country. Thus there must be a balance struck by a prime minister between political sensitivity and efficiency and between autocracy and democracy insofar as a prime minister's relationships with the cabinet are concerned.

It is essential that a prime minister value power but be able to use it without appearing to be dictatorial. Sir John A. Macdonald is quoted as having said, "I don't care for office for the sake of money but for the sake of power and for the sake of carrying out my own view of what is best for the country."[52] In order to exercise this power effectively Prime Ministers ". . . must enjoy extensive independent authority to take action and make commitments without being accused of ignoring, dominating or coercing their followers."[53] They cannot do so, however, if they stray too far from the accepted norms of their group — i.e., the cabinet and the party — and they must always be conscious of the expectations of the members of the group. "In fact, one of the few constants in leadership is the persistent preoccupation on the part of the leader with the impression he is making on other people and his unceasing efforts to adjust his personality and actions to conform to the expectations of the members of his group. The successes of great leaders in the past have been closely related to their ability to understand and express the sentiments of the followers."[54] Once having achieved the confidence of the group through adherence to their norms, the Prime Minister can then manipulate these norms to suit his own purposes.

These personal qualities and techniques affect the style of Canadian politics in three distinct ways. In the first place politics tends to be dull and unexciting because much activity must take place in secret in order that effective compromises be achieved, and consequently efforts are constantly made to depoliticalize sources of discontent. The second effect is that politics in Canada tends to be conservative; the necessity for compromise and the requirements that the leader adhere to the norms of the group ensure that radical innovators and policies are unlikely because of the disintegrating effect they may have on the stability of the country. Finally, the emphasis in Canadian politics is largely on maintaining the political system rather than resolving difficult problems or enhancing the moral development of the citizens or stimulating greater participation in political affairs by the average citizen.

NOTES

[1]Quoted by Robert Fulford in "Portrait of Lester B. Pearson". *Maclean's*, Vol. 76, No. 7 (April 6, 1963), p. 56.

[2]Canada, House of Commons, *Debates*. (May 14, 1956), p. 3867.

[3]Bruce Hutchison, *The Incredible Canadian*, p. 446.

[4]Quoted in Peter Regenstreif, *The Liberal Party of Canada, A Political Analysis*, p. 388.

[5]Dale Thomson, *Louis St. Laurent: Canadian*. (Toronto; Macmillan, 1967), p. 296.

[6]Quoted in Regenstreif, *The Liberal Party in Canada*, p. 387.

[7]Patrick Nicholson, *Vision and Indecision*, p. 31.

[8]Peter Newman, *Renegade in Power*, p. 92.

[9]Thomas Van Dusen, *The Chief*. (Toronto; McGraw-Hill, 1968), p. 50.

[10]Patrick Nicholson, *Vision and Indecision*, p. 31.

[11]*Interview*. (May 17, 1969).

[12]Canada, House of Commons, *Debates*. (September 11. 1961), p. 8174.

[13]P.V. Lyon, *Canada in World Affairs*, Volume XII, p. 37.

[14]Quoted in J.W. Pickersgill and D.F. Forster, *The Mackenzie King Record*, Vol. II, p. 463.

[15]Clark Davy, *Globe and Mail Magazine*. (November 9, 1968), p. 15.

[16]Thomas Van Dusen, *The Chief*, p. 92.

[17]Canada, *Commission of Inquiry Into Matters Pertaining to One Gerda Munsinger*. Report (Ottawa, 1966), p. 24.

[18]*Interview*. (June 13, 1969).

[19]Peter Newman, *Renegade in Power* p. 82.

[20]*Interview*. (January 3, 1970).

[21]*Toronto Daily Star*. (April 24, 1963), p. 5.

[22]*Toronto Telegram*. (April 26, 1963), p. 7.

[23]*Interview*. (August 18, 1969).

[24]Peter Newman, *The Distemper of Our Times*, p. 255-256.

[25]*Interview*. (August 18, 1969).

[26]Peter Newman, *The Distemper of Our Times*, p. 432.

[27]Quoted in "Two Canadian Prime Ministers Discuss the Office", in Thomas Hockin ed., *Apex of Power*, p. 197.

[28]Quoted in *ibid*.

[29]Canada, House of Commons, *Debates*. (August 31, 1966), p. 7905.

[30]*Interview*. (August 7, 1969).

[31]P.E. Trudeau, *Federalism and the French Canadians*. (Toronto; Macmillan, 1968).

[32]P.E. Trudeau, "Federalism, Nationalism and Reason", in *Federalism and the French Canadians*, p. 203.

[33]Gordon Robertson, "The Canadian Parliament in the Face of Modern Demands". *Canadian Public Administration*, Vol. XI, No. 3 (September, 1968), p. 275.

[34]P.E. Trudeau, *Federalism and the French Canadians*, p. xxiii.

[35]Walter Stewart, *Shrug: Trudeau in Power*, p. 189.

[36]Denis Smith, "President and Parliament", in Thomas Hockin ed., *Apex of Power*, p. 239.

[37]Ed Broadbent, M.P., *The Liberal Rip-Off*. (Toronto; New Press 1970), p. 8.

[38]James Walker, MP., "The Functions of the Whip in Canada". *The Parliamentarian*, Vol. LII, No. 4 (October, 1971), p. 261.

[39]Thomas Hockin, "Some Canadian notes on 'White House and Whitehall' ", in Thomas Hockin, ed., *Apex of Power*, p. 276.

[40]Richard Neustadt, "White House and Whitehall", in Thomas Hockin, ed., *Apex of Power*, p. 269.

[41]Douglas Fisher, "Trudeau in Action, Mackenzie King with Style" *United Church Observer* (October 15, 1968), p. 37.

[42]Ed Broadbent, *The Liberal Rip-Off*, p. 9.

[43]Thomas Hockin, "Some Canadian Notes on 'White House and Whitehall' " in Thomas Hockin, ed., *Apex of Power*, p. 247.

[44]*Interview*. (May 21, 1969).

[45]C.T.V. Interview, January 1, 1973, reprinted in the *Toronto Star*, (January 2, 1973), p. 8.

[46]Bruce Thordarson, *Trudeau and Foreign Policy*. (Toronto; Oxford University Press, 1972), p. 77.

[47]P.E. Trudeau, "For a Living Democracy", in *Approaches to Politics*. (Toronto; Oxford University Press, 1970), p. 89.

[48]P.E. Trudeau, "Contempt of the Legislature", in *Approaches to Politics*, p. 78.

[49]Arend Lijphart, "Consociational Democracy", *World Politics*, Vol. 21, No. 2 (1968-1969), p. 214.

[50]Jack L. Walker, "A Critique of the Elitist Theory of Democracy". *American Political Science Review*, Vol. 60, No. 2 (June, 1966), p. 291.

[51]Leon Dion, "The Concept of Political Leadership", p. 12.

[52]E.B. Biggar, *Anecdotal Life of Sir John Macdonald*. (Montreal; John Lovell & Son, 1891), p. 16.

[53]Eric A. Nordlinger, *Conflict Regulation in Divided Societies*. (Cambridge; Center for International Affairs, Harvard University, 1972), p. 73.

[54]Leon Dion, "The Concept of Political Leadership", p. 6.

Chapter IX

The Cabinet and Parliament

It has already been noted (Chapter I) that in theory the cabinet is responsible to Parliament but in effect the cabinet controls Parliament. There are, however, those who insist that Parliament somehow can do things on its own, without reference to the cabinet. Mr. Diefenbaker has frequently complained that "Parliament is being downgraded, undermined; its basic mission of freedom is being subverted."[1] It was only during the early years of Canada's history that Parliament was able to exercise some control over the cabinet. In fact, dominance of Parliament by the cabinet has been the norm in Canada rather than the exception. The development of political parties and the increase in the power of the cabinet have changed the relationship of the legislature to the executive and in the process the role of the private member has been substantially modified. The cabinet now usually controls Parliament because it is in control of its parliamentary caucus, it controls the House of Commons, and it is able to ignore the Senate.

Cabinet and Caucus

A parliamentary caucus consists of all the Members of Parliament (both in the House of Commons and Senate) of one political party, meeting to discuss matters of mutual interest. It should be pointed out that there is a basic difference between the caucus of a party in opposition and the caucus of a party forming the government. In an opposition caucus, all members, with the exception of the leader, are equal in status. The experience of former ministers may give them special influence, but by and large there is no difference in the responsibilities the various members bear. The situation in the government caucus is quite different, for in it the members of the cabinet have a very special status because of their responsibilities and their role in determining policy and introducing legislation. This special status affects the relationship between members of the cabinet and the party caucus.

Every cabinet has gone through the motions of consulting its followers on its plans and problems. Mackenzie King indicated that his government regarded the caucus as fulfilling a very important purpose. He described the caucus as ". . . the means whereby a government can ascertain through its following what the views and opinions of the public as represented by their various constituencies may be . . . a means of discovering the will of the people through their representatives in a manner which cannot be done under the formal procedure which is required in this chamber."[2] Several of King's biographers have suggested, however, that King did not rely on the views of the caucus as much as his remarks might indicate, but rather that he simply used caucus as the place to explain cabinet decisions and to develop strategy to be followed in Parliament.

The discontent of many government backbenchers through the years seems to indicate that while there may have been some consultation, little use has been made of the advice provided by caucus, and in fact the caucus has been more useful to the cabinet as a means of controlling the House than as a source of policy input. It is true, however, that no cabinet can afford to ignore the caucus, and there have been occasions when the caucus has rebelled and forced the cabinet to change a decision or alter a policy. It was, for example, the caucus of the Conservative Party that forced the appointment of Mr. Meighen as Prime Minister in 1920, even though the cabinet favoured Sir Thomas White. It was the caucus that rallied to Mr. Diefenbaker's support in 1963 and foiled the plans of those members who had hoped to unseat him. The conspirators had apparently not reckoned with the need for the support of the caucus nor had they taken it into their confidence; ". . . at no time was there liaison between the anti-Diefenbaker half of the Cabinet and the ungrouped dissidents on the back benches, which would be an essential prerequisite to a successful and smooth takeover of power."[3] These were, however, exceptional situations and the more usual situation was summed up by one member of the Conservative caucus under Mr. Diefenbaker: "We spent most of our time in caucus talking about secretarial service or parking space. We are never consulted about policy and hardly ever get to discuss it at all."[4] One of the problems under Mr. Diefenbaker was the enormous size of the caucus, which made it unwieldly and made it difficult to keep government secrets. Ministers who served during this period said they did find the views of caucus useful, mostly, however, because they had to defend their legislation in the caucus and this prepared them to meet opposition criticism. Thus legislation in final form did take account of caucus opinion, but mostly this opinion concerned details; by the time the policy proposal reached the caucus it was widely accepted and there was no great need for extended debate. One former minister in the Diefenbaker government noted that ". . . the backbenchers realized that a well erected wall existed between their group and the Cabinet . . . a backbencher often had to wait for the introduction of a measure into the Commons before he knew the exact nature of the government's plans. He was then expected to approve everything."[5]

But Mr. Pearson has noted that the caucus does have some influence with the cabinet. ". . . In my experience the Caucus — while often unaware of the actual terms of a Bill — has not only been kept aware of the policy decisions that had to be made but has influenced these decisions by the discussions in Caucus on the principles of the legislation. I think of two major matters in my administration — medicare and the flag — where the decision to proceed at a particular time was decisively influenced by caucus discussions."[6] One can assume that in the minority government situation in which Mr. Pearson had to operate, it was most important that considerable attention be paid to the views of caucus, as the bolting of only a few members could have had a disastrous effect on the government. Various observers have noted that during the minority governments of both Mr. Pearson and Mr. Trudeau, members of the Liberal caucus had much more influence than when the Liberals were in a majority and that, as a result, the influence of civil servants was sharply reduced.

This did not mean, however, that there was regular consultation with the caucus. One Liberal backbencher under Mr. Pearson has said that the cabinet did attempt:

> . . . to improve its own backbenchers' knowledge and understanding of proposed legislation, even allowing them on occasion to participate in the policy-making process. For example, Ministers and senior officials occasionally met with caucus groups to explain and discuss proposed policies before they were given first reading in the House . . . but these innovations, and others like them, although encouraged by the Prime Minister and a few other ministers, were never taken up gladly by the majority of ministers.[7]

The conclusion seems to be, then, that the caucus has had very limited influence on the determination of policy. Policy comes usually from the top (i.e., from the cabinet) to the caucus rather than the other way around, and this seems to have been the case with the Progressive Conservatives as well.

There are several reasons why caucus has been relatively unimportant in influencing policy. The great emphasis on secrecy is an important factor mitigating against government use of the caucus as a source of advice and policy input. Mr. Pearson has noted, "There is a very real difficulty in reconciling the necessity of the maximum amount of secrecy, while policy is being hammered out in Cabinet and the necessity of keeping the caucus informed of what is going on."[8]

A second explanation may lie in the types of problems with which the cabinet must deal. Many of the problems require a great deal of expertise that members of the caucus usually do not have. One former minister did note that where there was a considerable amount of expertise the caucus could be quite useful. "The ARDA program was to a large extent the product of a group knowledgeable in this field. Farmers are very effective in caucus when their particular area of interest is being discussed because they have expertise in it, likely more than the Minister has."[9] It may be that new members are not as knowledgeable of the problems facing government. The veteran Member of Parliament, Senator J.F. Pouliot, in reviewing his career in the House of Commons, said:

> . . . when I was first elected . . . I felt secure within the party because the party was doing nothing that was not submitted to and approved by caucus. No policy was enunciated until it had been approved by the party rank and file. . . . Since then because of a change in government in 1930 and due to war conditions, things have been different. For eighteen years I have been miserable. . . .[10]

In spite of all the criticisms, cabinets have made some use of caucus, but often this is for a reason other than to obtain advice from caucus on policy. The caucus supplies backbenchers with an opportunity to display their ability to either make or withstand criticism and as a result can be useful in identifying members who could usefully be promoted to the cabinet, although performance in the House of Commons is probably more useful in this regard than performance in the caucus.

The caucus can also act effectively as a brake on government proposals; that is, if the government puts forward a proposal that creates widespread opposition in the caucus, the cabinet may be forced to reconsider its plans. Under Mr. Trudeau, when Mr. Kierans submitted a plan to close a large number of post offices as an economy measure, ". . . so much opposition was raised in caucus that he had to revise his plans, reduce the number of post offices he was going to close and instead of closing a large number at one time, he changed his plans so that there was a gradual reduction rather than a wholesale one."[11]

ORGANIZATION OF THE CAUCUS UNDER MR. TRUDEAU

There is no doubt that over the years cabinets have not experienced a great deal of difficulty in controlling the caucus. Prime Ministers have been especially effective in keeping the caucus in line, since they appointed the officers of the caucus — that is, the chairman and the chairmen of caucus committees.

During Mr. Trudeau's first administration some effort was made to lessen cabinet control of the caucus. The chairman of the caucus was elected by the caucus itself rather than being appointed by the Prime Minister. The chairman of caucus in turn was empowered to appoint the chairmen of caucus committees, which had formerly been the prerogative of the Prime Minister. The caucus was organized into six subject committees that met on a regular basis with the appropriate ministers. Ministers were expected to discuss all major policy pronouncements and legislation with the committees, prior to second reading. Thus if consultation with the caucus moved a minister to change a bill he could do so and bring in appropriate amendments during his statement on second reading. The caucus was also provided with funds for research facilities, which was used to create a Research Bureau to assist individual members of the caucus, rather than caucus committees.

In some cases, copies of documents forwarded by ministers to the Privy Council Office regarding policy proposals were also forwarded to the chairman of the appropriate caucus committee, on the responsibility of the minister. By this means opposition to policy proposals in the Privy Council Office could be overcome by having the caucus bring pressure on the cabinet to adopt the suggestions made by ministers and their departmental officials.

In addition to these changes, efforts were made to require ministers to co-operate with caucus in a more concrete manner than before. The tendency has been over the years for ministers to ignore caucus as much as possible, either as the result of a deliberate choice or because they were overworked. In the Trudeau regime, the President of the Privy Council, who was also House Leader, is responsible for seeing to it that ministers co-operate with caucus and meet with caucus committees on a regular basis.

> The President of the Privy Council has been given a mandate to ensure the reluctant colleagues to cooperate and when Members feel that a particular minister has not dealt with them satisfactorily, the President of the Privy Council, as part of his responsibilities, is authorized to remind the Ministers of their duty. In addition, it is the responsibility of the House Leader to relay to those responsible complaints from members regarding offices, telephones, etc., to the responsible authorities such as, in some cases, the Speaker of the House or, in other cases, to the Cabinet itself.[12]

In addition the cabinet agreed to submit legislative proposals to the caucus before presenting them to Parliament in sufficient time to enable the caucus to discuss the proposals at some length. One backbench Liberal remarked:

> We are consulted a great deal and few policy decisions are publicly announced before we hear of them. I can think of three specific examples of consultation. The Cabinet consulted us before deciding to admit American draftdodgers into Canada. The caucus was responsible for important changes in the Tax Reform Bill of 1971 and we discussed the proposals regarding election campaign expense regulation before the Cabinet made its plans public.[13]

Another member who has served as a backbencher under both Mr. Pearson and Mr. Trudeau said:

> Caucus under Mr. Trudeau is consulted more than under Pearson. Trudeau does not have to contend with the situation Pearson did.

> Often under Pearson caucus would give an argument which Pearson would seem to accept, but circumstances might change which would require him to change his mind and then he would lose face with caucus. When Trudeau makes a decision in caucus you know it is not going to be changed.[14]

It should also be noted that during the first Trudeau administration caucus was subdivided into regional or provincial (Maritimes, Quebec, Ontario, Western, and British Columbia) caucuses, which also met regularly to deal with problems of special interest. These meetings were attended by the ministers from the areas concerned, and thus members were provided with an opportunity to discuss regional problems with the regional representatives in the cabinet. The Ontario caucus had a chairman and vice-chairman, as well as three directors, all elected by the members. Liaison was maintained with members of the Liberal caucus in the Ontario legislature and with other regional caucuses.

When Parliament was sitting, the caucus met on a regular basis on Wednesday morning at 10:30 for almost two hours. Unlike the government caucus in Great Britain, cabinet members were expected to attend. Prior to the meetings of the national caucus there might be meetings of the regional caucuses, which then reported to the national caucus. The meeting began with the President of the Privy Council and the Whip advising the members of forthcoming business in Parliament, following which the meeting was thrown open to members to raise subjects on which they had given advance notice to the chairman. Others who had not given notice could speak on the matter, but only for three minutes. The Prime Minister concluded the meeting by commenting on the matters discussed, after which it adjourned. On some occasions the caucus meeting was devoted to a discussion of a particular subject.

There is evidence, however, that the system instituted under Mr. Trudeau did not work as well as had been anticipated, in the sense that it provided members of the caucus with some influence in the policy process. The practice of having regular caucus committee meetings placed an additional burden on members who were also expected to attend meetings of parliamentary committees, in addition to being present in the House and attending to constituency responsibilities. One backbencher remarked that while there were opportunities for consultation available, many members ". . . found they simply did not have time to become sufficiently well informed to intelligently discuss proposed legislation or policy."[15]

A second reason why the system did not work was that while there was discussion before many policies were disclosed publicly or decisions taken, the cabinet did not necessarily take the views of the caucus into account, as in the case of protestations against the appointment of an ambassador to the Vatican. No motions were put in caucus and no votes taken; as a result the cabinet was free to interpret the opinion of caucus to suit its own purposes.

It has also been suggested that the new scheme did not work well because it was not to the advantage of an ambitious backbencher to fight the Prime Minister and cabinet too vigorously for fear of losing a promotion to a position of more influence and interest, since the Prime Minister appoints members of the cabinet, parliamentary secretaries, and the chairmen of parliamentary committees (in effect). One opposition spokesman noted in a debate on the Government Organization Bill in 1971: ". . . in the run of a four year Parliament 138 members supporting the government could have a paid position of one kind with the exception of committee chairmen. This is almost 90 per cent of the strength of the present crowd supporting the government."[16]

This figure was arrived at as follows:

Cabinet ministers	28
Ministers of state, five every two years	10
Parliamentary secretaries, 28 every two years	56
Deputy speaker, one every two years	2
Deputy chairman of the Committee of the Whole House	2
Whip, one every two years	2
Assistant Whip, one every two years	2
Chairmen of parliamentary committees, 18 every two years	36
Total	138

It is argued, then, that the ability of the Prime Minister and the cabinet to reward and punish a backbencher makes it possible for party discipline to be effectively imposed, thus enabling the cabinet to have its way. There is no question but that party discipline is effective; only once in the history of Canada has a government been defeated in the House of Commons as a result of its own followers voting against it. This was in 1873, when Macdonald's cabinet resigned after losing a vote of confidence.

But there is evidence that rewards and punishments may not completely explain why party discipline is effective in Canada. Hoffman and Ward discovered that, among the members of the House of Commons interviewed in 1965, ". . . only 24 per cent indicated that they would be interested in a Cabinet post at some time in the future; 50 per cent said that they had no interest in any public office(s) in future. . . ."[17] Assuming that these figures are correct, the promise of reward does not seem to be very effective in maintaining party discipline.

The threat of punishment in terms of expulsion from the party is probably not useful either. Government backbenchers who have spoken out against the cabinet or voted against it have rarely been expelled. There were serious disagreements among government backbenchers, for example, in 1944 over the conscription issue, when 41 out of 61 Liberals from Quebec opposed the government; none were expelled. Mr. Ralph Cowan, a member of the Liberal caucus under Mr. Pearson, spoke out against the cabinet frequently and was not expelled until the dying days of the 27th Parliament.

Party discipline, then, is probably effective because backbenchers tend to adhere to "rules of the game", one of which is that backbenchers of the governing party must support the party leadership, in the person of the Prime Minister and cabinet. It is understood by backbenchers when they are elected that they are to do this. One backbencher commented:

> I support the government consistently because that is the way politics operates in this country. I knew I had to do this when I decided to run for office, so did the people who voted for me. If I don't want to play by the rules I should get out of the party. But it is also clear to me that going along with the party does not mean I have to go against my own moral principles, party discipline does not make it necessary for me to sacrifice my principles. Where there is a conflict I am free to make my choice, without worrying that I am going to be punished.[18]

Besides rules of the game, peer pressure is also a factor in helping to ensure that party discipline is effective. The comments of the late Hon. Ross Thatcher made after he had left the C.C.F. Party in the House of Commons would probably be applicable to government backbenchers as well.

> Deviation in any party tends to cause hard feelings, resentment, and even bitterness among colleagues. Thus there is a very real, if indirect, pressure in Parliament to require a member to follow the party line on all occasions.[19]

The situation in Canada, then, is akin to that in the United Kingdom, where it has been concluded that ". . . there is not a very clear relationship between rewards and punishment and party cohesion. . . ."[20]

It can be argued that the provision of greater freedom and influence for backbenchers in caucus enhanced the cabinet's control over its followers in the House of Commons. Having at least been consulted by the cabinet before legislation was debated in the House, the opportunities for government Members to publicly dissent in Parliament were greatly reduced. Since consultation did take place in private, however, the opposition and press could still argue that government backbenchers were merely "trained seals" doing whatever the cabinet demanded. The procedure adopted during the first Trudeau administration did not provide the publicity necessary to overcome the charge and failed to substantially enhance the public status of government backbenchers.

The caucus then may be considered a source of influence in the Canadian political system, but it does not have as much influence or power as the civil service, the party, the personal staffs of ministers, and the Prime Minister's own circle of advisors. The function of the caucus under Mr. Trudeau has been very much the same as it was under Mr. Pearson. "For the Liberals the cathartic function of caucus ('letting off steam', in the words of most respondents) is clearly more important than for any other party. However the most important function of the caucus for the Liberals is to inform: 87 percent of the Liberals mentioned this function. . . ."[21] It does, however, enable a Member to present a case he believed had not been presented earlier. Thus when the then Minister of Labour, Mr. Mackasey, brought to caucus a proposal to increase the minimum wage to $1.65 per hour, one Ontario member argued that:

> . . . the figure should have been $2.00 an hour. The Cabinet's figure was too low in the light of economic conditions in my riding and I argued for the change as hard as I could. But members from other areas, especially in Quebec, said this would be bad for small business in their areas, so I lost the argument. But I had the chance to make my point, and when the matter came to a vote in the House I stayed away and I was able to explain to my constituents why.[22]

It is likely that the nature of the parliamentary system is such that it will never be possible to satisfy backbenchers in terms of providing them with great influence on the decision-making process. One veteran cabinet minister summed it up as follows:

> The complaints of backbenchers are numerous, varied and constant. They persist as a natural phenomenon of political life whether a party is on the Government or the Opposition side of the House. In my experience, there was always ample opportunity for a back bencher to advance an idea. Not all the proposals put forward were acceptable. Government plans for legislation may sometimes be submitted for scrutiny by back benchers sometimes because of the necessity for secrecy or because of pressure of time, that step has to be omitted. Much depends on the confidence of the elected members generally in the Leader and the Cabinet. . . .[23]

With a leader exercising strong control over the cabinet and popular with the electorate, it is unlikely that the government caucus will greatly influence the cabinet and Prime Minister.

The Cabinet and the Senate

One of the original purposes of the Senate was to act as the representative body for the various regions in the Canadian federation. It has failed in this role, and the fact that in cabinet construction the Senate is of little significance helps to emphasize this failure.

For some time after Confederation it was fairly commonplace for Prime Ministers to appoint senators to the cabinet, and two senators, Abbott and Bowell, served as Prime Minister for relatively brief periods. Neither held office for very long, but it seems unlikely that, had they had the opportunity to lead their parties in an election, their membership in the Upper Chamber would have been counted an advantage. Macdonald's first cabinet included five senators, and Mackenzie's had two. Until 1908 it was customary to have at least two senators in the cabinet, and these senators acted as department heads. Macdonald, however, was careful to ensure that "spending" departments were headed by members of the House of Commons. Frequently the portfolios held by senators were among the least onerous, but at times most of those considered to be the most difficult and the most important, such as Justice, Public Works, Trade and Commerce, and Interior, have been held by senators, indeed at one time or another almost every portfolio has been held by a senator.

The presence of senators in the cabinet was always a source of discontent, regardless of the party in power. As early as 1871, the Liberals introduced a bill that would have prevented senators from holding any office of emolument under the Crown, which would have prevented them from becoming cabinet ministers with portfolio, since portfolios always carried a salary. The bill was defeated by only one vote. Possibly because of the repeated criticism to which prime ministers have been subjected following appointments of senators to the cabinet, prime ministers in recent years have avoided appointing senators as department heads, except as a temporary measure. Since 1935 it has been the practice to appoint one senator who acts as Government Leader in the Senate and is included in the cabinet as a minister without portfolio, without departmental responsibilities. He speaks for the cabinet in the Upper House and acts as a link between Senate and cabinet. The last senator to hold a portfolio, the late Senator Wallace McCutcheon, acted as Minister of Trade and Commerce for three months during 1962 in the Diefenbaker cabinet. This was an unusual expedient, and Mr. McCutcheon resigned from the Senate in order to run for the House of Commons in the general election of 1963. It is worthy of note that for most of the period of the Diefenbaker government no cabinet member was a member of the Senate.

Up to February 1969, the Government Leader in the Senate, as a minister without portfolio, did not receive a salary equivalent to that of a head of a department. The Government Reorganization Bill of 1969, however, brought the Government Leader of the Senate under the Salaries Act, and he now receives the same salary as a cabinet minister in charge of a department, in addition to his Senate stipend. The Prime Minister explained at the time that this step was taken as a result of the expansion of the responsibilities and workload of the Government Leader in the Senate.

The Cabinet and the House of Commons

Writing in 1949, Robert MacGregor Dawson referred to the House of Commons as ". . . the body to which at all times the executive must turn for justification and approval."[24] In fact, for most of the time the House of Commons is controlled by the cabinet through party discipline, through control of the agenda, and through control of committees. Even in those cases where there is minority government, the rules of the House of Commons, the sheer necessity of government action in various fields, as well as the reluctance of opposition parties to force an election enable the cabinet to maintain a dominant position.

SPECIAL RELATIONSHIP OF THE CABINET TO THE HOUSE OF COMMONS

For many years members of the cabinet had a very special relationship to the House of Commons, in that they were the absolute exceptions to the rule that anyone holding an office of emolument under the Crown was disqualified from sitting in the House. A Member who accepted an office of emolument, such as a cabinet position, lost his seat at once and could resume it only after winning a by-election. Thus in 1926, when Meighen accepted Byng's offer of the prime ministership, he immediately lost his seat in Parliament and could not lead the government in the House of Commons. This procedure was abolished in 1934. Now other Members of the House, including the leader of the opposition, also receive salaries. The cabinet still has a very specific relationship because of its dominance over the Internal Economy Commission, which acts as an administrative board of directors of the House of Commons. The House of Commons Act specifies that the commission is to consist of five members, including the Speaker of the House plus ". . . four members of the Queen's Privy Council for Canada who are also members of the House of Commons. . . ."[25] The actual responsibility for administering the House of Commons (which now employs over 1500 people) is left to the Speaker and to some extent, the Government House Leader, who is a member of the cabinet. One would expect that the Speaker would see to it that the affairs of the House are conducted in a non-partisan way, but the fact that the Commission is dominated by cabinet members gives the cabinet powers which could be used in a partisan way. A Private Member's bill debated in 1970 would have reconstituted the Internal Economy Commission so that it would include members from all political parties, but the bill was talked out. None of the speakers in the debate[26] were able to cite examples of undue interference although several expressed fear of potential interference. The present membership of the Commission clearly indicates that the idea that the House of Commons is master of its own procedure is a ". . . transparent fiction."[27]

THE SPEAKER OF THE HOUSE OF COMMONS

The Speaker of the House of Commons occupies a particularly difficult position. He must enforce rules of debate so as to fulfil two contradictory aims. He must protect the cabinet so that the opposition will not prevent it from fulfilling its responsibility to govern the country and at the same time he must prevent the cabinet from becoming arbitrary and thus limiting the ability of the opposition to present its case. In theory, then, the Speaker must be impartial but in fact circumstances have made it very difficult for him to act in this way and have encouraged him to appear to favour the government. The speakership in Canada is still a political appointment made by the Prime Minister, sometimes after consultation with the leader of the opposition, but not necessarily always. As a result the Speaker cannot appear to function as an absolutely impartial chairman, and there is always present the suspicion that he can be pressured by the cabinet. The notorious pipeline debate of 1956 left many observers with the impression that the Speaker had at one point succumbed to pressure from the cabinet.

Several factors have made such independence difficult. In the first place, the speakership has been an explicitly partisan appointment; for many years his nomination was moved by the Prime Minister and seconded by a member of the cabinet. The speakership sometimes became involved in the process of cabinet making and was awarded as an alternative to a cabinet appointment; thus it came to be regarded as a form of political reward.

> When Mackenzie King was unable to find room for Rodolphe Lemieux in his first Cabinet, he persuaded him to accept the Speakership and there can be little doubt that it was only the excessive front bench strength from Toronto which placed Mr. Speaker Michener in the chair rather than in the Cabinet [under Mr. Diefenbaker].[28]

That this appointment is highly partisan is highlighted by the fact that almost every Speaker has been able to look forward to a reward in the form of a partisan appointment at the end of his term of office. Of the 27 Speakers who served prior to the present one, Mr. Jerome, only seven did not receive political appointments after having served as Speaker, and of these, six were members of parties which were defeated in general elections immediately after their term of office; thus there was no patronage available for them. Table 9-I indicates the subsequent appointments of Speakers of the House of Commons from 1867 to 1966.

TABLE 9-I

Political Appointments of Speakers of the House of Commons

Cabinet members	7
Senators	5
Patronage Positions (Collector of Customs, Chairman of Commissions)	3
Lieutenant Governors	2
Diplomatic Corps	2
Judge	1
No subsequent appointments	7
Total	27

A second reason why the Speaker has not been able to appear absolutely impartial is that he has remained a member of the party and has had constituency responsibilities that make him dependent on cabinet ministers for attention and favours and has had to fight election campaigns in a partisan context. There has also been a tendency for politicians to regard the Speaker as a partisan figure. Thus one former minister (Emerson, Minister of Railways and Canals under Laurier) said in a speech in the House:

> So far as it lies within his power he may seek to be immune from association with either of the political parties; but there is no use disguising the fact that the party which appoints a Speaker looks to him as one of its own, as a part of the Administration as it were.[29]

Mr. St. Laurent made this more explicit during the pipeline debate in 1956 when he implied in a speech that confidence in the Speaker and confidence in the government were almost synonymous, in that at that time the Speaker had not lost the confidence of the House since the Liberal majority still supported him.[30]

It is surprising that in spite of the partisan nature of the speakership, incumbents seem to have maintained a relatively good record of impartiality while in office, even when the nature of the position has emphasized the cabinet's control over the House of Commons. However, some recent changes have attempted to strengthen the concept of an impartial Speaker. From 1963 to 1974 the Speaker was nominated by the Prime Minister, with the leader of the opposition seconding the nomination, an approach that required consultation between the Prime Minister and the leader of the opposition. In 1974, however, Mr. Stanfield, the leader of the opposition, refused to second the nomination of Mr. Jerome, claiming that he had not been consulted on the matter, so that it would appear in this case that the Speaker was the personal choice of the Prime Minister. In 1965 the right to appeal decisions of the Speaker was abolished. There have been relatively few appeals over the years, but the small number may simply reflect the fact it was understood that the cabinet would have its way, since the majority — i.e., the government party — would inevitably support him. When appeals were made, however, there had developed a procedure whereby the opposition would make its case while the government would say nothing, and the Speaker would then give his ruling, a procedure that at times suggested that the Speaker was also the government's procedural authority. Since 1965 it has been customary for both opposition and government to state the case before a ruling is made by the Speaker, thus lessening the impression that the Speaker was the spokesman for the government on matters of procedure. In addition, in the general elections of 1968 and 1972 the Speaker ran as an independent Liberal, thus encouraging his image as a non-partisan figure.

It is too early to determine if these changes have made the Speaker more independent of the cabinet. Mr. Speaker Lamoureux, who served from 1963 to 1974, received the ultimate accolade from Mr. Diefenbaker, who stated that he was the best Speaker in his experience, but it is difficult to know whether this success was due to the Speaker's ability and personality or due to changes in his position.

OFFICERS OF THE HOUSE OF COMMONS

It is accepted practice in Canada that the officers of the House of Commons — that is, the Clerks, the Sergeant at Arms, etc. — are all, like the Speaker, politically neutral. Although these officers may conduct themselves impartially in the House, they frequently achieve their positions after some practical experience in politics. The present Clerk of the House, for example, is a former executive assistant to two Liberal cabinet ministers and was himself a candidate for the Liberal Party in two general elections. His predecessor in office was a former Liberal backbencher. Once appointed, such officers can be removed only with great difficulty, and given the Liberal dominance of the House of Commons in the 20th century, it is apparent that the senior officers of the House have been frequently politically congenial to the cabinet. In theory, they are neutral regardless of their political views, but there is some evidence to suggest that at times the Prime Minister or the cabinet can influence them. Mr. King's diaries indicate that on at least one occasion, in 1944, he insisted on overruling an official of the House. The Clerk of the House of Commons had said that General MacNaughton, who was then Minister of National Defence but not a Member of Parliament, could not bring advisors into the House of Commons with him. King was annoyed about this. "Finally found it was one of Beauchesne's troublesome matters. Told the Speaker they must be allowed to come in, that was arranged."[31]

THE GOVERNMENT WHIP

The government Whip is appointed by the Prime Minister after consultation with the cabinet. The Whip is responsible for attendance of members in the House of Commons and House committees; he also arranges office accommodation for backbenchers, and he usually makes up the list of speakers for each debate after consulting with the minister concerned. Presumably this means that the Whip and minister can arrange to have hostile government backbenchers left off the list and thus kept silent. In addition the Whip and the Government House Leader jointly decide on the composition of delegations, assignments to committees, and recommendations for committee chairmen. The Whip then is in a position to provide rewards and punishments to backbenchers, which tends to justify one former Whip's definition of his position as ". . . the Chief of Police of the Party."[32] Another former Liberal Whip stated that he had a great influence in determining who among Liberal backbenchers were permitted to go on trips and to receive coveted committee assignments. His judgment was usually based on the performance of a member first of all in committees, second in the House of Commons itself, and finally in the member's constituency. The cabinet may, by working through the Whip, influence to a considerable degree the behaviour of government backbenchers in the House of Commons, and obstreperous backbenchers are not likely to be kindly judged by the Whip.

THE ROTA SYSTEM

During the first Trudeau administration several important changes were made in the procedures of the House of Commons. One of the most important was the introduction of a rota system for cabinet ministers. Prior to 1968 cabinet ministers were expected to be in daily attendance in the House of Commons in order to answer questions. Under the procedure introduced by the first Trudeau cabinet, ministers were required to be present in the House only three days of the week. The Prime Minister normally attended the House every day, and the entire cabinet was to be present on Wednesday (the day on which the time set aside for questions is only forty minutes rather than the usual sixty), with half the cabinet present on the other days. This change illustrated the control the cabinet has over the House of Commons, in that it was made unilaterally despite the strong objections of the opposition parties and notwithstanding considerable criticism from the public and press. This change had two important consequences. Since members could no longer question ministers when they wished but only at times decided upon by the cabinet, the principle that the cabinet is responsible to Parliament was seriously diluted. The second consequence was that the position of the Prime Minister was further enhanced, since he appeared in the House every day and on occasion replied for an absent minister.

The rota system was introduced in order to give ministers more time to attend to other duties. The President of the Privy Council and House Leader, Mr. Macdonald, stated:

> During the 1960's usually fewer than a dozen Ministers were asked questions each day. This meant that on the average, more than half the Cabinet — indeed often two-thirds of the Cabinet — devoted up to two hours a day for questions which never came. . . . In other words, while formerly 60 per cent of the Cabinet had to waste its time preparing for Question Period when they did not receive questions the new system has reduced this figure to 30 per cent. Needless to say, this has given Members of the Cabinet invaluable additional time to administer the affairs of their Departments and to carry on their other important functions.[33]

The order of priorities of the Trudeau government was quite clear from this; responsibility to Parliament was ranked well below other responsibilities.

The election of a minority government in 1972 effectively abolished the rota system, since the possibility of a snap vote required ministers to attend the House of Commons on a more regular basis than had been the case from 1968 to 1972. A formalized rota system did not reappear after the 1974 election, when a majority government was elected, although members of the opposition have frequently deplored inadequate ministerial attendance in the House. The rota system attracted a great deal of criticism from the Opposition, press, and public, and its abandonment is probably a manifestation of the government's wish to de-emphasize administrative changes because of their adverse political impact.

COMMITTEES OF THE HOUSE OF COMMONS

Since 1867 the House of Commons has made extensive use of committees to scrutinize government activities and proposed legislation. For the first few years after Confederation there was no doubt that the government intended to dominate these committees, for it was arranged that cabinet ministers usually acted as chairmen of such committees. In those cases where they did not serve as chairmen they served as committee members and took a prominent role in committee activities. This practice continued for many years.

This practice of having ministers serve on committees was discontinued in the 1920s, and government backbenchers served as committee chairmen, except in the case of the Public Accounts Committee, which since 1958 has had an opposition Member as chairman. This did not, however, substantially diminish the influence of the cabinet or increase the efficiency of the committee, and consequently committees never were very influential in the policy-making process. Aside from the Public Accounts Committee, which has embarrassed the cabinet at times, committees in the House of Commons usually have not thwarted the cabinet or made any significant changes in proposed legislation. House committees have often been too large to be effective, and most important legislation was considered in the Committee of the Whole. There was a tendency to resist the notion that Members of Parliament should develop specialized interests, and committee membership changed frequently. Lacking expertise, committees did not challenge cabinet proposals and had little impact on the legislative process. Consequently committees have not seriously challenged cabinet proposals.

There have been important changes in the committee system in the House of Commons in recent years. In explaining the new system, the Government House Leader said that he believed that the changes would enhance the role of the House of Commons and increase its influence since the new system gave ". . . an entirely new status to the standing committees because the standing committees will be entrusted with the detailed examination of the estimates and will also have a new role in the examination of public bills."[34]

Under the new system, standing committees have been established along subject lines roughly parellel to the arrangement of government departments. The committees have been reduced in size to an average of about twenty members each. The rules of the House of Commons have also been changed, so that almost every bill is referred to a standing committee for consideration, although it is still possible for some bills to be referred to a Committee of the Whole. It is argued that under this system, with membership on committees remaining fairly constant over the life of a Parliament, committee members will acquire considerable expertise in particular areas. As a result, proposed legislation will be examined more carefully and with more competence and thus the end effect will be more effective and satisfactory legislation passed by a House of Commons whose members — both government and opposition — will have had the opportunity to examine it carefully and critically. It was thought that the establishment of a system that permitted committee members to become expert in a particular policy area would bring about new input into the policy-making process, with presumably beneficial results in the form of higher quality legislation. In addition the new system made it possible for committee members to move amendments to bills that the cabinet may not have anticipated or that the cabinet may oppose. Approval of these amendments by the committee does not imply a government defeat, however; their significance lies in the fact that this procedure is a means whereby pressure may be placed on the cabinet to change its original proposal. The cabinet, or individual ministers, aware of this potentially embarrassing position, might then be more willing to accept amendments from government backbenchers before the legislation reached the committee stage.

It has already been noted, however, that committees have been formed in the government caucus so that government members have already considered bills in caucus (before they go to a House committee) and usually have agreed with the cabinet on its contents. When this has been done, government members are then normally expected to support legislation in committee and in the House. The government majority in the committees usually then will only support amendments which by prior arrangements are acceptable to the cabinet or a particular caucus committee. It has been asserted, for example, that the recommendations made by the Commons Finance Committee in connection with the government's *White Paper on Taxation* in 1970 ". . . reflect prior understanding between Liberal committee members, and government. . . ."[35]

There is also evidence to indicate that the cabinet is *not* prepared to tolerate criticism from its supporters in committee sessions. One government backbencher, Mr. Steve Otto, advised his constituents in a letter in 1969 that "the government members of the committee have been instructed to make no change to the bills coming before the committee and to vote exactly as they are told by the government." On a subsequent occasion this same member stated in the House that cabinet ministers must realize that ". . . it is high time a backbencher's position meant something and that they and officials of their departments must consult with members of committees and advise them of government plans and policies."[36] The apparent reluctance of the present government ment to accept recommendations from committees confirms remarks made during interviews with present and former cabinet ministers regarding House committees. Former ministers interviewed stated that they felt that the nature of the system tended to make such committees relatively unimportant because of the fact that the government members dominate committee membership and thus the government controls the committees. One former minister stated that "Committees are arms of the government and this is true regardless of which party is in power."[37] This means that the committees will have at best only a minor effect on policy and that the cabinet is not overruled by House committees. Alterations in the committee system will not change this; the result of such changes has probably been more busy backbenchers rather than a new policy-formation process. House committee meetings have not received the attention from the press and the public that debates in a Committee of the Whole would receive, and a small number of committee members do not generate as much opposition as a large number of members operating in the Committee of the Whole.

There is also evidence to indicate that the government is not pre-pared to tolerate the presence on House committees of obstinate gov-ernment backbenchers. The rules of the House of Commons make it very easy to substitute members on committees. Standing Order 65 (4) (6) states: "Changes in the membership of any standing, joint or special committee may be effected by a notification thereof, signed by the member acting as the Chief Government Whip, being filed with the Clerk of the House who shall cause the same to be printed in the *Votes and Proceedings* of the House. . . ." Thus names of members can be added or deleted from committee membership lists merely by reporting from the Whip's office to the Clerk's office. References have been made in the House from time to time to roving "government goon squads" who move into committees when the government needs help. It would seem that in fact there are two types of goon squads, the quorum fillers and the voters. The quorum fillers are government backbenchers who are dragooned to attend committee meetings so that the committees can legally function with a proper quorum. Many such individuals do not actively participate in the committees' activities but their presence at the meeting enables other members to do so. The voters provide the government with a complement of loyal members on committees at the time of a vote, even though they may have not participated in the committee's deliberations. It should be pointed out that at times the government is forced to make alterations in committee membership in order to keep the whole system functioning. At one point twelve com-mittees were sitting concurrently with the House of Commons. This potentially could involve 240 members, more than the number available to fill committee assignments, and there can be no question but that some juggling of membership is required to keep the system going.

The cabinet also has other means at its disposal to ensure control of committees. The chairmen of committees are now elected by the com-mittee members, but these chairmen are choices agreeable to the cabinet. As one opposition Member remarked: "The chairmen are picked; they are chosen by the men in power, the executive. They know when they go in who is going to be chairman."[38] The influence of the government Whip has already been noted (page 195).

Some of the expectations regarding enhanced influence over the policy process as a result of the new committee system were based on observations of the committee system in the United States. Congres-sional committees are influential in the policy-making process, but this is in part due to the American system of government. The parliamentary system, which permits a government to be sustained in office only as long as it maintains a majority in the House of Commons, requires a heavy degree of party discipline and does not allow for the type of influence exerted by committees in the American Congress, and the cabinet retains control over policy making. In the Canadian system parliamentary committees may be expected to be influential in the policy process only when the cabinet has not taken a policy position. Policy positions already taken by the cabinet will not normally be discussed in committees on their merits *qua* policy, but rather in terms of their details. In the American system, with its separation of powers, Congress is expected to influence legislation, and to this end members of Congress are provided with large scale staff facilities and their congressional committees also have staff facilities. Members of the Canadian Parliament are provided only with secretarial service, and parliamentary committees themselves do not have research funds or staff available to them directly. Each committee has only one clerk, so that all research is done on a partisan basis, and this also affects the usefulness of the committee system. While it is true that the Trudeau government, in order to assist the opposition in dealing with the increased burden arising out of the committee system, has provided it with funds for research purposes, $350 000 in 1975 (the Liberal caucus receives $250 000 a year for the same purpose), this is a paltry sum in comparison with the manpower and resources available to the cabinet when it prepares its case. Under the circumstances the opposition is still at a great disadvantage insofar as successfully countering the arguments of the government is concerned. (In fact, it is not clear if these sums are being used for research purposes; it has been claimed that some of this money is being used to finance the cost of maintaining national offices and staff for the parties.)

The lack of research facilities for individual Members also poses a problem in that it is difficult for Members to adequately prepare themselves for committee meetings. The system itself tends to overwork Members; an analysis of the committee membership in October 1970 indicated that nine Members served simultaneously on five different committees, and one wonders how they could possibly be effective on all committees. Moreover the use of committees makes it very difficult for members of parties with a small representation in the House to take part effectively in committee proceedings; members of smaller parties must spread themselves very thinly in order to participate in the work of all committees.

Thus committees of the House of Commons have little influence on policy considerations and do not act as an effective check on the power of the cabinet. It may be that one reason why the system has not lived up to expectations is that the Prime Minister and the cabinet do not appreciate the difficulties of the opposition. In the case of the present cabinet (1975), the Prime Minister and almost all of his ministers have never served in opposition, and the three who have had experience in this sense served in opposition only briefly. This lack of experience of the Prime Minister and members of the cabinet may make it difficult for them to understand the difficulties and frustrations of backbenchers, and because of this they may have expected that various changes introduced over the years in the Commons committee system would be more acceptable and satisfactory than they in fact have turned out to be.

The argument that the House of Commons has been losing control over the executive and that the more vigorous use of parliamentary committees will restore some of this control simply does not hold true. In fact, Parliament has probably never controlled the executive. Parliament has rarely been able to assess and criticize government policy, and it has not controlled the cabinet, and when the President of the Treasury Board told the Commons Estimates Committee on February 25, 1969, that Parliament's power to control government spending was disappearing, he was describing a situation that had existed for many years. On this particular occasion the committee was studying supplementary estimates amounting to $122 million, including $105 million to go into the government's contingency fund to cover pay increases for civil servants. These pay increases were at that time the subject of negotiation and the Treasury Board, in preparing the supplementary estimates, had been deliberately confusing about the $105 million in order to avoid tipping its hand in advance of the salary negotiations. Mr. Drury told the committee that the loss of control was inevitable as government's role becomes more complex. "Parliament will have to pronounce itself on principle and leave the interpretation of the principles to the Government, subject to their auditing in the public accounts."[39] Mr. Drury then went on to say that Parliament's situation was similar to that of a shareholder in a private company, where the shareholder has had to abandon the idea that he can exercise managerial control.

> To put it in corporate terms, the shareholder of a large and complex corporation really had to abandon some years ago the notion that he can, at one stage removed, act as manager. He has to rely on enunciations of general principles and then decide, by detailed examination of the detailed accounts after the event, whether these have been satisfactorily carried out.[40]

It should be noted that these remarks did not cause any great alarm in the committee.

Committees, then, will be useful in permitting more informed criticism, but the cabinet will still remain in control of the House of Commons. Control over the cabinet depends more on public reaction to government plans than the House of Commons. When Mr. Drury reversed his position in the statement noted earlier and seemed to indicate that even the Auditor-General did not have the right to criticize policy and attempted to impose additional restrictions on the Auditor-General, the Opposition, supported by public opinion, managed to deter the government, but the revised committee system did not make this possible. The Opposition made use of other facilities always available to it — that is, debating time in the House of Commons and the question period.

It is clear then that the cabinet dominates the House of Commons and that this is inevitable under the parliamentary system of government. Provision of additional opportunities to criticize, evaluate and inform do not lessen this control, but they do ensure that the public is more informed about the legislative process and will be in a better position to judge at election time.

NOTES

[1]Canada, House of Commons, *Debates*. (February 17, 1970), p. 3694.

[2]*Ibid*. (February 12, 1923), p. 219.

[3]Patrick Nicholson, *Vision and Indecision*, p. 327.

[4]Quoted in James Eayrs, *Art of the Possible*, p. 115.

[5]Pierre Sevigny, *This Game of Politics*, p. 110.

[6]*Interview*, (August 18, 1969).

[7]Pauline Jewett, "The Reform of Parliament". *Journal of Canadian Studies*, Volume 1, No. 3 (1966), p. 14.

[8]*Interview*, (August 18, 1969).

[9]*Interview*, (July 17, 1969).

[10]Canada, House of Commons, *Debates*. (June 30, 1948), p. 6222.

[11]*Interview*, (October 1, 1971).

[12]*Interview*, (May 25, 1970).

[13]*Interview*, (August 2, 1972).

[14]*Interview*, (August 18, 1972).

[15]*Interview*, (August 5, 1972).

[16]Canada, House of Commons, *Debates*. (January 26, 1971), p. 2783.

[17]David Hoffman and Norman Ward, *Biculturalism and Bilingualism in the Canadian House of Commons*, p. 125.

[18]*Interview*, (August 18, 1972).

[19]Mr. Thatcher wrote as a guest columnist in "Gerald Waring Reporting", *St. Catharines Standard*, (September 27, 1955), p. 6.

[20]R.J. Jackson, *Rebels and Whips*. (London; Macmillan, 1968), p. 21.

[21]David Hoffman and Norman Ward, *Bilingualism and Biculturalism in the Canadian House of Commons*, p. 162-163.

[22]*Interview*, (October 1, 1971).

[23]*Interview*, (June 3, 1970).

[24]Robert MacGregor Dawson, *The Government of Canada*. (Toronto; University of Toronto Press, 1949), p. 358.

[25]Revised Statutes of Canada, 1970, Vol. IV, Chapter H-9, Sections 15-18, p. 3765.

[26]Canada, House of Commons, *Debates*. (February 24, 1970), p. 4035-4044.

[27]J.R. Mallory, "The Financial Administration of the House of Commons". *Canadian Journal of Economics and Political Science*, Vol. XXIII, No. 1 (February, 1957), p. 108.

[28]J.R. Mallory, *The Structure of Canadian Government*. (Toronto; Macmillan, 1971), p. 246.

[29]Canada, House of Commons, *Debates*. (March 25, 1913), p. 6313.

[30]*Ibid*. (June 4, 1956), p. 4659-60.

[31]J.W. Pickersgill and D.F. Forster, *The Mackenzie King Record*, Vol. II, p. 239 (Beauchesne was Clerk of the House of Commons and an authority on parliamentary procedure.)

[32]James Walker, "The Functions of the Whip in Canada", p. 260.

[33]Press release, (November 4, 1969).

[34]Canada, House of Commons, *Debates*. (Dec. 19, 1968), p. 4166.

[35]C.E.S. Franks, "The Dilemma of the Standing Committees of the Canadian House of Commons". *Canadian Journal of Political Science*, Volume IV, No. 4, (December, 1971) p. 470.

[36]Canada, House of Commons, *Debates*. (July 22, 1970), p. 2707.

[37]*Interview*, (July 17, 1969).

[38]Canada, House of Commons, *Debates*. (October 30, 1970), p. 761.

[39]Canada, House of Commons, Committee on Miscellaneous Estimates, *Minutes*, (February 25, 1969), p. 97.

[40]*Ibid*.

Chapter X

The Cabinet and the Party

The representation principle adhered to in cabinet construction has been duplicated quite substantially in party organization. The pattern has developed whereby cabinet ministers have responsibility and authority for political and organizational matters in their own regions, with the Prime Minister being the only truly national figure in the party and, as in the cabinet, exercising ultimate control.

In the early years following Confederation, political parties as known today did not exist in Canada. The parties were in fact loose coalitions of various groups, with each group having its own leader to whom the group members were loyal. It was the task of the cabinet, and especially the Prime Minister, to persuade the leaders to support government measures in Parliament. In addition to the various groups, there were many Members of Parliament who refused to commit themselves to any particular group in order to be in a position to support any government that would provide well for their constituents. As a result, the cabinet, in addition to assuming the responsibilities of lawmaking and administration, had to devote much time and energy to holding together a majority in the House of Commons, and this involved making generous use of the patronage available to the government, a task for which Macdonald was especially well suited.

As the parties coalesced over the years, the cabinet became the most powerful element of the governing party because of its control over patronage and also because of the fact that, while a national form of organization was slowly superimposed over the various groups and sectional factions, their leaders still represented these groups in the cabinet and dominated the party program and planning. The federal pattern in the cabinet tended to be duplicated in the party, and the ministers assumed responsibility for the party in their own areas. Members of the cabinet were important in the party because of their role as representatives of various groups. The function of the party itself was twofold — to recruit men into political roles on the federal level and to provide labels that enabled the voter to choose one candidate over another. Parties were not the integrating force they might have been because they were controlled on a regional basis and because they were active usually only during elections.

The Liberal Party

Laurier was very appreciative of the use of patronage as an aid in controlling the party. He appointed Tarte as Minister of Public Works and ". . . Tarte with the magic wand of the patronage and power of the public works department began to make over the party organization in the Province [of Quebec]."[1] While the ultimate control over patronage remained with the Prime Minister, the pattern developed that individual ministers assumed responsibility for the party in specific areas; the Prime Minister, being the only national figure, dominated the party at all levels. It is important to note, however, that the party was not controlled by the cabinet as a collectivety, but rather by individual ministers working under the direction and supervision of the Prime Minister; the cabinet as a body did not direct the affairs of the party. Each minister had a great deal of autonomy in his area, as reflected in a letter from Laurier to the Hon. C.S. Hyman, who was the minister responsible for the Liberal Party in Western Ontario: ". . . I have it [sic] an invariable practice never to interfere with the choice of candidates."[2]

King continued Laurier's practice. One minister from each province was made responsible for the national party organization in his province, and in the case of larger provinces the area was subdivided into districts, thus ". . . as Mackenzie King's senior minister from Western Ontario, Elliott had a special responsibility for the constituencies in that area."[3] When Mr. Power took over responsibility for the Quebec City area, he had to find ". . . funds to put the organization to work and to pay the wages of the employees. Then I had to find suitable candidates. The next and perhaps most important step was to find funds to place these candidates in the field. . . ."[4] In some instances one provincial leader would find himself with a surplus of funds, and this would be loaned out or transferred to another area in need of help. Power, for example, was able on one.occasion to borrow $25 000 of Saskatchewan Liberal money from Gardiner, the minister responsible for that area.[5]

The result of this technique was that there was no effective national organization of the party except at election time. Between elections Ministers dealt mainly with provincial party officials and the central office became important only at the time of a general election. This was a constant source of concern to King who was always conscious of the need for an active organization at the federal level. In Senator Norman Lambert, King found a person with considerable organization talent and under him the nucleus of a small national organization was formed. Lambert was appointed secretary of the National Liberal Federation and was quickly involved in one of its most important tasks, that of raising money for the party, for one of the causes of King's concern was the chronically woeful condition of party finances.

One of the methods used by the Liberals during this time to finance the party was to solicit contributions from companies which had received contracts from the federal government and here certain Cabinet ministers could be useful by providing information as to which companies were doing business with the government. At one time Lambert told the Toronto bagman to ask for donations amounting to ". . . one and a half to two per cent contributions to campaign funds on federal contracts in Ontario".[6] Some supporters gave more than one and a half per cent or two per cent; Lambert noted in his diary that one Toronto firm gave eight per cent. King also brought Vincent Massey into the National organization as President of the National Liberal Federation. Massey was anxious that he be appointed High Commissioner to London and he was told by Lambert that King ". . . expected him to attend to business (sic) end of things and in effect that was to be the price of London appointment."[7]

Lambert's functions were potentially a source of embarrassment to King and his cabinet and as a result they never really became deeply involved in the operations of the National Federation, fearing apparently that to know too much insofar as party finances etc. were concerned might cause them difficulty later on. This in turn caused resentment on the part of Federation officials and Lambert, himself politically ambitious, was especially annoyed. "I had felt and still feel that one's identity with political organization was regarded as a stigma and a barrier by the Prime Minister and his colleagues to any form of service."[8] Thus, in spite of the fact that the Liberals were elected in 1935 and 1940, Lambert bitterly noted that on election night in 1935 he ". . . did not hear from King at all. He (King) was at Laurier House for the returns."[9] It was the same in 1945.

The situation thus existed where the humdrum and more mundane aspects of party work were left to others, and the members of the cabinet concerned themselves with policy formation and patronage. Although party officials were consulted, their suggestions and opinions did not seem to be very significant. The task of organizing the party was as thankless as it was difficult. In 1940 King told Lambert on January 23 that he would announce an election on the 25th, giving Lambert very little time to prepare. Once the election was held, however, the role of party officials greatly diminished. One disgruntled official, Senator Peter Campbell, noted in 1940:

> One's experience since the election would suggest that everybody in the Government ceased to have a thought about party organization or those connected with it the moment it was over. . . . The government is now seeking for somebody to keep its federal party fences up. It wants somebody to do something for it; what arrangement is the government going to make and guarantee; that it will reciprocate in a more systematic form of cooperation than has been seen during the past year."[10]

During the King era some ministers played a more important role than others in party matters. The fact that each member had a certain responsibility in specific areas of the country tended to perpetuate divisions among the ministers. One writer has stated that after 1935 the Liberal party became ". . . a coalition of sovereign powers . . . Gardiner managed agricultural policy under almost exclusive jurisdiction, often disregarding the views of the Prime Minister and Cabinet,"[11] and King's diary in the closing years of his term of office indicates that Gardiner rarely even bothered to attend cabinet meetings. Nevertheless, recognizing his efficiency as a political organizer, King appointed Gardiner national organizer of the party in 1943. C.D. Howe was an important contact man for funds, both through his own efforts and also by way of supplying Lambert and others with lists of firms that had received contracts from his department. (Some of these lists may be found among Senator Lambert's papers.) Later King assigned one of his ministers, Brooke Claxton, to act as the link between himself and the party organization. But King was still not satisfied with the state of the federation and frequently called in those ministers most concerned with party organization to give them a blast on the poor state of the organization. King reflected that, "No Cabinet ever had a more indifferent lot of Ministers when it comes to matters of organization."[12] He overlooked the fact that one of the reasons for this was his own shabby treatment of Lambert. It is clear then that during this period cabinet members dominated the party, and the party's influence on policy was insignificant.

Under St. Laurent, the pattern begun under Laurier and King continued. Cabinet members continued to dominate the party in matters of policy, and this seemed to be acceptable to the rank and file, as evidenced by the fact that none of the resolutions passed by the 1948 convention implied any serious criticism of the cabinet's policies.

Under St. Laurent, Claxton remained the member of the cabinet primarily responsible for party affairs. Howe also remained important. Just as Howe was the "minister of everything" on the administrative side of government, so his interests were wide and varied in the political domain. As the senior minister from Ontario he was automatically in charge of party matters in that province, although he delegated regional responsibility to other ministers. Each minister was responsible for a group of constituencies, and their duties included ensuring that the best possible candidates were selected, that good relations were maintained with the press, and that they kept in touch with the grass-roots party workers in the constituencies. Thus ". . . Walter Harris (then Minister of Finance) was the minister responsible for southern Ontario. . . . He was the man through whom we in the regions, and our members of Parliament. . . communicated with Ottawa's hierarchy."[13] An election organization was called into being by a few senior party officials after the Prime

Minister decided on the date of an election. The party's funds were raised in the main by anonymous party men (bagmen) with considerable aid from various members of the cabinet, and these senior officials disbursed the funds, although regional party chiefs retained tight control over funds raised in their own areas.* The cabinet *per se* did not have close relations with the party but individual ministers did, subject always to the control and direction of the Prime Minister. Policy rarely, if ever, originated from the lower levels of the party, but came from the top. Aside from campaign periods, no one had any particular responsibility for the health of the party, and often there was great frustration among the rank and file. Public participation was not encouraged in any organized way except at election times, when each regional or special interest group leader took responsibility for persuading his own constituents on the basis of their own interests and prejudices to vote for the party.

Canadian parties have not been typical of parties in consociational democracies. In the Netherlands, for example, the parties are almost exclusively representatives of particular class and religious segments of the population and receive very little backing from other segments. The Liberal Party in Canada has not acted as the organized representative of any particular group but rather as an election machine. The party thus did not help to integrate Canadian society in that it has stressed particularism and regionalism rather than contributing to the development of a pan-Canadian political culture.

The cabinet itself has had no direct and formal relationship with the party, but individual ministers did. The party organization tended to strengthen the position of the Prime Minister greatly; politically it was an "umbrella name" for a group of ministers each responsible to the Prime Minister. The Prime Minister determined the organization of the party, gathering around him in the cabinet sectional leaders who were also committed to the maintenance of the federal political system. The party at the provincial level produced regional leaders of varying ideological background who could still come together as Liberals and function as cabinet ministers. ". . . There are ample historical cases, from Joseph Howe onwards of provincial politicians with no more attachment to the federal system than the mass of their constituents being transformed in Ottawa into Cabinet ministers intent on making the system work."[14]

It should be noted that World War II led to tremendous changes in the way the cabinet operated with regard to the party. Due to the exigencies of war the cabinet to a large extent ceased to be a body of regional representatives and concentrated on the politics of the country

---

*For a description of the Liberal Party's financial situation, see K.Z. Paltiel, *Political Party Financing in Canada*. (Scarborough; McGraw-Hill Ryerson, 1970), pp. 19-46.

as a whole. One former minister noted, "In the process many ministers lost the habit of politics and began to think more of themselves as administrators."[15] The result of all this was serious for the party, because the influence of civil servants increased as that of party officials waned and the party organization rusted and ran down. This condition persisted until the election of the Diefenbaker government, and it was the normal state of the affairs of the party for it to be run by a director appointed by the Prime Minister and responsible directly to him.

The defeat of the Liberal Party in 1957 led to some important changes in the party. More members of the rank and file became involved, mainly because, being out of power, it was necessary for the party to operate far differently than when it formed the government. There was little pressure to make decisions quickly, and party organization became more relevant. The experience influenced the party when it regained power. When the Liberal Party was returned to power, cabinet members once again assumed responsibility for ". . . campaign finances, for short term policy and for *most* long term policy, but there was some policy input from the party outside the Cabinet, a residue of the days in opposition."[16] The cabinet as a body, however, was not greatly involved in party activity.

> We often talked of setting aside a special Cabinet meeting to deal with political organization and with problems of a partisan nature. . . . It can come as no surprise that not once in those five years did the people who were supposed to be the leaders of the Liberal Party ever formally discuss its own affairs. Further we had very little contact with the national party organization and its officers itself.[17]

Even if members of the cabinet favoured such discussions, there was never time available for them. It was also discovered that the pressures in a minority government, combined with the normal pressures on the cabinet to make decisions, made it impossible to consult to any large extent with party members outside the cabinet. Improvisation became necessary for survival, and this precluded continual consultation with the grass roots.

There have been attempts recently to make the Liberal Party leadership (i.e., the cabinet) more responsive to the rank and file, to transform the party from a cadre party, little more than a framework dominated by the cabinet and oriented solely towards the winning of elections, towards a more popular type of party midway between Duverger's mass and branch types. The aims of the party, according to the former national president are, among others, to:

(a) involve as many people as possible to as great a depth as possible in the public affairs of the country
(b) to act as the major link between the people and the government.[18]

This involves taking away from cabinet members, as much as possible, the control of essentials, including policy, organization, and finance, and building a party organization not for election purposes alone, but one that will enable many more people to participate in dealing with problems of government.

Since Mr. Trudeau became leader, several changes have been made to make the party more influential. Head office facilities have been improved and the staff enlarged after consultations with a management consultant. A second step was to create a provincial advisory group for each province, consisting of a cabinet minister, a representative of caucus, and a representative of the provincial party organization. The "troika" is responsible for consultations and recommendations on all political and organizational matters concerning the province. The advisory group can make recommendations only, however, and apparently it is not intended that it replace existing channels of contact between Members of Parliament or party officials and members of cabinet.

There is also a National Advisory Group composed of a minister appointed by the Prime Minister, the chairman of the parliamentary caucus, the president and the national director of the National Liberal Federation, and the principal secretary to the Prime Minister. There is also a "political cabinet", which is the cabinet meeting, without civil servants being present, with the members of the National Advisory Group. The political cabinet usually met weekly.

Various other steps have been taken to ostensibly diminish the influence of the Prime Minister and his colleagues over the party. The president and treasurer of the National Liberal Federation are no longer the personal choice of the party leader but are elected by the party. Senator Richard Stanbury was elected president of the Liberal Party in 1968 during the national convention, prior to the election of Mr. Trudeau as leader. An important development took place in1975, when opposition arose within the Liberal Party to the election of Mr. Trudeau's personal choice, Senator Keith Davey, as president of the party. As a result of this opposition (which attracted considerable publicity), Senator Al Graham was acclaimed as president, even though the Prime Minister had not initially approved of his selection. This is one of the few concrete manifestations of successful mass pressure on the party leadership and may reflect increased confidence among party members arising from the changes noted above. It may also illustrate some of the difficulties mass participation causes leaders as they seek to maintain their control over the party.

The party has also established a standing committee on policy to ensure that the results of various policy conferences are communicated to the cabinet, and for a time after the 1968 election cabinet documents usually contained a reference to convention decisions, thus reminding cabinet members of the relationship between policy and official party decisions. There is a clause in the party constitution requiring the leader to be accountable to the party membership concerning policy decisions taken at conventions.

It remains to be argued if these arrangements have in actual fact limited the power of the cabinet and if the result has been that more people have been "plugged in" to the policy-making process. The answer seems to be that in fact very little has changed. The power of the Prime Minister over the party depends on his standing with the electorate, and it is unlikely that, while he is in power, he need take account of party suggestions that run counter to his own wishes. Often there is no time for the cabinet to consult with others before making a decision, and it is doubtful if rank-and-file party members have access to the information the cabinet has, so that their opinion on many matters is simply not valuable. The old system of having one minister direct party activity in one region still exists, with the larger regions having been subdivided into smaller ones, each under a particular minister. It is also important to note that the party has continued to play a very active role in staffing the office of the Prime Minister, which ensures that the Prime Minister's control and importance have not diminished. Regional desks help to ensure that the Prime Minister is constantly informed on political matters, but they also enable the Prime Minister to inform party members as to what he has in mind. Cabinet members still assume responsibility for election campaigns, as in the past. Hon. Robert Andras, Minister of Consumer and Corporate Affairs, was responsible for the Liberal campaign in English Canada in the October 1972 election, and Hon. Jean Marchand, Minister of Regional Economic Expansion, had the same role in Quebec.

In a letter to a delegate to the November 1970 Policy Conference of the Liberal Party, the Prime Minister dealt with the question of to what extent the government would be influenced by the decisions and recommendations made at the conference. Mr. Trudeau pointed out that ". . . difficulties can be encountered in attempting to carry out the will of the Policy Convention . . . for various reasons but whatever the government's position however, it should be communicated to the delegates and the constituency organizations in accordance with the principle of accountability. . . ." In other words, there is no commitment on the part of the cabinet to react positively to suggestions emanating from the party, although it would seem that many party members anticipated this would be the case.

The new system raises several serious problems. The first has to do with the government's providing information to enable rank-and-file party members to make intelligent decisions. So far this has not been done; cabinet decisions are still being made in secret and with political expediency in mind. The second problem is that of keeping the people in the party outside of government interested and stimulated so that they will want to participate in the decision-making process. If such people feel their advice is being ignored, they are not likely to give it, even when attempts are being made to stimulate their interest.

An even larger question is whether or not the Prime Minister and the cabinet really desire a great deal of participation by party members. The Prime Minister has made clear, as previously noted, that he expects only general guidance, not specific advice on policy matters.

> We are like the pilots of a supersonic airplane. By the time an airport comes into the pilot's field of vision, it is too late to begin the landing procedure. Such planes must be navigated by radar. A political party, in formulating policy can act as a society's radar.[19]

It is likely that the effort to involve party members in policy making is really a response to changes taking place in society whereby people are becoming less deferential to political elites and less apolitical. This means that the old concept of elite deference no longer applies in this light, and the actions of the Liberal Party may be seen as a response rather than a bold initiative.

It is interesting to note that among the various former cabinet ministers interviewed, almost all felt that cabinet domination of the party in terms of policy is inevitable under our system of government. Some felt that this had to be so because there simply was not time for the cabinet to consult the party; others felt that with the information available to it the cabinet had to take the lead in formulating policy, although in some instances it could consult the party. Some felt that it was impossible to construct a mechanism that would make effective consultation possible. Others felt that, given the large cabinet typical of Canada and assuming that ministers kept in contact with caucus and party officials, additional consultation was not necessary. It was also pointed out that in a minority government, when the government must at all times be extremely political and at the same time move very quickly, it is virtually impossible to carry on any large scale consultation with the party rank and file.

The consociational model stresses decision making by elites, which in the Canadian context has meant that control of the two major parties has rested almost exclusively in the hands of the parliamentary leadership, which has had the responsibility for creating policy. The transformation of the Liberal Party from a cadre form of party to a mass party implies mass participation in the policy-making process. This would require a drastic reorganization of the Liberal Party and a great change in attitude among party members. It would be necessary to greatly strengthen the linkages among local, provincial and federal bodies, and party members would have to identify first with the party rather than with their language, economic, or geographic groups. Given the strength of group loyalties in Canada, it is not likely that this will develop. Consequently,

> . . . the decline of 'elitism' in Canada and a growing popular acceptance of the Jacksonian myth of popular or participatory democracy may be detrimental to the maintenance of Canadian federalism if it leads to a situation in which the mass of the people are unwilling to accept the inter-elite accommodations made by their political leaders. If inter-elite accommodations must be popularly ratified they may be impossible to achieve.[20]

The attempt to develop mass parties may create even greater friction among the Canadian political subcultures as they come into more contact with one another. This may eventually lead to the fragmentation of the Canadian party system, for parties might well find it difficult to respond to diverse electoral needs and demands without creating great internal strife. The political apathy of Canadians in the past may have helped elite accommodations to be made, widespread public interest and a deepening of divisions in Canada may well force changes to be made in the party system with consequent effects on cabinet government in Canada. A multiparty system may thus be more appropriate to a divided society in which divisions appear to be becoming less susceptible to compromise.

The Progressive Conservative Party

The Progressive Conservative Party has in the past been organized much like the Liberal Party. Bennett was very much the master of the party while he was Prime Minister, possibly because he personally paid most of its expenses. Since he was master of both party and cabinet in an absolute sense, neither had much influence on the other.

Under Mr. Diefenbaker the Progressive Conservative Party was very much dominated by ministers rather than by the cabinet as a whole. The Prime Minister saw the national director of the party ". . . almost every day he was in Ottawa".[21] The Prime Minister adhered very strictly to the doctrine of cabinet secrecy and never "revealed to the Director anything discussed in Cabinet unless it had first been made public, even when it would have been to the advantage of the party to have had such information in advance."[22] For example, when it became necessary for the cabinet to agree to the devaluation of the Canadian dollar during the election campaign of 1962, the national director, who was chief party strategist and who was in daily contact with the Prime Minister, ". . . knew nothing about it until the decision was made public."[23] This event illustrates the difficulty a party will experience if it attempts to keep party members informed of the government's plans. It can happen that to consult the party meaningfully, the cabinet would be required to divulge information which, under the rules of cabinet secrecy, it cannot properly divulge. The result can be a very disillusioned party rank and file, for having been assured that they will be involved in the policy-making process, they will not realize their expectations because of the circumstances under which the cabinet must work and because of the great mass of expert information available to the cabinet. This is disappointing and frustrating to them.

Under Mr. Diefenbaker, the Progressive Conservative Party had a committee in each province that dealt with the regional minister on local matters. As a result, the party director had nothing to do with ministers on political matters. Like his Liberal counterpart, he would make suggestions regarding appointments, etc. but this advice was not necessarily accepted. He never met with the full cabinet, and the vast majority of his contacts were through the Prime Minister's Office.

The method of raising funds was very similar to that of the Liberal Party. The national director and the members of the cabinet had no idea as to the source of party funds, although one minister did say that while normally the party bagman did not attempt to see ministers or to make appointments for others, the minister assumed that ". . . if the bagman contacted a minister and said that a certain person wished to see the minister, the minister could draw his own conclusions."[24] Like the Liberal Party, the Progressive Conservative Party has relied on the business community for the bulk of its funds.

Unlike the Liberals, the Progressive Conservatives did not staff the office of the Prime Minister. The director felt that this was a mistake on the party's part in that the Prime Minister, having only three executive assistants, was greatly overworked.

Conclusion

The picture that emerges of the two parties is one of an organization that until very recently has been dormant and ineffective between elections, coming to life only at intervals to act as an election vehicle, under the direction of cabinet ministers. Control of the party has been exercised, not by the cabinet as a collectivity, but by individual ministers who draw their power from the groups which they represent. The dominance of the ministers is subject to the pre-eminent influence of the Prime Minister, who is at the apex of the party both within Parliament and outside, making him by far the most powerful man in the Canadian political system.

NOTES

[1]John W. Dafoe, *Laurier, A Study in Canadian Politics*. (Toronto; T. Allen, 1922), p. 107.

[2]Quoted in Neil McKenty, *Mitch Hepburn*. (Tonto; McClelland & Stewart, 1967), p. 7. (fn.)

[3]*Ibid*. p. 22.

[4]Norman Ward, ed., *A Party Politician*, pp. 127-128.

[5]*Ibid*.

[6]McKenna, *Mitch Hepburn*, p. 168.

[7]Queen's University, Archives, *Lambert Diaries*, (September 11, 1934).

[8]*Ibid*. (March 9, 1945).

[9]*Ibid*. (October 14, 1935).

[10]Peter Campbell, Memo to Senator Lambert, *Lambert Papers*, December 3, 1940.

[11]Bruce Hutchison, *The Incredible Canadian*, p. 214.

[12]Quoted in J.W. Pickersgill & D.F. Forster, *The Mackenzie King Record*, Vol. II, p. 280.

[13]Judy LaMarsh, *Memoirs of a Bird in a Gilded Cage*, p. 140.

[14]S.J.R. Noel, Political Parties and Elite Accommodation", p. 137.

[15]*Interview*, (August 24, 1971).

[16]*Interview*, (April 10, 1969).

[17]Judy LaMarsh, *Memoirs of a Bird in a Gilded Cage*, p. 140.

[18]Richard Stanbury, *The Liberal Party of Canada – An Interpretation*. Unpublished paper, p. 19.

[19]*Notes for Remarks by the Prime Minister at the Harrison Liberal Conference, Harrison Hot Springs, B.C., November 21, 1969*. Press release, Office of the Prime Minister, (November 21, 1969), p. 4.

[20]S.J.R. Noel, "Political Parties and Elite Accommodation", p. 139.

[21]*Interview*, (July 9, 1969).

[22]*Ibid*.

[23]*Ibid*.

[24]*Ibid*.

Chapter XI

The Cabinet and the Civil Service

There are two theories regarding the relationship between the cabinet and the civil service. One theory states that policy making is the sole prerogative of the cabinet and it is the responsibility of the civil service to administer policy once it has been determined. This theory is based to a large extent on explanations of government practice in Great Britain. One scholar has said that: "The traditional view of British Government was that all decisions on matters of policy were taken by the Cabinet or by individual ministers so that the civil service merely carried out instructions."[1] The second view is that our society has become increasingly subject to administrative control and the real initiative in policy formulation has tended to pass from the hands of politicians to those of civil servants. Each theory has an element of truth in it. The senior civil servant, in addition to his administrative duties, is involved in policy making, and the more senior his position the more time he spends on policy matters. ". . . In fact the deputy [minister] spends as much of his time on policy advising and devising as he does on implementation."[2] It is therefore incorrect to assume that the business of government is conducted on two distinct planes, policy and administration, with the cabinet or individual minister being responsible for the former and the civil service for the latter. It is equally erroneous to assume that the civil service exclusively dominates the policy-making process in Canadian government, for no matter how decisive the advice of the civil servant, the ultimate responsibility, and hence power, rests with the minister.

While the senior civil servant is involved in both administrative and policy matters, the converse is not quite true of members of the cabinet, as there has been a very strong tendency in Canada for the cabinet to leave responsibility for administration almost exclusively to civil servants, a tendency reinforced by the pattern of recruitment of cabinet ministers, which does not give priority to administrative ability.

The Policy Influence of the Civil Servant

It has already been noted that because the cabinet is the significant federal body in Canada, it has had to function much more as a collegial body than cabinets in other countries. As a result, although civil servants have had considerable influence on policy formulation at the departmental level — i.e., influence over their ministers individually — their influence has been somewhat reduced at full cabinet level. At this point their advice and recommendations have been subjected to the scrutiny of a large number of ministers. Sectional and group interests serve to limit the authority of ministers over policy even within their own departments, and ministers have a very strong voice in policies influencing their areas or groups. As one experienced public servant has noted: ". . . C.D. Howe, J.G. Gardiner and other monarchs of sovereign areas brooked little interference with what was theirs."[3] This practice, similar to that of senatorial courtesy in the American Senate, has tended to limit the policy influence of Canadian civil servants.

On general issues, however, the policy influence of the civil service has been quite significant; civil servants could influence a minister to favour a particular policy, and the minister could have his way in the cabinet simply because he was frequently the only one present who had all the facts on a particular issue. Countervailing influences, where they did exist, would not be as informed and consequently not as effective. One cabinet minister who served for a time in the public service has commented:

> We have tended in the past to rely on the public service to do all the choice-making, the internal trade-offs and to present the government with a ready made program . . . an option which would appear to somebody in the public service as the most attractive would be presented first to the government and then to the public and all the discarded options wouldn't be mentioned at all.[4]

The influence of the civil service over policy making is not necessarily harmful if it is sensitive to the particular needs and aspirations of various groups within the country, but this does not seem to have been the case in Canada. The civil service has not been a representative body, however; the principle of representation followed in cabinet building has not been followed with regard to the civil service, unlike the situation in the Netherlands, where the composition of the civil service is patterned after the relative strengths of the blocs among the general population. That this has not been the case in Canada may have been a disadvantage and a handicap in maintaining the unity of the country. This is not to suggest that a strict rule of proportionality in the civil service is desirable, but dominance by one particular group is likely to have a dysfunctional effect on the stability of the state, in that the civil service may not be sufficiently sensitive and responsive to group or sectional needs. It has also been argued that if members of various groups, and especially minority groups, are given an opportunity to serve as full partners in the administration of the country, they are more likely to develop a sense of commitment to the country. In fact one of the major groups, the French-speaking group, has not had this opportunity. This was vividly illustrated in a study prepared for the Royal Commission on Bilingualism and Biculturalism, which clearly shows that few French Canadians have occupied influential positions in the Canadian civil service (see Table 11-I).

TABLE 11-I

**Proportion of Francophones in the Federal Public Service
by Salary Grouping (1965)[5]**

Annual Salary	Percentage of French Canadians in Salary Group
Below $6 000	23.1
$ 6 000 — $ 7 999	16.4
$ 8 000 — $ 9 999	15.0
$10 000 — $11 999	12.8
$12 000 — $13 999	9.1
$14 000 — $15 999	9.7
$16 000 — $17 999	9.0
$18 000 — $19 999	5.0
$20 000 and above	16.5

In the early years appointments to the civil service were made on the recommendation of politicians, so that most appointments went to friends of the party in power. This tended to create a cycle of appointments and dismissals as parties succeeded one another in office. Over the years various efforts were made to root out patronage in the civil service, but it was not until 1918 that almost the entire civil service, with some exceptions, was placed under a politically neutral Civil Service Commission, which was given the power to make virtually all appointments based on open competitive tests administered by the commission itself. While patronage has not been entirely eliminated, the civil service is fairly well protected from political influences and pressure, and patronage is no longer a major factor in appointments to or promotions in the federal public service. The abolition of patronage relieved ministers of one of their most time-consuming activities and permitted more time for other matters.

The existence of patronage had insured that the civil service was favourable to the government of the day. It also stimulated inefficiency and nepotism, and its abolition has been regarded as a positive step. While the abolition of patronage undoubtedly increased the efficiency of the civil service, it may also have had undesirable side effects in terms of a consociational democracy, in that with patronage it was possible for members of the cabinet to appoint people drawn from their particular areas or groups to the civil service. In one sense, then, the merit system has had dysfunctional effects on the Canadian federal system, especially since merit and the ability to speak English seemed to be equated, resulting in a low level of participation by French Canadians in the federal civil service. In an attempt to correct this imbalance, in recent years merit and the ability to be bilingual seem to have been stressed, which has the effect of limiting participation by citizens from parts of Canada where French is not emphasized in the educational system. The element of proportionality in the civil service, which appears to be typical of other consociational democracies, is thus lacking in Canada. It can be argued that as government increasingly affects the lives of citizens, proportionality becomes more important. But proportionality can lead to inefficiency, so that dissatisfaction for one reason may be replaced with frustration as the result of another. This is the dilemma of the Canadian federation and one that probably cannot be resolved satisfactorily.

The Responsibility of Ministers and Civil Servants

In theory a cabinet minister is responsible to Parliament for everything done in his department, and departmental officials are in turn responsible to the minister. The representation principle and the growth of governmental responsibilities have altered this theory considerably in the case of the Canadian cabinet.

One of the effects of the representation principle in Canada is a tendency to resort to Orders-in-Council rather than to ministerial directives for executive action. Thus it is often difficult to hold a particular minister responsible in cases of alleged maladministration. Consequently, it is even more difficult for Members of Parliament to single out officials for criticism.

It has been noted that one of the effects of the representation principle was a tendency to have a larger number of departments than the business of government actually required. However, as the responsibilities of government grew, there were times when the creation of a large number of departments would have created problems in preserving sectional and group balance. Consequently, extra tasks were assigned to existing departments rather than creating new ones. Immigration, for example, has at times been the responsibility of the Departments of Agriculture, Interior, and Mines before becoming a separate department. Thus some departments have become responsible for the administration of a conglomeration of responsibilities that bear little relationship to one another. This increases the problems of effective co-ordination and also helps to increase the immunity of cabinet members and the civil service from effective criticism. An exasperated Member of Parliament once complained:

> We now have four ministers dealing with problems in respect to the wheat board. . . . The Minister of Industry, Trade and Commerce is still involved with problems of wheat sales. The new Minister without portfolio is charged with responsibility for the Wheat Board. We also have the . . . Minister of Transport . . . who is interested in moving grain. The Minister of Agriculture would naturally be interested in the welfare of the agriculture industry.[6]

The growth in governmental responsibilities has also tended to increase the immunity of the civil service from criticism. The doctrine of ministerial responsibility, which still exists in theory, has actually added to the power and invulnerability of the civil service simply because the increase in governmental responsibilities has become so great that no minister could possibly be aware of everything done in his name by the officials of his department. Although at times ministers appear to be immune from criticism, as noted above, at other times they must take responsibility for acts of civil servants who remain untouched. Thus in 1952 the Minister of Agriculture was severely criticised for administrative acts in connection with an outbreak of hoof and mouth disease in Canada when he could not have been aware of the early errors made by his officials in connection with the situation. In 1969 the Minister of National Defence was criticised when expenditures on a hydrofoil ship exceeded original estimates by 51 million dollars and the cost of refitting the aircraft carrier *Bonaventure* turned out to be 13 million more than had been estimated. While some civil servants were transferred into other positions, the minister bore the brunt of the criticism and had to take full responsibility. In 1972 the Minister of Manpower and Immigration complained that many of his officials were not enforcing immigration regulations properly but there is no evidence that such officials were disciplined, and the minister continued to receive criticism in the press and in the House of Commons. The impossibility of supervising the activities of civil servants has led to the situation where ministers find themselves being held responsible for matters over which they have no control. However, even though the doctrine that ministers are responsible for policy and civil servants only for executing it is no longer valid, the distinction in function is useful in that only on the basis of this doctrine can Members of Parliament question a minister and hold him responsible for the actions of civil servants.

The Prime Minister and the Civil Service

Another result of the principle of representation is to enhance greatly the role of the Prime Minister. He is the only minister with a truly national constituency, and his ministers inevitably depend on him for their own political survival. Since both cabinet ministers and deputy ministers are appointed by the Prime Minister, it is likely that his will prevails in cases of conflict over issues of policy formation or execution. Although the deputy minister is the personal appointee of the Prime Minister (and Prime Ministers have jealously guarded this prerogative), in the event of conflict with a minister ". . . the Prime Minister will likely back the Minister rather than the deputy since deputy ministers are easier to replace than ministers."[7]

Although the civil service is now politically neutral, there are still certain appointments that can be made by the Prime Minister and the cabinet. There are certain appointments made via Order-in-Council, some of which are made by the Prime Minister alone, others after cabinet consultation and approval. In addition each minister is permitted to appoint a personal staff to assist him in his duties.

Order-in-Council Appointments

In the case of Order-in-Council appointments to the civil service that are the prerogative of the Prime Minister, two lists of prospects are prepared. One list is prepared in the Privy Council Office and consists of names of persons already in the civil service who are deemed qualified. The second list is prepared by a special section in the Prime Minister's Office which advises him and the cabinet on appointments. This second list consists of names of qualified people from outside the public service. These names are obtained in one or two ways:

(1) they are suggested by outside individuals or groups; for example, the Canadian Medical Association might suggest an individual for the position of Assistant Deputy Minister of Health;

(2) the individuals themselves make it known that they are interested in a government position.

The section in the Prime Minister's Office prepares background information on the people on its list, as does the Privy Council Office for its list, and the names are considered by the Prime Minister, the Clerk of the Privy Council, and the Principal Secretary to the Prime Minister. In the process no attempt is made to establish a regional or group balance, except that an attempt is being made to appoint as many qualified French Canadians as possible. Outside pressure groups may be consulted but there is no regular procedure for doing so. About 25 per cent of these appointments have been awarded to persons outside the public service. "The experience has been that those appointed to operating departments have done well, those appointed to coordinating departments have performed badly because they are not familiar with the system."[8]

The rotation of senior officials such as deputy ministers is decided upon by the Prime Minister, the Clerk of the Privy Council, and the

Principal Secretary to the Prime Minister, based on information supplied by the Privy Council Office. The evaluation of an official's performance is based on:

(a) his performance in cabinet committee meetings;
(b) his performance during personal contacts with the Prime Minister and other officials;
(c) the opinion of his minister;
(d) the opinion of other senior civil servants.

For Order-in-Council appointments to positions outside the civil service, such as membership on various government boards and commissions, judicial positions, lieutenant governorships, and others, a list is prepared each month of those positions to be filled during the next sixty days, and this list is circulated to all members of the cabinet. If the appointment is the prerogative of the Prime Minister, he will consult with the ministers concerned, receive suggestions, and then make the decision. Thus, for example, if a Lieutenant Governor is to be appointed for British Columbia, the Prime Minister will consult with the ministers from that province and provincial party officials before making his decision.

When appointments are to be recommended to the cabinet by a particular minister, that minister will advise the other ministers of the qualifications necessary for the position; since one of the qualifications usually is a regional one, only a few ministers are involved in the actual appointment. Thus if a vacancy arose on the board of Air Canada, for example, one of the requirements of the position would be that the prospective board member come from a particular area. If this area was Ontario, only the Ontario ministers would be expected to submit names to the Minister of Transport, who must make a recommendation to the cabinet. Unless there are strenuous objections to his nominee in the cabinet, his recommendation is accepted as a matter of course. The role of the Liberal backbencher is negligible in this process, and such appointments are almost a monopoly of members of the cabinet. One backbencher commented, "We can make suggestions if we hear of the vacancy but they don't seem to count for much and we are not asked for recommendations."[9]

The Minister's Office Staff

Prior to the abolition of patronage in the civil service, it was possible for ministers to surround themselves with close associates who could assist them with their political responsibilities and provide advice independent of the influence of permanent civil servants. Abuses led gradually to the creation of a non-political Public Service Commission, which limited the ability of ministers to appoint people to the civil service. For many years a minister was permitted to hire from outside the civil service only a private secretary and a limited number of clerical employees; any other individuals in his office who were not members of the civil service had to be paid from non-public funds.

In 1950 ministers were permitted to employ a total of eight persons from outside the civil service — an executive assistant and seven clerical employees, including a private secretary. Various other changes were made to increase the number who could be employed in this way, and in 1962 the Civil Service Act provided that all persons in a minister's office were exempt from the Civil Service Act and there was to be no limit as to the number of people a minister could employ, except that the cabinet had to approve the appointment of persons other than the executive assistant and the minister's private secretary. Normally this would be a formality, although it is possible that the cabinet would question an inordinate number of appointees. As a result, each minister now has his own personal office staff, appointed by him and paid out of public funds. Such a staff can insulate him from his department and at the same time provide him with policy advice independent of the civil service. Consequently, as of November 25, 1970, a total of 224 persons were on the staffs of federal cabinet ministers (excluding the Prime Minister's Office), and only 112 of these were appointed by the Public Service Commission.[10] Those appointed by the Public Service Commission were mostly clerical employees. It may be assumed that the most important persons in the minister's office are not civil servants, are not politically neutral, but are appointed directly by the minister, are personally and politically congenial to him, and their tenure of office depends on that of the minister. It should be noted, however, that Section 71 (31) of the Civil Service Act of 1962 provides that:

> A person who, for at least three years, has held the position of Executive Assistant to a Minister or the position of Private Secretary to a Minister is entitled to be appointed to a position in the civil service for which he is qualified, not being lower than the position of head clerk.

The original idea behind the establishment of the positions of executive and special assistant (the position of executive assistant is senior to that of a special assistant in terms of both salary and responsibility) seems to have been to provide the minister with a source of political, rather than administrative, assistance. It would seem, however, that quite frequently the duties and responsibilities of these people have exceeded the political boundaries originally established, and executive assistants have become involved in administrative duties and in policy planning.

The position of the assistant (executive or special) depends on his minister. Among their varied duties assistants have been known to ". . .

parcel out patronage, mend political fences and even make the occasional political speech. . . . They have been known to run errands for their ministers, visit the liquor stores, carry luggage, ghost write speeches, answer mail and issue press statements."[11] A more precise description of the duties of a special assistant is provided by the Dorion Commission. Discussing the duties of one special assistant, the Report noted:

> His work consisted of handling relations between the Minister and the departmental staff, seeing for instance that a file reached the Minister on time, together with a memo summarizing the contents of the said file for the Minister's information. He had also been asked to handle the Minister's correspondence, to read it, and distribute it to the different offices within the Department. Quite frequently he drafted acknowledgments of receipts of letters. He added that all files going to the Minister were handed to him beforehand, so that he could check and see that they were complete and in order.[12]

There is no doubt that the creation of these positions has provided some important advantages for ministers. Often a minister will select as an assistant a person who complements his own personality, who has strength where the minister has weakness; for example, a shy minister may employ an expert in public relations. The assistant can provide the minister with new ideas and can also serve as a reliable sounding board for the minister's own ideas, ideas a minister might be reluctant to discuss with his senior officials. The assistant can also help manage the minister's office, organize the flow of work, and maintain a balance between political and administrative chores. He may also assume personal responsibility for looking after the minister's own constituency, keeping him in touch with local party and community leaders, etc. The trend seems to be now, however, for many ministers to maintain offices in their own constituencies; in 1970 it was reported that "Thirteen Cabinet ministers maintain offices in their constituencies at an annual cost to the public treasury of up to $101,535."[13] Since, as a result of the representation principle, ministers have certain responsibilities connected with their areas or groups, the assistant can provide liaison with other departments through the assistants of other ministers and thus keep the minister regularly informed of situations relevant to his area or group.

One former executive assistant has commented, however, that while the performance of all these functions may be useful to a minister, none help ". . . the minister with his most difficult task, understanding and controlling the Civil Service. . . ."[14] It is argued that a minister can easily become the prisoner of his departmental officials and that he must have alternative sources of advice. There seems to be a tendency among many assistants to feel that one of their chief tasks is to exercise a surveillance role over the civil servants in the department on behalf of the minister. Not suprisingly, civil servants often resent this role, possibly because of the tactics used by the assistants, who often antagonize civil servants and create friction. Thus, while the position of executive assistant can be a great help to the senior civil servant in relieving him of many quasi-political responsibilities, it can also create problems for him, especially when an executive assistant insists on being the sole channel of communication between the minister and departmental civil servants or when he bypasses normal departmental channels to achieve results. Civil servants have tended to resist intrusion into what they consider their domain by assistants who are prone to believe that unless they ". . . are used as an active instrument for the surveillance of departmental activity few ministers will be in effective control of their departments."[15]

It is probably true that the civil service can become the master of the minister and that this should be prevented. (Mr. Diefenbaker has suggested that one of the problems he encountered when he first took office was that civil servants exercised undue influence over new ministers.) The problems that arise between assistants to the minister and the civil servants seem to frequently be the result of the way in which assistants deal with bureaucrats. Often the people who become executive assistants are young, inexperienced, impatient, and brash. They do not have the sense of professionalism and the sense of duty that often characterize civil servants. Too often their attitudes, rather than their objectives, are the cause of friction.

There is probably also resentment in the civil service because of the special privileges accorded to assistants who can use a minister's office as a means of entry into the higher levels of the civil service. They are paid at a higher rate than many experienced civil servants and are guaranteed after three years a position in the civil service at a salary level most civil servants take many more years to reach, and no doubt this encourages ill will.

It may well be that the friction that has been generated between executive assistants and civil servants has been the result of particular political conditions. The first loyalty of the executive assistant is to his minister. In the post-St. Laurent period, when the office of executive assistant became quite visible, there existed a difficult situation; where a new party was in power, ministers were especially anxious to make a mark and were unaccustomed to dealing with the civil service. Toward the latter part of the Pearson era, the Liberal Party leadership was at stake, and executive assistants fought hard to advance the interests of their ministers. Now that the political situation is less exciting, executive assistants appear to be more involved in relieving the minister of many administrative burdens and performing less dramatic, newsworthy duties than was the case prior to 1968.

The Effect of War on Civil Service-Cabinet Relations

Prior to World War II the limited functions of government and the consequent small size of the civil service made it possible for ministers to closely supervise the work of their departments and still determine policy as a group. Moreover, the large number of ministers in the cabinet resulting from the representation principle assured that no particular minister (with the possible exception of the Prime Minister) was overworked. The advent of World War II, however, completely changed the cabinet's method of operation and affected its relationship with the civil service. The enormous number of decisions that had to be taken necessitated much more independence for the civil service. The volume of business conducted is illustrated by the fact that in the period 1939-1945 over 60 000 Orders-in-Council and over 60 000 Treasury Minutes had been passed.[16] This average of over 10 000 per year can be compared with the number for 1968, 2352 and 1230 respectively.[17]

Although the influence of Parliament over policy making had never been supreme, the emergency conditions of wartime hastened a shift of power into the hands of the executive — both cabinet and civil service. It should be noted that during World War II the War Measures Act was in effect, which enabled the cabinet to govern without recourse to Parliament. "The public began to look to the Prime Minister and the members of the Cabinet, they — and they alone came to be regarded as responsible for everything concerned with the war. This increased the prestige of the Cabinet and Government enormously and correspondingly decreased that of Parliament."[18] During this period cabinet ministers could not possibly supervise the government carefully, and much power was, of necessity, delegated to civil servants, the senior ones becoming almost a second cabinet. Thus, during this period, many policy decisions were determined largely by members of the civil service. One of the mechanisms utilized during this period was interdepartmental committees made up of senior bureaucrats. These committees enabled senior civil servants to become well acquainted with one another, providing them with a sense of solidarity, a common point of view and a unique knowledge about the major problems of government. Thus there developed considerable cohesiveness and a common orientation to problems among the various bureaucrats, which tended to increase their influence on policy.

Post-War Developments

At the conclusion of the war, civil servants in policy making continued to be deeply involved in policy making. The problems of post-war reconstruction and the continuing evolution of the welfare state imposed a heavy burden on the cabinet and prevented a complete return to pre-war practices. Moreover, much of the planning for the post-war period was done, on the instructions of the government, by civil servants, who thus acquired a great store of technical knowledge. This knowledge was indispensable to the cabinet and it came to rely more and more on the civil service. The fact that the cabinet had a virtual monopoly on the technical knowledge and ability of the civil servants had the effect of making the cabinet more dependent on them and consequently increased the influence of the civil service. The civil service thus became a very important source of policy input.

A second factor tending to enhance the power of the civil service was the long tenure in power of the Liberal Party. A very close relationship grew up between ministers and senior civil servants, since they served together over a long period of time. Furthermore, the party's long tenure meant that ministers began to think less in regional and group terms and almost exclusively in national terms. In this they were encouraged by civil servants, who tended to spend most of their working lives in Ottawa and hence had little inclination to think in other than national terms. Senior civil servants came to share the same outlook; as a consequence civil servants became increasingly involved in matters formerly left to the politicians, and the distinction between the civil service and the Liberal Party became blurred.

It is possible that this development had an adverse effect on the Liberal Party. Its lengthy term in office brought about a situation in which group and sectional influence was to a large extent neutralized. Policy making was left more and more to the civil servants, reaching its zenith under Mr. St. Laurent, when it was alleged that the cabinet tended to take little initiative in policy matters, leaving the civil servants to take the lead. This *national* type of thinking may well have contributed to the defeat of the Liberals in 1957.

Under Mr. Diefenbaker, who tended to distrust the civil service, the pendulum began to swing back the other way. In his period the cabinet did assume more control over the policy-making process, and the influence of the civil service was reduced. Opinions varied as to whether or not Mr. Diefenbaker's distrust was merited. Shortly after taking office Hon. Howard Green remarked that ". . . we have had the finest assistance from the members of the Canadian civil service."[19] Another former minister noted, however, "Almost all officials were co-operative, indeed many were glad that the change in government had taken place. But there were enough men in certain important departments and especially the department of Finance, to make Mr. Diefenbaker very nervous about the influence they might exert."[20] Mr. Diefenbaker noted:

> When we first came to office I appointed several ministers to departments who had been very critical of their departments' policies when we were in Opposition. I found that in several cases after only a brief time in the department these same ministers ceased to be critical and argued against making any changes, changes which we had promised to make during the election campaign. These ministers were completely turned around by the departmental officials and were now supporters of the same policies they had criticized earlier. The only way to get around this was to make policy in the Cabinet and force the officials to carry them out, but when I insisted on this I was accused of excessively interfering.[21]

One minister, General George Pearkes, V.C., the Minister of Defence, held a press conference shortly after taking office. He was asked what changes he planned to make in Canadian defence policy and he said none. When he was reminded that he had been a strong critic of Canadian defence policy when in opposition and that as a result it had been anticipated he would be making changes, he replied, "I have learned more about the defence situation in the last eight days than I had been able to learn in the preceding twelve years. I now see that some of my criticisms were ill founded."[22]

There was another reason for Mr. Diefenbaker's distrust of the civil service. Under Mr. King and Mr. St. Laurent the dividing line between the Liberal cabinet and the civil service had become blurred and several senior civil servants, such as Mr. Pearson and Mr. Pickersgill, had passed from the bureaucracy directly into the cabinet. Inevitably such moves encouraged the opposition to distrust the civil service, and this was evident when the Progressive Conservatives came to power in 1957.

The return of the Liberals to office under Mr. Pearson did not restore the civil service to its earlier pre-eminence. While the Pearson government contained several ministers who had been civil servants at one time, such as Mr. Sharp and Mr. Drury, its being a minority government tended to prevent a return to the type of situation existing under Mr. St. Laurent. Thus the influence of the politician over policy continued. The cabinet was no longer always in control of the House of Commons and was continually in danger of defeat. The House was aware of this, and members tended to display considerable determination in respect to influencing policy.

The system of decision making instituted by Mr. Trudeau has greatly changed the situation. The system makes it more difficult for a minister and his officials to force a policy through, because other ministers are now much more informed on matters outside their own departments. The Privy Council Office can submit policy proposals on its own or submit proposals contrary to those coming from departments. Many policy proposals go to ministers for study well in advance of a discussion, and thus ministers have time to prepare arguments and questions.

The influence of departmental officials as opposed to other officials would seem to vary with the minister involved and with the department. One parliamentary secretary who has served in several departments since the Trudeau government took office commented:

> A strong minister will resist a great deal of influence or pressure from the Privy Council Office and they will usually leave him alone. There are certain departments, such as Finance, which require a certain amount of expertise not normally found in the P.C.O. and these departments are not influenced much by the P.C.O. or by other ministers. There are other departments such as Indian Affairs and National Health and Welfare which are responsible for matters on which everyone has an opinion and these departments do get a great deal of flack from the P.C.O., the P.M.O. and other ministers.[23]

Thus departmental proposals regarding the legalization of marijuana and the new Unemployment Insurance Act were fought vigorously in the cabinet.

The net result has been not so much a reduction of the influence of the civil service in policy making as a shift in influence from departmental officials to officials in the Privy Council Office. The role of the departmental official will now be restricted, to a large extent, to:
(a) assisting in the preparation and development of policy proposals;
(b) advising ministers in cabinet committee meetings (thereby eliminating many interdepartmental committees utilized since 1939);
(c) implementing cabinet or cabinet committee decisions.
It can be seen that this role more closely approximates the traditional view of the civil service.

These changes have evoked considerable resistance and resentment among certain ministers and civil servants. The changes have required ministers to some extent to give up some authority within their own departments in order to facilitate better co-ordination. Many departmental civil servants are resentful of the power in the Privy Council Office and the Prime Minister's Office. They frequently dislike the fact that other civil servants have a voice in determining policies for which they have responsibility. One senior departmental official stated: "It is folly for me to quarrel with the people in the Privy Council Office because they have so much influence with the Cabinet committees, because they can delay policy and because I have to live with them."[24] An official in the Privy Council responded to this by saying, "There is no question but that people in the P.C.O. have tremendous influence because they are close to the policy makers and know everything that is going on. Consequently, other civil servants fear us and this is bad, what we need is respect, not fear."[25] Apparently it is hoped, as the process becomes better known, and as civil servants acquire experience in the Privy Council Office before going on to other departmental positions, that this fear will disappear. Thus tours of duty in the P.C.O. are deliberately kept short, so that the time spent there will be seen as part of a program of career development. If the situation develops whereby there are in the departments a large number of officials who have had an overview of policy planning while serving in the Privy Council Office, more cohesion may develop among civil servants, with a greater appreciation for the virtues of centralization and with more knowledge as to how to get around obstacles raised by the Privy Council Office.

Since Confederation the cabinet and the civil service of Canada have worked well together. The cabinet has relied heavily on the civil service for advice and information on policy matters but has, in the main, made the final decisions itself. The special circumstances of World War II necessitated the devolution of additional responsibilities upon the civil service and set a pattern that was difficult to dissolve in the post-war period. If it can be concluded that during this latter period the civil service exerted undue influence, the cabinet, rather than the civil service, was responsible for this situation. Although in recent years there has been a reduction in the influence of the civil service on policy making, this change has not resulted from the provision of poor advice or undesirable policies by the civil service; rather it has resulted from the government's desire to admit other groups to the decision-making process and to return the prime role in policy making to the political executive. In spite of these changes, however, the number and complexity of the demands placed on government today ensures that the civil service will continue to have a great deal of influence on policy making.

NOTES

[1]John P. MacKintosh, The British Cabinet. (Toronto; University of Toronto Press, 1962) p. 453.

[2]A.W. Johnson, "The Role of the Deputy Minister". Canadian Public Administration, Vol. 4, No. 4 (December, 1961), p. 363.

[3]Gordon Robertson, "The Changing Role of the Privy Council Office", p. 498.

[4]Hon. C.M. Drury, quoted by Peter Desbarats, "Bud Drury — A Uniquely Canadian Type". Halifax Chronicle-Herald, (May 23, 1972), p. 7.

[5]C. Beattie, J. Desy, and S. Longstaff, "Bureaucratic Careers: Anglophones and Francophones in the Canadian Public Service". Internal Report for the Royal Commission on Bilingualism and Biculturalism, p. 211, quoted in Van Loon and Whittington, The Canadian Political System. (Toronto; McGraw-Hill, 1971), p. 357.

[6]Canada, House of Commons, Debates. (October 29, 1969), p. 254.

[7]Interview, (January 7, 1971).

[8]Interview, (June 29, 1972).

[9]*Interview*, (June 27, 1972).

[10]Canada, House of Commons, *Debates*. (May 31, 1971), p. 6199 (starred question 520).

[11]Peter Dempson, *Assignment Ottawa*, p. 40.

[12]*Report of the Commissioner*, the Hon. Frederic Dorion, Chief Justice of the Superior Court for the Province of Quebec (Special Public Inquiry 1964, P.C. 1964-1819) (Ottawa; Queen's Printer, June 1965), pp. 81-82.

[13]Canada, House of Commons, *Debates*, (April 13, 1970), p. 5758.

[14]John Roberts, "The Executive Assistant" *Globe and Mail*, (August 8, 1969), p. 6.

[15]*Ibid*.

[16]Canada, House of Commons, *Debates*. (October 31, 1945), p. 1681.

[17]*Ibid*. (November 19, 1969) p. 985.

[18]C.G. Power, "Career Politicians: The Changing Role of the M.P." *Queen's Quarterly*, Vol. LXIII, No. 4 (Winter, 1956), pp. 488-489.

[19]Canada, House of Commons, *Debates*. (November 15, 1957), p. 1211.

[20]*Interview*, (July 28, 1969).

[21]*Interview*.

[22]Quoted in Blair Fraser, *The Search for Identity*. (Toronto; Doubleday, 1967) p. 172.

[23]*Interview*, (June 27, 1972).

[24]*Interview*, (September 8, 1971).

[25]*Interview*, (January 7, 1972).

Chapter XII

Conclusion

This study has been an attempt to describe the Canadian cabinet as the supreme decision-making body in Canadian government and to demonstrate that as such it fulfils four distinct roles. In the first place, it is not only the vital connecting link between the executive and legislative parts of the Canadian federal government; it dominates Parliament. Under normal circumstances Parliament can only criticize and scrutinize the cabinet rather than control it. In the second place, the cabinet is at the apex of the party system in Canada, determining the conditions of the party struggle. Third, as the highest organ of administration, it assumes responsibility for the supervision of its own policies. Finally, the cabinet acts as a mechanism of accommodation, serving as the chief vehicle for group and regional representation at the federal level, making possible sufficient integration to keep the federal system operating but without impairing the diversity and regionalism the Canadian people seem to desire.

The study has also attempted to demonstrate the formidable power of the Prime Minister over the cabinet and to show that the primacy of the Prime Minister in the Canadian political system is not a recent development; the Prime Minister of Canada has been far more than first among equals almost continuously since 1867.

There are, however, two major checks on the Prime Minister — the representation principle and the electorate. The representation principle is a distinctive feature of the Canadian cabinet and clearly distinguishes it from its counterpart in Great Britain. The principle imposes limitations on the Prime Minister's ability to appoint and dismiss ministers because it requires that he constantly avoid offending one bloc or segment of the Canadian community and thus may require him to take in the cabinet people who are objectionable to him or who are his personal enemies. This characteristic is in distinct contrast to the situation in the United Kingdom, where one authority has noted that ". . . there is not a single case in this century of a man whom the Prime Minister wishes to exclude from office forcing his way in. . . ."[1] In addition, because of their regional or group base, Canadian cabinet ministers are not as much at the mercy of the Prime Minister as is the case in Great Britain. It would no doubt be impossible in Canada for a Prime Minister to dismiss a large number of ministers as Mr. Macmillan was able to do in 1962.

In spite of these limitations, however, prime ministers rarely lose their positions as the result of difficulties with the cabinet. The prime ministerial careers of Mackenzie, Tupper, Laurier, Meighen, Bennett, St. Laurent, and Diefenbaker were all terminated by the electorate. Abbott, Borden, King, and Pearson all retired voluntarily, and Macdonald and Thompson died in office. The House of Commons dismissed Macdonald (in effect) in 1873 and Bowell was replaced in 1896, mainly as the result of discontent in the cabinet, but these are the only two examples in 106 years of prime ministers being successfully challenged other than by the electorate, although it could be argued that the Governor General forced King out of office in 1926. It is true that prime ministers have had difficulty with the cabinet, but aside from Bowell none were removed from office for that reason.

The study has also discussed the innovations made in the Canadian cabinet by Mr. Trudeau and has shown that these are not as radical as some critics have suggested, but rather that they have evolved from innovations made over the years and especially during Prime Minister Pearson's term of office.

Proposals for Reform

The various innovations that have been made over the years have had as one of their chief objectives improving the efficiency of the cabinet. There can be no question but that the cabinet is far too large to be efficient in decision making or in supervising administration. Two authorities have commented on this. Former Prime Minister Diefenbaker has stated:

> . . . today the Cabinet is too large for the effective carrying out of the business of the nation. . . . I think one of the major reforms which must be brought about is to ensure a reduction in the number of ministers and to divide these ministers into two classifications, those of the Cabinet and those of the ministry.[2]

Mr. Pearson, when asked if the cabinet was too large, replied:

> It is too large and not large enough. The work of government has grown so much that there is room for more members of Parliament with ministerial responsibility. But the time is coming when we should have to decide that while there should be more members, there should perhaps be a smaller executive committee inside a larger Cabinet.[3]

Not only the size of the cabinet has caused concern. There has also been concern about the work load of various ministers, who often appear to be so busy that they do not have time to think out policy properly, leaving civil servants and other sources of policy input with excessive influence. It has been suggested, then, that what is needed are some senior ministers (senior in terms of ability and experience) without departmental responsibilities who would have more time to think out government policy and co-ordinate it.

The fact that not always the most able people are appointed to the cabinet has also caused concern. As long ago as 1928, Agnes MacPhail advocated changing the system. "The time will come when the Cabinet will be a committee of the House of Commons. The Cabinet will be chosen from the House and be responsible to it."[4] Under this scheme members of the cabinet would be members of the House of Commons elected from among its own ranks. This scheme, which was favoured by the members of the Progressive Party, assumed that party differences would not come into play and that the most able members of the House would become members of the cabinet, regardless of their party preference.

There have been other suggestions for reform as well. Several observers have suggested that cabinet responsibilities be divided into functional groups, with a cabinet member responsible for each group, supervising a number of departmental ministers who would not be of the cabinet. Hon. Alvin Hamilton has suggested:

> . . . that the Cabinet could be grouped into four groups. The three main groups are first, human resources, second material resources, third . . . all those things dealing with the monetary and fiscal side of government and fourth, the grouping of those ministers who do not fit into those particular categories.[5]

There would be a cabinet minister at the head of each of these groups, with a minister not in the cabinet heading each of the administrative departments within each group. The cabinet member would be responsible for general supervision and co-ordinating the work of the departments.

A similar scheme, advocated by David Lewis, would create ". . . two classes of ministers, one belonging to the Cabinet and having the general responsibility of government and the other a class of junior ministers not belonging to the Cabinet but having responsibility for the administration of a department."[6] A variant of these schemes, suggested by Peter Stursberg,[7] would allow for, "a small executive committee of government, without departmental responsibilities, for policy making and general supervision of functional groups of ministeries."[8] Under this scheme there would be ten Secretaries of State who would oversee functional clusters of ministers, while a larger group of departmental ministers would be responsible for the administration of the various departments. The ten groups would include National Resources, Transport and Communications, Manpower and Social Security, Commerce and Industry, Finance, National Security, External Affairs, Justice, Cultural Affairs, and Common Services. Such an arrangement would leave the Secretaries of State free from day-to-day problems and presumably give them time to concentrate on long term policy.

Reform and the Representation Principle

There is some merit in each of these proposals, but they all collide with the basic problem of Canadian federalism — that is, the problem of providing each major group and area with adequate federal representation and influence. It has already been demonstrated that the cabinet is the chief vehicle for such representation, but each of these schemes would require that some areas or groups be under-represented in the cabinet. For example, if the Stursberg scheme were implemented and there was a Secretary of State from each province, French Canadians would be under-represented. If the scheme were amended to provide for satisfactory representation for French Canadians, more cabinet members would come from Quebec. Ontario would then demand at least equal representation, which would result in other areas being under-represented.

Possibly this would be a good thing, and it may well be true that "efficiency in government is more important than provincial prides. . . ."[9] By eliminating the regional and group emphasis in the cabinet a sense of pan-Canadian consciousness would be stimulated, with consequent beneficial results for Canada as a whole. It is argued from time to time that regional and group representation is detrimental to the development of Canadian nationalism. However, the recognition of particularism and regionalism is possibly more significant than efficiency in the context of the Canadian federal system, and the accommodation of these factors in the Canadian federal cabinet may well account for the successful functioning and continued existence of the system.

Resorting to a form of populism or a participatory form of democracy in cabinet formation, as advocated by Miss MacPhail, could result in minority groups being excluded from the cabinet and thus being placed at the mercy of numerically superior ones. A variant of the scheme advocated by Miss MacPhail has in the past been practised in Australia.

> When Labour is to take office, the leader announces to a party meeting (caucus) the number of posts there will be in the Cabinet. Nominations are made and an exhaustive ballot . . . is taken to elect the members of the Cabinet. The allocation of portfolios remains in the hands of the leader . . . he cannot refuse to accept those whom caucus has chosen, once the ballot is concluded.[10]

Such a practice would inevitably have an adverse effect on the principles of cabinet responsibility and of loyalty to the Prime Minister; loyalty to party and caucus would replace cabinet solidarity and result in seriously weakening the position of the Prime Minister.

The schemes involving an inner cabinet consisting of ministers supervising a group of non-cabinet ministers also raise the question of responsibility. Who would be responsible in the final analysis for policy innovation and administration? It is unlikely that a non-cabinet minister would assume responsibility, if, when differences of opinion arose, the co-ordinating ministers, as is likely, would successfully insist their will prevail. The proposal was briefly experimented with by Sir Winston Churchill in 1951, when he appointed two co-ordinating ministers who were included in the cabinet while the ministers whose departments they co-ordinated were not. However, departmental ministers who resisted a co-ordinating minister's suggestions always had access to the cabinet.[11] The experiment was short-lived because of friction between ministers and cabinet members.

Premier William Davis of Ontario instituted a variant of this scheme by appointing several "super-ministers" who had no administrative responsibilities and who were thus free to concentrate on policy formation in the fields of social development, environment and resource development, and justice. However, all ministers in the Ontario government remained in the cabinet, whether they had departmental responsibilities or not. As in Great Britain, this produced friction among ministers, in that, according to one cabinet member, ". . . super-ministers were often caught between the Premier's office and the departmental Minister's office and there was considerable bickering over proper channels of communication and so forth."[12] One of the side effects of this conflict was to force policy ministers off the front pages of newspapers and from news broadcasts; they almost disappeared from public view. Some of the super-ministers were concerned that in accepting their new positions they ". . . may have committed political suicide.".[13] The Ontario experiment indicates that the super-minister arrangement may not make possible the high degree of visibility necessary for the successful performance of the role of group and regional representative in the federal cabinet. If either of these experiments were attempted at the federal level in Canada, an imbalance of group or regional representation among policy or co-ordinating ministers and the loss of opportunity for participating in general policy making would cause discontent among those under-represented in the cabinet. Schemes for reform that fail to take into account the representation principle are not likely to be satisfactory to Canadians.

The Trudeau Innovations

During his first administration, Prime Minister Trudeau attempted to make more moderate changes than those described above. These changes stressed a rationalist approach to decision making and to politics generally in Canada, an approach that ran counter to the pragmatic tradition in Canada and created serious problems. Pragmatism takes the attitude that ". . . if a programme does not work in practice there must be something wrong with the theory, the rationalist will retort that what is true in theory must be true in practice — that is, the practice, not the theory must be wrong."[14] This attitude may have affected Mr. Trudeau, his cabinet, and advisors and may have contributed to a dogmatic and doctrinaire approach to Canadian politics; it may also account for the charge heard frequently during the 1972 election campaign that Mr. Trudeau and the Liberals were "arrogant".

There are two other obstacles to the rational approach to decision making in Canada in addition to the pragmatic tradition: Parliament and the federal character of Canadian government. For example, it was suggested to one official of the Privy Council Office that the decision-making process in Canada was no more efficient now than it was before the Trudeau government took office, as evidenced by the government's seeming lack of preparedness for both the October 1970 crisis and for the economic policies announced by President Nixon on August 15, 1971. The official argued in reply that in fact the cabinet had anticipated the October crisis,[15] but that an alternative to the War Measures Act had not been passed into law ". . . because the government was afraid of the reaction of the House of Commons and thus did not introduce any legislation because it was felt that, in the absence of an emergency, Parliament would debate the proposal endlessly."[16] The efforts made to program Parliament (see pages 59 ff.) through the office of the President of the Privy Council seemed to have been made with this situation in mind, but since Parliament is the final stage in the policy-making process, it can react "irrationally" (in the minds of the policy planners) and thus the process cannot be completely rational, since all reactions from Parliament cannot be anticipated.

With regard to President Nixon's economic policies of 1971, it was argued that a reaction could only be organized with the approval and participation of the provinces, and that while the federal cabinet was aware that Mr. Nixon would have to take action eventually, it had not been able to get approval in advance from the provinces for a suitable response. Thus the country was not prepared with specific plans when the President did take action; this would have had to be the subject of federal-provincial negotiations. Again, rationality is impeded by the federal system of government.

On the other hand, while not contributing to "rationality", the growing importance of federal-provincial conferences has contributed to the centralization of decision making and a new role for the Privy Council Office and the Prime Minister's Office in the formation of policy. There are clear signs that many crucial and important political decisions will be taken, not by the federal cabinet alone, but rather at federal-provincial conferences. The Canadian political system may respond to contemporary stresses, not by modifying the cabinet, but by in effect producing a new consociational body. As of June 1970 there were 467 different federal-provincial committees functioning.[17] The role of the Prime Minister and his staff has thus been enhanced, for the Prime Minister must act as chief spokesman and prime bargainer at such conferences.

The Decline of the Cabinet as an Instrument of Accommodation

The shifting of the policy-making centre from the federal cabinet to federal-provincial conferences will alter the consociational model but still maintain it, and may help to maintain the stability of the Canadian political system. If one defines a stable democracy as ". . . one in which the capabilities of the system are sufficient to meet the demands placed on it. . . ,"[18] the shift to federal-provincial conferences may represent an adjustment in the system to accommodate new demands on it. One scholar has noted that ". . . the pattern of English Canadian-French Canadian bargaining through Federal-Provincial meetings closely approximates what Arend Lijphart has called consociational democracy."[19] This means that the important political elite for the purpose of bargaining may be changing and in future will consist of the Prime Minister and the provincial premiers. If this is the case, then the development of federal-provincial conferences as consociational bodies will make it possible for representative elites to continue to participate actively in the decision-making process.

There is some evidence that the cabinet's function as a consociational body is changing. The cabinet as a collegial body is disintegrating; it has, to a considerable extent, become a large committee that deals only with problems other smaller committees have not been able to resolve. The power of the Prime Minister and his staff over cabinet committees may serve to discourage dissent in them and thus further reduce the collegial aspect of the cabinet. Another manifestation of the decline of the cabinet is the fact that cabinet secrecy seems to be collapsing because of the large number of people now involved in its operations. Secret bargaining is typical of consociational democracies and of most federal-provincial conferences. The element of secrecy has been highly important to the successful functioning of the cabinet to date, but numerous leaks of information that have become quite typical of the Trudeau cabinets may be a sign that it cannot function in secret any longer. However, the decline of secrecy may also be simply a sign of the times:

> Rejection of secrecy as essentially wrong, skepticism about established authority and impatience with the slowness of government processes for decision can readily lead to the conviction that revealing a document

can be the best way to force the hand of government and to foil the plots of those who are thought to be frustrating government action.[20]

This is all not to suggest that a change in the role of the cabinet will make it unimportant. The representational role is still important, interdepartmental conflicts still must be settled, large policy issues will still have to be discussed, and situations will still arise that do not lend themselves to the usual policy-making procedures. An example here is the Trudeau government's ". . . action in March 1970 to prevent the sale of Denison Mines to an American company [which] had to be decided at an emergency full Cabinet meeting, without discussion in a Cabinet committee and without the context of an overall Government policy toward the problem of foreign ownership of strategic resources."[21] The cabinet will still have a role to play in accommodation, but it will no longer be the only mechanism for that purpose.

It will possibly become more an instrument of administrative co-ordination, approving decisions taken elsewhere and co-ordinating their implementation. The development of other political decision-making bodies, such as federal-provincial conferences, may help to hasten this change.

NOTES

[1]John MacKintosh, The British Cabinet, second ed., p. 622.

[2]Canada, House of Commons, Debates. (May 9, 1966), p. 4876.

[3]"Blair Fraser, "Your Guide to the Split Level Cabinet", Maclean's, Vol. 77, No. 7 (April 4, 1964), p. 18.

[4]Canada, House of Commons, Debates. (February 28, 1928), p. 842.

[5]Canada, House of Commons, Debates. (May 9, 1966), p. 4906.

[6]Ibid. (May 24, 1966), p. 5437.

[7]Peter Stursberg, "Badly Needed: A Reform of the Federal Government", Commentator, Vol. 10, No. 10 (October, 1966), p. 7ff.

[8]Ibid., p. 7.

[9]Ottawa Journal, (September 21, 1967), p. 6.

[10]J.D.B. Miller, "Parliamentary Institutions in Australia" in S.D. Bailey ed., Parliamentary Government in the Commonwealth (London; Hansard Society, 1951), p. 93.

[11]R.S. Milne, "The Experiment with Co-ordinating Ministers in the British Cabinet", 1951-1953, Canadian Journal of Economics and Political Science, Vol. XXI, No. 3 (August, 1955), p. 367.

[12]Interview, (December 3, 1972).

[13]Interview, (December 5, 1972).

[14]Giovanni Sartori, *Democratic Theory*. (Detroit; Wayne State University Press, 1962), p. 332.

[15]George Bain, "Cabinet Leak Reveals War Measures Studied Five Months Before October Crisis", *Globe and Mail*, (December 23, 1971), p. 1.

[16]*Interview*, (January 7, 1972).

[17]Gordon Robertson, "The Changing Role of the Privy Council Office", p. 497.

[18]Arend Lijphart, *The Politics of Accommodation*, p. 71.

[19]Richard Simeon, *Federal-Provincial Diplomacy*, p. 291.

[20]Gordon Robertson, quoted by John Bird in "Too Much Unnecessary Secrecy in High Places". *Financial Post*, (July 6, 1972) p. 5.

[21]Thomas Hockin, "Prime Minister and Political Leadership", in Thomas Hockin, ed., *Apex of Power*, p. 15.

Index